PAT ROACH'S
BIRMINGHAM

PAT ROACH'S
BIRMINGHAM

Pat Roach and Shirley Thompson

BREWIN BOOKS

First published by
Brewin Books Ltd, 56 Alcester Road,
Studley, Warwickshire B80 7LG in 2004
www.brewinbooks.com
Second Impression February 2005

ISBN 1 85858 252 0

A Cataloguing in Publication Record
for this title is available from the British Library.

Typeset in Baskerville
Printed in Great Britain by
Warwick Printing Company Limited.

CONTENTS

ACKNOWLEDGEMENTS

*(for providing interviews, photographs,
encouragement and numerous other favours)*

The Birmingham Post and Mail Ltd; Birmingham Reference Library - Local Studies and Archives; Carole Bailey; Kenny Baker; Norman Bartlam; Peter and Cynthia Berrington; John Bevis; PC Michelle Birch; Pat Bowen; PC Phil Burlace; Alan and Alistair Brewin; Bill (a.k.a. Wayne) Bridges, and Sarah Bridges; Ronnie and Alison Callow; Professor Norman Cherry; Professor Carl Chinn; Johnny 'Brough' Cloves; Ken and Barbara Collins; Gordon Cull; Ed Doolan; Alton Douglas; Nicol Dwyer; Len Edwards; Chris Fairbank; Don, Eddie and Gordon Fewtrell; Geoff Field; Eric and Ken Goodby; Mark and Marie Haddleton; Thomas Paddy Hallett (a.k.a. 'Big Paddy'); Val Hastings; Johnny Hayles (a.k.a. 'Killer Kowalski'); Georgie James; Norma Knewport; Robert Knight; John Landon; Mike Long; Chris Millard; Peter Mulroy; Jean and Bernard Newbould; Roy O'Neill; Jackie Pallo; Wayne Pell; Jack Perkins (a.k.a. Little); Janet and Lynn Perkins; Inspector Sean Phillips; The Reverend Tom Pyke; John Rischmiller – (former Chief Inspector); Dolly, Doreen, Mark and Patrick Roach (Junior); Walter Roach's family: Frances, Frank, Glenys, Helen, Ruth and Tom Roach; Josie Rudge; Ian Sandy; Ken and Linda Schofield; Dara and Randhawa Singh; 'Smudge' Smith; Timothy Spall; Geoff Staley; Billy Sutton; Jack Taylor; Joyce Taylor; David Thompson; Albert Townsend; Andy Townsend (a.k.a. Hudson Shaw); Rob Turley; Shirley Underhill; Julie Vincent; Brian and Merle Webb; Jim White; Paddy and Jill White; Krys Zalewska.

Also, the cast and crew of canal production, *So Far So Good*: Blue Spirit Productions August 2002: (actors): Marie Blount; Alison Carney; Litha Efthymiou; Liam Jarvis; Geoffrey White; (and both co-authors). (Actor/assistant director) Jacqui O'Hanlon; (actor/producer) Claire Turvey; (composer) Nick Price; (designer) Amanda Grist; (director) Jonathan Holmes; (musician/stage manager) Katherine Palmer.

Please forgive any possible omissions. Every effort has been made to include all organisations and individuals involved in the book.

For my grandson

Patrick Roach Junior

I think it's every man's dream, that someone should follow in his footsteps – emulate him, or at least aspire in his own way – although I'm sure that he has the ability to do so - in his own right. When I look at my big grandson, (I have to call him 'Big Grandson', otherwise he tells me off!), I can see that he has qualities, beneath the surface. It would be lovely to think that I would be around long enough, to help them come to some sort of fruition. Sometimes I try to explain to Patrick, that it's quite a good thing to listen to someone who has made mistakes in his life - and learned by them.

FOREWORD

Dear Readers,

I think it's absolutely bostin' that my old mate, Pat Roach, should ask me to write a few words for the 'Foreword' to his book about Brum. I was tickled pink that he should wish me to use my, not inconsiderable literary skills, to pen a few lines. Ironic – don't you think? Considering that he and I (in a manner of speaking), have swapped identities, in terms of 'Brummie' and 'Southerner', for 'Auf Wiedersehen Pet'. Although, strictly speaking, Barry's more of a 'Black Country' boy, really.

I believe that some 'radish', a few years back, had the temerity to suggest that there were more miles of canal in Birmingham than in the whole of Venice put together; the gentleman in question hastily withdrew his words, a short while later! Strange as it may seem, I do know whereof I speak. In real life, my wife Shane's family hail from the West Midland areas of Walsall and Cannock Chase, whereas I'm a Londoner, born and bred in Battersea, just a 'stone's throw' from Clapham Junction.

Pat's book is packed to the gills with 'duckers-and–divers' and dodgy situations, so I'd strongly advise you to hide all the best silver and lock up your jewellery, before you commence reading! As the story unfolds, you'll discover that, to cope with the uncertain environment of his youth, Pat was obliged to hone two essential survival skills, which eventually became second nature to him. The facility to make a swift assessment of individuals, (those he could trust and those he couldn't), combined with a talent for 'playing his cards close to his chest'.

Pat and I first met in the early 1980s, on the morning of the first read-through, for the very first series of 'Auf Wiedersehen Pet'. You couldn't have assembled a more diverse bunch of people, although, fortunately, no one was trying to play ego games. We filmed in some very odd places. I remember Pat looking at all these great big diggers, with a kind of glow in his eyes, and saying: "Oh, I love plant!" I know he's had scrap-yards, and he always has various business deals on the go. You never quite know. Occasionally I'll get a call from him, about some deal or other.

I've always thought of Pat, although it's a cliché, as being a big, gentle, giant. He has that kind of street wisdom that he never foists on you - and you can always rely on him to get you out of trouble. I think he's brought such charm to the character of Bomber, and a Burt Lancaster-type quality, especially in the way he delivers his lines.

I remember one day, on set, we had to keep repeating a pub scene, in the second series, over and over again. Pat had to get up, and I was supposed to sit in his seat. I didn't hear the director say: "OK, can we go from the top please?" I was chatting, to Jimmy, and all of a sudden I was in the air. I thought, 'My God, what am I doing up here?' Pat had picked me up, like I was a piece of paper – and I'm no lightweight! Then he put me down. He said: "Alright our kid?" I said: "I'm sorry." He said: "Don't worry kid – OK?" There's something very charming about him, and a shyness that has tremendous audience appeal. We've come a long way since the first series, and have just finished filming the fourth. The seven principal actors who started out together, in that first 'Auf Wiedersehen' could not have foreseen the tremendous impact it was to have, on all of our lives.

Like the 'Gentle Giant', I reckon there must be something of the water gypsy in me too, because one of my favourite pastimes is taking narrow-boat holidays, to get away from it all. Although he's a very personable, amiable man, Pat's always had that mysterious air of the 'gypsy' about him…

Timothy Spall - (a.k.a. Barry Spencer Taylor).

Chapter One –

THE LUCKIEST PEOPLE

George James, (my friend Georgie's dad), was a hawker. His family lived two doors away from us. George would trundle down Shakespeare Road every Sunday with his barrow, crying: "Pennywinks!" He had periwinkles for sale, and bits of lettuce, celery and the occasional tomatoes. The odd 'winks' - when he stopped abruptly - would roll off, onto the ground, and we'd chase them down the street, because they used to roll down like marbles. Chasing a periwinkle down the street for about twenty yards, picking it up and secreting it in our pockets; trying to get three or four, so that we could make a meal of it!

Throughout the book, unless otherwise stated, the passages in italics are Pat's words. One of his early pleasures was a visit to the cinema: three-pence for a seat in the main auditorium, or 'stalls', and four pence upstairs.

That was the 'Four-penny Crush', of course – the 'Saturday Menu'. But when you got really serious about it, I think it was eight-pence and 1/6d – the old 'Ledsam'. My Granny used to take me there. She'd sit at the front, because she couldn't see. I'd sit in the middle, I suppose, and she'd shout at half-time, as loud as she could: "D'you want an ice-cream Paddy?!" It was so funny. God bless my poor old Gran! So I'd go down to the front of the cinema - I can't remember how much an ice-cream cost in those days.

Then we'd go back to Shakespeare Road, and that would be it. We'd go to bed, and the door wouldn't be locked 'til ten o'clock – it would be pushed to - (in the summer of course); it would be ajar otherwise. Then at eleven o'clock, we'd actually lock it. That's how life was. No one burgled your house – or stole anything; everyone knew everyone else – and life was fairly jovial – it really was.

That's what we used to do. That was our life, and that's what this book's all about – I suppose - my life - and the life of people in Ladywood, Balsall Heath, and similar areas. How normal and naturally they lived, under those conditions – because that's all there was. Despite our arses hanging out, and no boots for our feet - (the stories which are untold, about free boots, and how we used to get whacked, for having dirty feet!). But that will all come out later – if you're interested enough to read the book – it will all come out…

Pat's mother, Doris Bevis, was born in the Scarlet Buildings, Garbett Street, Ladywood, in 1915, close to Birmingham's Gas Street Basin, nucleus of the English canal system. Her parents, Bill and Amelia Bevis, christened her Doris, but everyone knew her as 'Dolly'. She was the second youngest of two boys and two girls. Her mother, Amelia, was sole witness to the canal side murder of her mother, allegedly by one of her own gypsy clan; although at the age of three, she'd been too young to give evidence. Kindly Grandfather Jackson, whom we assume was her mother's father, had taken Amelia (known to her friends as 'Milly') under his wing, raising her as a water gypsy. The two of them plied their trade, up and down the Birmingham canals, until Amelia was well into her teens. She was thought to have the 'sixth sense' of the gypsies, telling people's fortunes by reading tea leaves and cards.

Our story begins on 19 May 1937, in Park Road, Hockley, when Amelia's daughter, Dolly, gave birth to her first-born son, Francis, Patrick Roach. The coronation of King George VI and Queen Elizabeth, (the Queen Mother), was only a week before. The celebrations continued for a week - culminating in Pat's birth.

As our story progresses, we will take you on a tour of suburban Birmingham, spanning three centuries. It will include areas such as the Jewellery Quarter, Aston, Newtown, Ladywood, Lozells, Balsall Heath, Winson Green, and several others - all having strong associations with Pat and his family.

When I was born I was 12½lbs, can you imagine? Mom tells me that they couldn't weigh me on the hospital scales: they had to weigh me, suspended from a hook, on an enormous pair of scales, borrowed from the butcher next door!

His head and body were unusually large. Dolly stared at him in disbelief: "I've just never had that!" she gasped. It had taken two exhausting days and nights to deliver him.

Pat's own memories, combined with those of relatives, friends and neighbours, provide a valuable insight into his early years. We are particularly grateful to Walter and Hilda Roach's family. Also, to former Ladywood residents, Georgie James, Ken Collins, Brian Webb, Josie Rudge and three of the Berrington family - Peter, Norma and Carole; sisters Pat Bowen and Shirley Underhill (née Smith); Geoff Staley and Johnny 'Brough' Cloves, for their kind assistance. Apart from Josie, they were originally children of a similar age to Pat, growing up in the same neighbourhood.

Pat renewed his acquaintance with Ken, Pat, Johnny and Geoff, at a bi-annual meeting of *OLRA* – the *Old Ladywood Reunion Association*, on Sunday 6 October 2002. The two of us were special guests at the meeting, held at the Clarendon Suite, Edgbaston, in Birmingham. Brian Webb and his wife Merle, and Peter Berrington and his wife Cynthia were familiar faces at the meeting, as Pat's co-writer had interviewed them some weeks previously, and Pat had already met them again, at the launch of his first book, in March 2002. At a subsequent *Ottakars* book signing in June 2002, attended by both authors, Pat was reunited with Josie Rudge. It had been many years since they last met, but he recognised her immediately.

At the *OLRA* meeting, in October, we were asked to say a few words to a hall-full of members. Pat later mingled with the guests, while his co-writer fronted an *If Exhibition*, consisting of posters relating to *If – The Pat Roach Story*, plus copies of the book - (one was auctioned later that afternoon). Poppy Brady, of the *Birmingham Mail*, interviewed Pat. The association is always pleased to welcome new members. Gordon Cull, the organiser, may be contacted on 02476 746 886, or by e-mail: oldladywood@ntlworld.com. Alternatively, phone Norman Bartlam, at the *Ladywood History Group*, on 0121 455 0663.

Pat's mother, Dolly Bevis, continued to live in Garbett Street, Ladywood, during her teens, in the late 1920s. Two of her close friends, from that period, were Lily Savigar, who became Lily Webb, on marriage, and Rose Fowler, daughter of Albert and Mary, (she lived in a neighbouring street, and later became Rose Collins). Sadly, all three women were eventually either widowed, or separated from their husbands. Difficult to imagine, in those early, impoverished years, that Dolly's eldest son would become a celebrity. Or, that with the 21st century under way, Rose and Lily's sons, Ken Collins and Brian Webb would be helping Pat's biographer to supply some of the missing strands of his life story, for this book. Brian and Ken also happen to be cousins: Ken's father was Lily's stepbrother.

Pat's father, Frank Roach, born to Nellie and Walter Roach in 1905, was the third youngest, in a family of three sons and four daughters. The family lived in a large house, at 3 back 90 Tower Street, just off what was later to become infamous Summer Lane, in the Newtown district of Birmingham, a short distance from the city centre. Frank's youngest sister, Nora remembered her brother as a 'tough nut', who enjoyed street fights. Although you needed to be tough to survive in those days, such fights would probably have been far less serious than many which hit the headlines today.

Frank had two older brothers, Walter and Peter. Pat's friend, and Best Man at his wedding, Roy O'Neill, met both brothers; his father later became a close friend of Frank's. "They were at my dad, Tommy's yard, in Bridge Street West: he was a scrap dealer, in antiques. Frank and his brothers lived down the same opening as my gran. The first time I met Frank, he came into the yard, on his own, to see my dad," recalls Roy. "He bought a big handcart with two wheels, off my dad, that a horse could be harnessed into, and said he was going to collect it – but he didn't."

Roy's father decided to teach Frank a lesson. "Tommy Barrett, one of the dealers, took it round to Frank's shop in Hamstead Road. That would be in about 1938, because Frank had recently married Dolly. Tommy Barrett tipped this cart up, on its end, and put it against the doorway of Frank's shop, when Dolly and Frank were in the back place. Dolly was blonde at that time - always dressed up. They managed to escape – eventually! Frank sold the shop later to a chap named Plotnik."

Pat's early years were very traumatic. His parents separated when he was just four years old. In our previous book, *If – The Pat Roach Story*, Dolly explains: "I took all my bits and pieces to my friend Maggie, to sell up. I had a 'sell-up' from Park Road." She and Pat moved back to Garbett Street, Ladywood, to live with Amelia for a while. Pat describes his childhood as "very dis-jointed". There can be no doubt that he and Dolly share a close and loving mother-son relationship. However, as a child, growing up in what would nowadays be termed a 'single-parent' family, and sometimes as a 'foster-child', he experienced several traumatic incidents, which were to have a profound influence upon him. He moved several times during his childhood. In an effort to trace his movements around Birmingham, I asked: "You were born in Park Road, then moved to Tenby Street North, followed by Garbett Street?"

But my life was so dis-jointed, so dis-jointed. Although I did move to Tenby Street North, my mother could still have been living there and I was living in King Edwards Road – somewhat divorced from the situation. I mean, I don't know.

I always seemed to be living apart from my mother and father – with someone. I remember once, somewhere between the ages of five –seven; it must have been Christmas or my birthday - my mother bought me a hat and coat. I think I was living with my Aunt Edna, or someone – at the time. My father arrived on the scene about the same time as my mother, who had come to see me, and presented me with this hat and coat. I thought it was marvellous. My father just threw it on the fire: I stood there and watched this hat and coat burn on the fire. It was the first new coat that I remember having. I suppose I cried – I don't know. But I remember that very vividly.

Such was the confusion in young 'Paddy's' life, it's hardly surprising to learn from Dolly that the relatives Pat was staying with, at that time, were Frank's older brother Uncle Walter, and his wife, Aunt Hilda. "I was there", explains Dolly, "and poor momma bought the hat and coat for Paddy, because I lived with her. I took it round - she was golden – our momma. I think Frank had come round to sort me out."

Pat is delighted to have renewed contact with Walter and Hilda's family, whilst researching this book, following the chance discovery that they are related to the co-author's youngest sister, Julie Vincent! Michelle Roach married Steve Brason, a nephew of Mike Vincent, Julie's husband. Thanks to Julie, and Michelle's aunts and uncles, we discovered that Michelle is Uncle Walter's great granddaughter!

Furthermore, Walter's family has provided us with documentary evidence, from the 1881 Census, proving that a certain Mary Roach, from Galway, is Pat's great grandmother, on his father's side. To the best of our knowledge, she and her husband, William, (Pat's great grandfather), emigrated from Southern Ireland, in the 1860s.

Mary Roach is designated 'Head of the Family', because William, as evidenced in a further document, had moved into lodgings, in nearby Cecil Street. James Roach, the oldest son was nineteen at the time, which means that he was born in 1862. He was a bricklayer, (as his younger brother, Walter – Pat's grandfather – was later to be).

Fortunately, Tom's wife, Glenys, has correlated these additional details, in a Roach Family File. Included in this collection, is a letter from Pat's cousin, Colonial Walter's wife, Ruth Roach, whose son-in-law, Dr. William Neville, provided the research. Ruth writes:

'Herewith the start of the Roach Family Tree … As far as the 1881 Census, I wonder why William and Mary were living at different addresses? Also, why William (my son-in-law), didn't write to County Mayo, where William was born. The town where the Roaches were rumoured to have come from, was Tuam.'

Tuam is to the southwest of Roscommon. Sadly, Walter is now deceased, but all of his younger brothers and sisters have, to date, survived him. Great Grandmother Mary came from Galway and Great Grandfather William, from County Mayo. Looking at the map, Galway is situated south of Tuam, and Mayo to the north. Galway's the nearest of the two counties to Tuam, but both counties are within a reasonable distance, so logic dictates that they probably *did* live there.

At the time of the Census, Mary was thirty-nine, (born 1842), so she and William were probably in their late teens when they married, and came to England. William was just a year older: forty in 1881. Research by the co-author, into her mother-in-law Ellen's family, (Tom's daughter), has revealed that the Roaches hailed from an area bordering Roscommon, which substantiates Dr. Neville's findings.

Glen is compiling a 'Generational Chart'. County Mayo William (Pat's and the family's great grandfather), born 1841, is at the top; one step below, and to the left is Pat's grandfather, Walter Roach, (born 1874). Below that is his Uncle Walter (Frank's brother – and father to those present – Frank, Helen and Tom); on the bottom step is Pat's cousin, Walter, John Roach (older brother of those present), Colonial Police Walter, born 2nd March 1920. We reveal more about him, in a later chapter.

At a recent meeting with Glen, and Pat's cousins, Tom, Helen and Frank, we agreed that William and Mary's eight children were probably born in England, although as James (or Jim) was born in 1862, he *may* be the exception. We have only just discovered that Pat's grandfather, Walter had a sister, Mary, in addition to six brothers!

This new family connection enables us to revise the description of Pat's Uncle Walter, contained in our previous book. His daughter, Helen, explains: "My father, Walter Roach, was a gentleman. He had his problems, because of the war, but he certainly wasn't violent – he was quite a man! We always used to have a laugh. He took us to many of the musicals, and variety shows at the *Birmingham Hippodrome*. Then we'd come out, and have baked potatoes. That's the kind of dad he was – he used to take us out. We weren't rough you see; we were looked after. And he liked cricket – he was always at the cricket grounds." Her brother, Pat's cousin, Frank, confirms: "He used to take me to the Warwickshire Cricket Ground in Edgbaston; we'd sit on the grass bank."

It's funny that, many years later, when they tried to close the 'Hippodrome' down, I was Chairman of 'Equity', and we picketed that very same theatre, for several weeks, finally managing to keep it open.

In Chapter 8, assisted by Len Edwards, Birmingham Branch Secretary of *Equity,* and former Secretary, Val Hastings, we take a closer look at Pat's involvement with the union.

"My mum, Hilda, was lovely," Helen continues. "She was eighty-five when she died. We got on well together. She always worked hard and looked after us. She had to compensate for dad, when he wasn't well." She particularly recalls her grandparents, (and Pat's) - Walter and Nellie, "... because I was Nellie's favourite. I went to stay with Nora and Grandma: they lived together in Weoley Castle." Built in the 1930s, this was a popular place for Ladywood people to move to, following a round of slum clearance.

Helen confirms that Walter, died in 1930, and Nellie, in 1935. "I was five when my granddad died. I can remember the funeral, and wearing a little black serge dress." Joyce Taylor, Agnes' daughter was there too; at four years old she was even younger than her cousin, Helen. "He was a beautifully big man – a handsome man," comments Helen. "My brother Walter was a handsome man too: he was the *image* of Grandfather Walter."

Nellie had two businesses: a second hand shop and tailoring, and could make a suit to the correct size, simply by looking at someone. Helen recalls: "Grandma was poorly for ages – she used to walk with a limp. There was a park facing Tower Street, and Granddad would stand on a step and watch me on the swing. Nellie was small and dainty." Interestingly enough, that *seems* to be a family trend. Grandfather Walter was very tall and his wife was dainty; the same applies to Pat and his wife, Doreen. "My dad and Hilda were the same too," adds Helen, – "mum was only small. Grandmother Nellie still had jet-black hair 'til the day she died. I used to plait it for her, down to her back - the same as my dad, Walter, and Grandfather - he always had jet-black hair. I was only ten when Nellie died, but I can remember Walter's funeral as plain as anything – he was only fifty-five."

Pat treasures a photo of Grandfather Walter, (as it was the first that he'd seen), given to him just four years ago, by Pete Mulroy, Nora's son. He's seated between two other men, with a large house in the background. "Granddad

Walter's death was very sudden," explains Helen. "He died of pneumonia. My Grandma Nellie told me that an insurance man came to visit Walter, but he was in the front room, in his coffin. Grandma hadn't realised that the insurance man didn't know that Walter had died. So she said: 'Oh yes – he's in the front room!' Well, he walked in the front room, took one look at him, and when Nan looked, he was half way up the road, running for dear life!"

In 1881 Mary and her eight children, (including Walter and Tom), were living in Summer Lane Court 52, House 1. When Walter and Hilda married, they stayed very close to the family home. Pat's cousin, Frank, confirms that, for many years, their mutual branch of the Roach family, (William and Walter's), continued to live around Summer Lane, Hospital Street, and Tower Street, Aston. Having scoured church records for information about Walter's offspring, it seems quite strange, to be actually seated in their dining room - talking to them!

"Hospital Street got bombed out," Frank explains, "then we moved into the Lozells area – to Lennox Street. I was in the army, and was called from Germany, to come home on Compassionate Leave, but it was too late." Helen observes: "Walter died in Lennox Street, in 1948, at the same age as his own dad, fifty-five, of the same disease – pneumonia." On marriage, Walter and Ruth lived in Hong Kong, Frances and Ken resided in Kent; Frank and his wife, Barbara, moved to Castle Bromwich, while Helen and family, plus Tom and Glenys, set up home in Shard End.

Glenys explains: "Walter and Frank were really good friends: they got on well together. But Walter wouldn't allow Frank to work with him, because he said he was too 'light-fingered'. But they were *always* together." "Yes – Uncle Frank and Dad," continues his namesake. "I've been in the coffee house on the corner - *Jones's*. Uncle Frank loved his bacon and eggs and fried bread. The coffee house was on the corner of Buckingham Street and Hospital Street. Frank was always round at our house." The family collectively confirms that Frank was a well-spoken person and, despite being very tall, was very upright. "He wore a trilby most of the time," adds Frank. "In those days we all wore a collar and tie, to go to work."

Tom's siblings recall that, being of a similar age, Tom and Pat would play together - sometimes by the canal. "My memory of that period is vague," explains Tom. "I remember him being there, but no distinct details, except that his hair was blond – the Shirley Temple look!" When Pat visited their family home – at 56 Hospital Street, he was only about two or three years old. "But as soon as he came into the house," recalls Helen, "my mother would take one look at him. Then he'd be washed, changed – some clean clothes put on, and have his hair washed (he was quite lousy!). He was a handsome boy. I was only young myself, but I remember." She confirms the views of several others:

"He wasn't unruly or anything: he'd got *used* to people. I think it was because he'd become accustomed to being pulled 'from pillar to post' really - by people - all the time. But the first thing my mother used to say, because she was very particular: 'Come on then Paddy – let's have you!' " According to Glenys: "Hilda said, Pat said to his dad: 'I'm not going there any more, because she keeps cleaning me up!' "

When the school nurse arrived, she'd take one look at me, gingerly take one mucky sleeve of my shirt between her thumb and forefinger, muttering: "I don't think so!" Then she'd have nothing more to do with me.

When I was doing some charity work for Moseley Hall Hospital, they told me that one of the Roach aunts, or Great-aunts, had spent her last years in the hospital. She died in her nineties.

"What you must realise," explains Frank, "is that with Frank and Dolly splitting up, it took Pat away from *our* side of the family. We never saw him." Helen elaborates: "After he moved back with his mother – or whoever – Frank never brought him again, you see?

Pat - just to tell you that you're not the only one who didn't see your grandfather. Wal would have done, and Frances and I, but Frank and Tom didn't. And if you could have seen him ... in Tower Street ... when I was in the park, and he had to stand on the step, and watch me, as I was swinging. A great big man he was – very striking, with his collar and tie: a big, good looking, handsome man. In those days, we hadn't got much. Then some houses were knocked down, and they put swings on there. The Roaches lived right on the front, facing the 'rec'. A nice big house it was, next to the vicarage. When they had parties at the vicarage next door, I used to sit on the wall and watch them.

"The other place you mentioned in the previous book, was the Settlement, down in Summer Lane. It's been there a long time; we played netball there – Fran and I; it was a Learning Centre as well." Frank adds: "Nowadays, it's an Advice Centre, for people in financial trouble; it's on the corner of Tower Street and Summer Lane."

Shortly after losing contact with Walter's family, Pat met Ken Collins' cousin, Brian Webb. The two of them were evacuated, as four and five-year-olds, to a large farm, at Litmarsh, near Whitegate, Hereford, following the bombing of the corner pub, in Tenby Street North. Brian recalls: "That was in about 1941 or '42. Pat and I both remember Ginny the Pig - it was always in a bad mood! Pat's mother and my mother came over to visit us the one time; having grown up in Garbett Street together as young adults or teenagers, they remained lifelong friends.

"My mother and father split up, and Doris and my mother - Aunt Doris, I should call her - used to go on holidays quite regularly – to Spain or somewhere. Our family lived within a short distance of Pat, in Anderton Street.

During our younger days, just after the war, both mothers took us on holidays to Stourport." Parochial though this may sound, Pat recalls that even a bus trip out to Harborne was quite an event - in those days! "It was supposed to be a caravan," continues Brian, "but in fact it was a converted, single-decker coach. All the seats had to be taken out and beds and tables put in. There were no services – we had paraffin lights and no water.

"There was a natural spring in the next field. Pat and I, being the eldest, used to go over and fetch water every morning." Brian is just a year younger than Pat. One particular holiday remains forever etched in his memory. Pat's stepbrother, Rickie, born 18 May 1946, was on holiday with them and had just begun to speak, so it seems likely that it was in late 1947. Brian's younger brother, Terry, was also there.

The two older boys were collecting water. "There was a log in front of this spring, where you could kneel down and get a bucket of water," Brian explains. "Pat, being the big chap he was, just leapt across. I was only half his size – and still am. I thought, 'I'm never going to get across this' - it was like a lake to me, but it was nothing to Pat. Anyway, I took a flying leap, got about halfway through the air, and went down like a stone, into the spring - I sank. It was quite deep. I was *terrified* – and freezing cold! All I remember is shooting out. Pat had leaned down, grabbed hold of me under the water, and just dragged me out by my hair. I'm sure he saved my life. I'll never forget that! It was just a natural reaction to him – an *immediate* reaction; he held on to something, leaned down into the spring. That's the sort of kid he was: a really great friend. We never had our fathers with us, but the two ladies – Doris and Lil, used to pop out of an evening to the local pub together, in Stourport - and have a little bit of a 'knees-up', on their own."

Brian remembers Pat as a very sensitive, deep feeling person. "He was very fair with us – he didn't put on airs and graces. Despite his size he was never ever a bully. I've seen him insulted: you know what kids are like – they can say nasty things sometimes. He never lost his temper. Sometimes I could see that Pat was hurt – and he'd just walk away. But other times, if he met them again, he'd just stand there and stare. They never said anything else: they used to quake in their boots, in case Pat *did* lose his temper! But he never did."

Pat saved his friend's life on a second, even more 'hair-raising' occasion: "He was always very faithful – always protecting us. I remember Pat, Terry and I were on another countryside holiday. We got stuck in a field of horses. The horses got really excited and started charging towards us. We were only 'nippers' and Pat said: 'Run!' So me and Terry were away – got to the fence, and Pat was standing there, waving his arms like this (demonstrates) with these horses, running towards him! And they all split. Pat just walked back and said: 'It's alright now, they've gone away; they were frightened – that's all!' I remember that, as clear as anything. He could only have been about ten or eleven then." This self-confidence which Pat exhibited from an early age, is another aspect of his character, which several people have referred to.

"He went to live with Amelia at 180 King Edwards Road at first, where some of his friends were my friends as well," explains Brian. "Malcolm Cabey and his sister, for example: like Pat, they lived opposite the 'rec'. Later, they used the Beehive pub in Garbett Street. That's where I last saw them – just before they knocked it down." Titcher Coates was another mutual friend, (or 'Titchy', as Pat calls him). He became Ken Collins' friend too, when Ken moved from Steward Street School to Barford Road. Ken explains: "I met Leslie Coates or 'Titchy' Coates, (so-called because he was so small, he couldn't get in the army to do his National Service). We ended up sitting next to each other at the desk in Mr. Bradley's class. He was pretty good at Mathematics – I wasn't. I was good at English, so I swapped notes about English; he let me look over his shoulder when he was doing his 'sums', as they used to call them.

"During the war, Ladywood children used to play in the streets, sometimes with torches," elaborates Ken. "Most people can see in the dark: everyone has 'night vision'. When you're in the dark long enough, your eyes become adjusted to the darkness and you can see – to an extent. It depended upon the game you were playing. One of our favourites, which we played using torches for ray guns, was based on *Flash Gordon*."

Ken was born in 1930. His parents rented an attic room at number 21, Shakespeare Road, which was the sweep's house. " My grandmother told me that I was born with the chord around my throat, so I could have been strangled," he explains. "Some people say I should have been! My grandmother shouted to my father George to go and get the midwife." He was the oldest of four children. A few weeks after his birth, the family moved to Sherborne Street, in Ladywood, then returned to live at 2 back of 19, Shakespeare Road. "Being a bit older I had my set of friends," he recalls. "Pat would be with a younger group.

"There was one individual who always had the 'little ones' around him, instead of people of his own age." As he was 'holding court', the older children couldn't resist calling out to him, in the Birmingham vernacular, 'Here comes the King of the Babbies!' "This was Maurice Evans," Ken continues. "He played games like that, but he also played with us; he couldn't boss us around like he could with the little ones. He'd be about ten or eleven and the little ones would be about five or six, you see? I should point out that Maurice Evans was a very dear friend of mine. He was a bit of a risk-taker, and although I lost contact with him, I have many fond memories of the wonderful times and the funny incidents we were involved in together."

Rose Collins had several jobs, but still found time to socialise with Dolly. "My mother spoke very warmly about her friendship with Doris. I'd be about five or six at the time when I first remember Rose speaking about her." Ken recalls having Sunday afternoon tea in Park Road, Hockley, with his sister Jean and Aunt Lil' (before Brian was born). This was the same, long and winding road, where Pat had spent the first four years of his life.

Ken describes the Shakespeare Road sweep, Charles Greenwood (their former landlord), as a grumpy old man. "One of our favourite pastimes, at ten or eleven years of age, was to sit on his doorstep with my friends and pass the time of the evening or the time of day; we'd be joking and so forth. The sweep had a very subtle way of getting rid of us. He used to gently pour a bucketful of water, so that it ran underneath the door; we all ended up with wet bottoms and wet trousers! Everyone seems big when you're small, but I remember him as a burly kind of fella, with a walrus moustache."

Ken has very positive memories about his childhood. "I had a marvellous time; there were so many games we could play." One of the games that both Pat and Ken used to play, albeit separately, was 'Up and Over'. A brick wall separated every courtyard, all the way down Shakespeare Road. "We'd start by climbing over the *one* wall of the *top* courtyard," recalls Ken, "then into the next courtyard, then the next and the next – and so forth, until you'd reached right to the end of Shakespeare Road and climbed *every* wall. It was a wonderful game to play. You had plenty of energy in those days, and were just out to have a good time."

Around 1948, Pat joined that same community, when he moved with his gran, from around the square, in King Edwards Road, to 68 Shakespeare Road. "I think that Shakespeare Road was the most settled part of his childhood– because he was there quite a few years," comments Brian Webb. "He used to come round to our house. We were ten or eleven, and old friends, by that time." It was at this stage that Pat first met the other Ladywood people featured in this chapter, and the one that follows.

Pat's first school was Hope Street Infants', in Balsall Heath. Then he attended Nelson Street School, when he moved to King Edwards Road, but being a year ahead of Brian, didn't see much of him. Pat left Nelson Street School a year before his friend, moving to Steward Street Junior School, followed by Barford Road Secondary School. Normally, he would have gone to Hope Street Secondary School, near the family home in Balsall Heath, (he'd also attended the junior branch of the school for a while; a photograph shows him in the football team). But he had problems with Harry Meakin, his step-father, so preferred to return to live with his grandmother, for substantial periods of his childhood; he could always to turn to her, when things became too difficult at home.

Saturdays were a special occasion for Pat and Brian: "We'd have to go to Monument Road Baths first, for our weekly scrub," explains Brian. "Afterwards, we'd go home, have a couple of sandwiches, then get down to the *Lyric Cinema*, for the 'Crush' on a Saturday morning." A series of photographs from Brian's private collection, show the sequence of events. "That's the *Lyric Cinema*. We used to queue round here; there were hundreds of kids. We watched Johnny Mack Brown, Roy Rogers, Gabby Hayes, Hop-along-Cassidy, Flash Gordon – three-pence it used to cost us. But it was a riot: it wasn't a cinema show at all; they used to play about, screaming, while the films were on. We'd come out of there, and start playing here (moves on to the next photo), at the Sandpits." There is an Orthodox Church in the background. The car in the photograph marks the spot where the boys used to play.

"This is Summer Hill Passage," continues Brian. "All this was a garden, in the late 40s and into the 50s. Cinema times were from 1.30pm to about 3.30pm. We'd come out to the Sandpits afterwards and play Cowboys and Indians in these bushes, then work all the way round – for about an hour; one of us would be Hop-along-Cassidy. There was a little Herbal Shop over here. We'd get a penny stick of liquorice root - Pat, and my younger brother Terry; we were always together – the three of us. If we'd got the funds we'd have a stick of troche, which was dark brown, and shaped like piece of seaside rock." Ironically, 'Stick of Troche' was Frank Roach's nickname! "The gardens used to finish up at Powell Street, just before the Ice Rink." They couldn't afford the entrance fee, and every so often, would sneak in the back way!

According to Brian: "It was a place we got to know quite well, because there were steps there, leading up to the door, we used to get our girlfriends in there, in later days. But there'd be someone inside, who'd open the doors in Goodman Street for us. They used to let us in – they weren't too bothered. I tried ice skating a couple of times, but I wasn't any good. I can't remember Pat having a go, although he used to go down there quite a lot. I was more into roller-skating at the Embassy, Sparkbrook. But *this* became a roller skating rink eventually. The building is still there, but it's a big stationery and computer showroom now. That factory's still there, to the left of the Ice Rink, and there's King Edwards Road; the 'rec' was on the left."

We moved on to another photograph: "That's the *Crown Cinema*, where we all used to go as well. That was a bit posher than the *Ledsam*. We'd be about thirteen or fourteen by that time. If you were taking a young lady out, you'd go to the *Edgbaston*, because that was the posh one. (My cousin, Ken Collins worked there as a projectionist, at the age of fifteen). "But if we were on our own, we'd go to the *Lyric* or the *Ledsam*."

Shakespeare Road is no longer there. I was happy, I suppose. We had our little pleasantries and games, particularly in my early days, when there was no television. We did all sorts of things. We used to swap cigarette cards. Georgie James and myself used to stand in an entry, when it was pouring down with rain.

It was one of the old air-raid shelters, with a roof on it, which remained after the war; they used to run and hide in it.

We stood between the walls, which were sort of entries. We had packs of cigarette cards and we'd draw for the highest card. Whoever won had the pick of the other's cards. I found out, after about two years, that George had a secret slip-pocket, where he used to hide 'Drummer Boy', which was our prized possession. And the crafty devil used to hide it off me.

Georgie, a Smethwick garage-owner, recalls: "I first met Pat when I was eleven years old. He moved in two doors away from my house, in Shakespeare Road, to live with his grandma, who was old and infirm. She lived at number 68 - I was at 64. We just palled up. The old man took a shine to him. He said, 'Come and live here,' because Pat's grandma *was* old. He used to come in and have something to eat. One Christmas, when Pat came in for dinner, the old lady," (George's mother), "put him a chicken leg, on his dinner plate, and he picked it up and said: 'Can I wrap this up and give it to my mom, because she hasn't got none?' He used to be at our house an awful lot, and eat with us; sleep over occasionally. He always went back to his nan, because he used to worry about her, even though she was only two doors away.

"I really shouldn't tell you about *some* of the things we used to do! We'd go all down Ledsam Street, of a Sunday morning. Nip in the shops – and nick a few cigarettes – and then I used to go and sell them to me relations. Pat used to keep his eye open, while I did it, because he was tall, wasn't he? Then we'd have a 'split-up' afterwards."

At one time, (although they cringe, simply *thinking* about it now!), Pat and Georgie stole flowers from private gardens, on the Hagley Road. "We'd pick the flowers, get them all bunched up, then stand outside Dudley Road Hospital and sell them," Georgie explains. However, their antics came to an abrupt end! "We'd been up there to get some, and we're both cycling back, down Shakespeare Road. I fell off the bike, the bicycle wheel cut off the flower heads, and all my money fell out of my pockets. They carried me up to the house because I was knocked out. Pat collected all the bits of flowers and the money, took them to my dad, and said: 'This is his.' Of course, the old man wanted to know where all the money had come from - he was a bit strict!

"He had a horse and cart down at the Blue Gate, in Smethwick, at one stage. After that, he used to push a wheelbarrow around the streets of Birmingham, of a Sunday: stopping at all the pubs, selling periwinkles, in Edgbaston, Ladywood, and Smethwick. At the time, they were a 'seller', because you couldn't get them: they were *allocated*, when they bought them, down the Bull Ring. My grandfather would buy them, then boil them in the boiler at the wash house; they used to squeal when you cooked them!

'Pennywinks!' I'd sit there, on the horse and cart, knicking the 'winks' and throwing the empty shells back in, with the rest! You'd scoop them out in a pint glass, and put them into a paper bag - a shilling a pint.

"The way they used to go on in those days - my God! My grandfather wouldn't give me a penny. He once gave me a three-penny bit for Christmas, and they never stopped talking about it for three years! My mum's brothers used to count the loads of money, of a Sunday. They'd all meet, when they finished, and count it out to the old boy; he ruled with a rod of iron. I used to treat the old man, when we went out, with the money I'd knicked!"

Ken Collins describes how the betting slips in Billy Lowndes' betting shop were laid out in neat rows, with winnings placed on top, ready to be wrapped up, for lucky customers. *The Buff* was a popular racing paper, because, unlike some of the others, it was also available during the week. There was also a side entrance to the premises. "When Pat and I had a bet, as teenagers," Georgie explains, "we'd just write it on a piece of paper. The betting shop was a backhouse, about thirty or forty yards down the road. So we'd watch the television, (before anyone realised we'd got one), write the bets out, and Pat would 'leg' it down there. Give it to a bloke called Eddie Callaghan, who was older than us, and lived on the corner of Shakespeare Road. He'd put the bet on and collect the winnings. Then we'd share it out. Eddie couldn't understand why we kept getting winners!" They stood for it about four times times, then realised what was happening. Brian Webb recalls that later, someone else bought a set, involving several others in a similar scam.

Georgie's father must have been doing pretty well; the family's television was the first one in Shakespeare Road. "Yes – he worked seven days a week," recalls Georgie. "He worked in a factory during the week – then on weekends he'd do this other. It was my grandfather, Fred Wilson's business. He used to pay George for going out and selling the 'winks' as well. Fred was my mother's father."

Yeah – Ladywood. I suppose when you think about it, everything that happened there was perfectly normal. I mean, you went to school – like everybody else. My poor old Nan, Amelia, who I lived with, went to work until she was seventy-two, in fact. And you just lived your life. In the evenings, you sat in someone's house, as kids do - perhaps visiting. I remember Raymond Green, who lived in the last house at the top of one of the entries; if he lived fifteen feet from the rail track, that's as much as he lived! We would sit in his room, talking. We couldn't watch television, because there wasn't any. There we'd be, rocking with the vibrations of the train. I dunno, four, five or six hundred-ton of train, whizzing by at ninety miles an hour. It was probably the Royal Scot – that was our number one favourite train.

In those days, we were all train spotters. You'd sit in the room, rocking backwards and forwards, to the vibration of the train. Everything rocked – it was as 'normal' as when we used to go swimming in the canal, which ran parallel with the rail tracks. On odd occasions, I slept at Ray's house. The whole household would wake up with a start, at five o'clock in the morning, (with the exception of me, of course); not because the train whizzed by at ninety miles an hour - all two, four, or six hundred-ton of it - but because it was two or three minutes late. There's some irony in that, isn't there?

The things you used to do down Ladywood: Hopscotch, Tipcat, Marlies ('Glarnies', as we called them). We'd sit outside the pubs, waiting for people to go in or come out. That's where the jollifications were. People always used to be laughing, when they came out of a pub. We never really understood why; we were too young to realise that alcohol stimulated - and gave people all sorts of different senses of freedom and happiness.

Pat has always placed great value upon *genuine* friendship; it's an important feature of his life, and a central theme of our book. If there were a song, capable of capturing the essence of this book, it would be Burt Bacharach's *People*; in particular, the opening verse:

> *People, people who need people,*
> *Are the luckiest people in the world.*
> *We're all children, needing other children*
> *And yet letting our grown-up pride*
> *Hide all the need inside*
> *Acting more like children, than children.*

Following hot-on-its-heels for his theme song, must surely be Rodgers and Hammerstein's *Climb Every Mountain*! Such relationships, with Pat, have always been very much a 'two-way street'; without any prompting, *several* people have emphasised how much they value his friendship. In those early days of his unsettled childhood, he instinctively realised the importance of those friendships that he could *rely* on; they provided a vital support system for him, both physically and emotionally.

The following selection of Ladywood children's street games, has been compiled especially for us, by Ken Collins; no doubt, they were popular in other areas of Britain too:

"There was a game where we all stood in a line; the aim was to find the weakest link, jump on his back and break the line. Some called it 'Molly on the Mop-stick'; the Shakespeare Road boys called it 'Sugar Pudding'. "We also played 'Tip-Cat'," explains Ken. "You chalked a circle in the road, sat on the footpath and threw the 'tip', or the 'cat', into the circle – a shaped piece of wood. If the piece of wood ended up with any part of it touching any part the circle, (you only had one shot), you got the bat – whack! You hit the piece of wood, and then wherever it landed, you had to try to stride from the circle to where the piece of wood had landed. So you'd say to your opponent, if for example it was twenty yards away, you could be facetious and say: 'Five.' Well, it was impossible to do it in five strides. But if you were playing the game as it *should* be played you'd say something like 'Ten.' If they could do it in ten, then it would be their turn to have a go with the bat. There was also marbles – in the gutter.

"Like Georgie and Pat, we'd play card games with cigarette cards (packets of cigarettes in those days, always contained a 'cigarette card'); it would either be about ARP, cricketers, footballers, golfers or other sportsmen. If you found enough cigarette boxes on the ground, you could save the cards and play a game with them. The game I played, was where you stood a card up on one of its ends, leaning the other end against the wall. Each player would have a second card, and you'd flick your card towards the one that was standing up, against the wall. The first one to knock that card down, picked up all the other cards that had been landed around it before."

Pat eventually returned to live with Dolly, his step-brothers, Pete and Rickie and step-father Harry Meakin, in Belgrave Road Balsall Heath, completing his education at Hope Street Secondary School. Pat and Brian remained in touch. "Pat's father had a big house on Hamstead Road. It was like an empty shop, in a row of shops. There was a blonde lady, who must have been his partner." The lady in question was Adele (the mother of Pat's stepsister, 'Frankie').

I used to go down to see him, every Sunday. He lived in Hamstead Road, Handsworth. He'd give me four bob – two, two shillings – two florins, and take me to the pictures. Then I wouldn't see him for another week.

"Pat and I would sometimes walk down there together and visit, at the age of eleven or twelve," explains Brian. "I called Pat's father, 'Uncle Frank'. He'd say: 'How are you? Come on in!' We'd have a cup of tea and a slice of cake. After we'd been fed and watered, he'd put us in the front room, in the abandoned part of the shop and give us a magnet each. He had a box of old scrap cufflinks, and we had to sit there, dipping these magnets into the cufflinks, and anything that stuck to the magnet was put into another box. We'd get fed up with this after a while. Then we'd play at the back of the house, where there were some chicken coops. It was quite safe to *walk* back, in those days – not like it is now."

In the following article, published in Carl Chinn's 'Old Brum' supplement of the Birmingham Mail, 9 September 1996, Brian, (who has very generously granted us permission to reproduce it in this chapter), writes about his 'diamond polisher' (window cleaner) father, Wally Webb, still remembered affectionately by Pat as 'Uncle Wal'.

* * * * *

On the Ladders with Dad

'Just after the war we came to live in Anderton Street, Ladywood. In 1947 the old man, known as Wally Webb, started window cleaning. He built up quite a round. When I was eleven, during the school holidays, he let me help him. I cleaned the downstairs of course. He worked six days a week and loved his pint, so I never really saw much of him until I became his apprentice, and then I got to know him.

He was a short, dapper individual, very fit, had a great sense of humour and became quite popular in old Ladywood. He worked Sherborne Street, the Shipyard in Ledsam Street- a little town on its own – Shakespeare Road, Anderton Street, Alexandra Street, Barker Street, Garbett Street and Nelson Street.

Dad had this uncanny knack of always finishing the pub windows bang on opening time! Then I knew we were finished for the day. I would disappear until closing time, then go back to help take the cart back home. I always felt quite proud coming down Shakespeare Road, in control of the cart, with the old man slightly the worse for wear and a bit wobbly - holding on!

It was a bit rough in the winter, but the people of old Ladywood were great. We could always get a kettle of hot water to wash the leathers and numerous cups of tea. On Saturdays we did Nelson Street, starting at the faggots and peas shop, by Hickman's the greengrocer - that took all day. At 1.30 p.m. the old man went collecting, starting of course with a few quick pints in 'The Edward'. I'd see some sights – especially on Saturday afternoons – when I was left alone with the ladders! Then he'd come back and we'd finish the work. The main collecting time was a Friday evening when dad would always wear a suit, collar and tie and would finish up in 'The Commercial'. His only real 'sports', as he called them, were Crib and Dominoes and he taught me those games at an early age, until I became quite proficient.

I learned a lot with my father: respect for other people and their property, manners and how to handle money. It was a sort of education in itself - getting to know the real people of old Ladywood. Maybe some of your readers will still remember dad – known as Wally Webb – and his young assistant Brian? The son of a diamond polisher.'

*   *   *   *   *

Local author Norman Bartlam, mentioned earlier in the chapter, is also Housing Education Officer for Ladywood and has expert knowledge of the area. He observes: "As a generalisation, people say that Ladywood turned out to be a bit of a slum, but that's only the case in certain streets. Even in the so-called 'backstreets', certain individuals I've come across were extremely proud of their possessions and their particular house. People had still got a lot of respect for themselves, even though the area was in decline." He recalls how, when redevelopment began, in the 1960s, much of the community spirit inevitably disappeared, as people moved away, or were re-housed in tower blocks. He and Pat were eventually involved in the Ladywood Redevelopment Project.

The Smith family lived at 52, Shakespeare Road, Ladywood, just eight doors away from Pat and his grandmother, on the same side of the street. There were three children: Shirley, her sister Pat, and their brother, John. On marriage, Shirley became Shirley Underhill; Pat's married name is Bowen. To avoid confusion between the two Pats, we'll refer to Pat Smith as 'Patricia'. The two sisters were born either side of Pat: Shirley is just a year older than him, and Patricia a year younger. Patricia recalls: "We had a lovely childhood, really, although we didn't have a lot. What I remember about Pat is him wearing his short trousers."

They both recall Pat's grandma, Amelia. During her childhood, spent as a water gypsy, she became deaf, through washing her hair in the canal. "She was a frail little lady really and Pat used to shout and bawl at her," recalls Patricia, "because he knew she couldn't hear him! What I remember about Dolly, his mom, is that she used to wear quite short skirts, above the knee, but she had very muscular legs. She always wore dark clothes." The sisters recall that every now and again, Dolly would visit Pat, in Shakespeare Road, although they never have occasion to speak to her. Shirley confirms: "Pat *had* used to play his Nan up; he'd pull faces, when her back was turned, and shout at her, because she couldn't hear what he was saying. She didn't know that he was 'taking the mickey' out of what she was saying to him! I think he used to do it, more or less, because *we* were there – and he knew we were watching."

Chapter Two –

FROM LADYWOOD TO HOLLYWOOD

"Pat wasn't a quiet boy. I'd say he was a bit mischievous." Although her nieces, Norma Knewport and Carole Bailey, (née Berrington), remember him as being quiet, Josie remains adamant: "I think he was a bit mischievous! He always had that 'whatsit' about him: you could always have a laugh with Pat – it's the way he looks sometimes."

Josie Rudge

Josie Rudge (née Usher), had lived in Shakespeare Road since birth, and was a young married woman, with children, when she first met Pat. She remembers that his gran, who sometimes wore a little black beret, always looked quite smart, even 'regal', but kept herself to herself. "She wasn't a 'down-and-out' person, although you *did* get those kind of people in Shakespeare Road. Amelia was never like that: she was a 'stately' person. Pat used to sit on the low windowsill of the Thomas's - their next-door-neighbours." Her niece, Norma adds: "That's when he had lots of blond curls."

Shirley Underhill, née Smith, recalls: "Amelia would come down the road, do her shopping, or whatever she'd got to do, and then more or less go straight in." Although it was difficult to communicate with Amelia, Brian and Terry Webb managed it, provided she bent her head down close to them. They had a strong incentive: being of a generous nature, she sometimes gave each of them a three-penny bit! Conversely, Shirley comments: "Amelia was a nice lady, but you just couldn't communicate with her, and with us being young – we didn't really understand. I mean, my dad was deaf, but not as bad – through the aeroplanes." Shirley and Patricia were very friendly with Norma's sister, Carole, whose mother, Winnie, was Josie's sister. The two families lived next door to each other, in a backhouse and a front house respectively, each with two bedrooms and an attic.

Patricia spent a lot of time at Carole's. "We used to go over the wall, take a picnic and go train spotting, at nearby Monument Lane Station." She recalls sitting on the railway embankment there, with Carole. Pat enjoyed train spotting too, with Carole's brother, Pete Berrington, and was 'thrilled to bits', when he first saw the Royal Scot.

Most families in the immediate area had little money, although there *were* exceptions. Norma and Carole, like many inner city children, were Means

Tested, then subsequently awarded Birmingham Mail boots and jumpers. The Smiths, however, were more fortunate. Patricia explains: "They used to call us 'The Rich Family'; there were only three cars in the road, at the time - my dad's, another outside Sid Butt's, across the road from where Pat lived, and the bookmaker's car up the road, Billy Lowndes; my dad had two cars. He and my mum worked for the Post Office. He also had a radio shop and used to charge accumulators." Their father eventually closed the shop, when one of his sons died, changing it into a front room, to provide extra living space.

There was no television, just the radio, with 'Much Binding in the Marsh', Dick Barton (Special Agent); 'Billy Cotton's Band-show'; 'Round the Horne', with Kenneth Horne and his group. People used to gather round their radios. That's after we'd gone down to the Smith's accumulator shop, just down the road, to get the accumulator charged up. I always used to think in those days, that an accumulator-driven radio played different music to the electrically powered one; and a battery-driven one played different music again. I didn't realise that it was just a source of power. No one told me!

The Smith's grandmother owned a fish-and-chip shop, at number 86. Patricia recalls: "We had a good gran – she used to buy all our clothes – of a Christmas. Her friend made all our Christmas dresses – in red velvet." Although it's interesting to compare the families who Pat grew up with, those who knew him say that he seemed totally unconcerned about any financial differences between himself and his neighbours. Patricia remembers: "When Pat was young he always used to wear trousers with the knees hanging out, or the soles hanging off his shoes. He used to look really poor, but it never seemed to bother him. He went around and he was friends with everybody. Everybody liked him, so they just used to take no notice; he was just from one of the poor families." There was at least one exception to the rule. Pat recalls that Colin Evans' mum stopped her son from playing with him, on the grounds that he was too scruffy. Patricia adds: "But usually, Pat was a friend of everybody's; alright - he'd got nothing - but we felt sorry for him really."

Shirley explains: "When things were rationed, a woman over the road, called Mrs. Mole, who lived next door to the draper's shop, would come over and ask our mom: 'Do you want to buy some coupons?' Because you could only get a pair of socks, or other clothes, with the books of coupons. As soon as she'd got them, mom would say to us: 'Here you are, go and get yourself a pair of socks from Sid Butts.' Of a Sunday, the shop was supposed to have been shut. But we used to knock on the door, and he'd open it and let us in!"

Pat recalls that the Moles were a very sociable family. Every evening, when the Smiths gran had finished serving fish-and-chips, she used to wrap whatever was left in the chip pan, for Mrs. Mole to give to her children. "Her husband was different again to *Mrs.* Mole," explains Shirley. "He used to be really smart. You could see your reflection in his shoes – they were that highly polished."

Patricia adds: "Then again, I remember going in there. They had a big table – it was clean and scrubbed. All the kids used to go in there, you know? They'd got no milk - just these tins of condensed milk on the table. You used to have that in your tea!"

Shirley visited the *Longbridge Social Club,* just a few weeks before our conversation: ex-residents of Shakespeare Road, and other parts of Ladywood, meet there, including Tony Palmer and Eddie Callaghan (mentioned on page 18 of *If,* and in our previous chapter). Pat said recently that he knew Tony as a boy, but hadn't seen him for fifty plus years!

Sid Butts is a name that crops up several times, in connection with Ladywood. Business must have been good. Many of Pat's neighbours were Sid's customers, although Amelia only bought from him occasionally; what little clothing she could afford, for herself and the family, usually came from one of her favourite haunts, the Rag Market - (or 'Rag Alley', as Dolly calls it) - behind St Martin's Church.

Patricia recalls that, even as a boy, Pat was a budding performer: "He used to tell us a lot of stories that he'd made up. He used to make us laugh – he was a right comedian!" Shirley agrees: "Even if we hadn't been to see the picture, we'd know what it was about! His hands were a-going, you know? We used to all sit on the corner step of *Eborne's,* a sweetshop, on the corner of Alexandra Street and Shakespeare Road. Pat would stand in front of us, telling us all about the different films he'd seen – with the actions. He'd be about twelve or thirteen - he hadn't got a girlfriend at that stage." Although Pat is also a good mimic, it's his comedic and storytelling skills that the two sisters most remember: "He used to come out with these gags – not just the films he'd been to see," Patricia recalls. "He used to make up jokes himself and funny stories – anything to make us laugh."

Research and posterity confirm that this was, indeed, a classic case of 'a chip of the old block'. Pat's cousin, Frank, recalls that his Uncle Frank (Pat's father's) favourite 'party-piece' was *Dangerous Dan McGrew*: "I always remember that – and the way he put it over - reciting at parties. Frank was an entertainer. He'd got all the actions, and was a good speaker." His fellow dealers confirm that he would keep them enthralled for hours at a time, in *Shay's Café,* with various tales – especially about Canada. Pat's cousin, Helen, interjects: "Well, funnily enough, all the Roaches, (if you'd ever met them), were like that – with regard to their attitude – and speaking; the sisters were too … if you'd ever met Nora. They weren't rough, like you might expect in those days. You saw a lot happen in those days, but it never happened to us." According to Pat's cousin, Joyce Taylor, her mother Agnes and Aunt Cissy were also natural performers and musicians. Agnes enjoyed reciting lines from Shakespeare. Dolly was an accomplished storyteller too – as the next chapter reveals. What a pedigree!

Glen explains: "My brother-in-law used to meet Frank when he was home from the forces and go for a drink with him. Wal used to talk about Frank a lot: he was really impressed with him; he thought he was 'the biz'." The family consensus about 'Colonial Walter', is that he was well spoken, with an air of authority about him – a trait which he greatly admired in his Uncle Frank, (Pat's father).

As evidenced by success in his military and police careers, Wal was obliged to be more of a 'systems man' – and more 'correct' than his uncle. Pat's father, as Pat confirms, had less respect for authority. However, according to Glen: "Wal said that he modelled himself on Frank, when he was younger, and was very impressed by the fact that he could keep everyone's attention, for hours."

Geoff Staley's first memories of Pat date from the late 1940s, when Amelia first moved in to Shakespeare Road. Like Brian Webb, Geoff lived around the corner, in Anderton Street. Although he was Pat's senior by two years, he comments: "He was always a bit bigger than me! There was a 'gang' from Anderton Street and a gang from Shakespeare Road. We used to be standing around and all of a sudden, the gang was coming from Shakespeare Road. We'd say: 'OK – let's get going!' We'd all get our dustbin lids and our sticks and we used to fence each other. I don't think we ever drew any blood! It was all just a bit of fun really, although it *seemed* very serious – until Pat came out; then it was: 'Oh - the giant's arrived!'- and we all 'scarpered'. "

Like Patricia and Shirley, he remembers the Moles, (or 'Moulds', as they were sometimes called). "They lived just across the road from Pat, and were ridiculed a bit. We weren't bullies in those days, but we were cruel." Johnny 'Brough' Cloves was a close neighbour of the Moles. He also lived opposite Pat, at 3 back 71, near to Sidney Butt's shop. Johnny's gran's surname was 'Brough' – hence the nickname. Johnny was a similar age to Pat. They shared a common situation, because he lived on and off, with *his* grandmother too.

The Mole family's house fronted on to Shakespeare Road, but Johnny's house was behind that, at the back entrance to the terrace, just three houses away from the railway line. A group of them used to play together, Johnny and Paddy, (as he calls Pat), Ray Green - (he of the vibrating house) - Peter Berrington and Georgie James. If their football went on the railway line, one of them had the pleasure of retrieving it. As if that wasn't dangerous enough, sometimes they'd put a penny on the line! Bill Codling, featured with Pat in an *Evening Mail* article, in 2002, was another train-spotting friend, who used to go to local dances with Pat, when they were youths.

Ken Collins recalls that his access to the railway line was even more hazardous, via the next courtyard down Shakespeare Road, in the direction of Garbett Street. "There was a sheer drop of at least twelve feet. To train-spot you sat on the wall. If you wanted to put a penny on the line, you had to climb over the wall, using the footholds left by perished mortar. The fare from Monument Lane to New Street was a penny, because it was only a short ride. There was a long curving tunnel under St Vincent Street. Once you were in the tunnel, all hell broke loose. You got used to it, because you knew what was coming. It was pitch-black, so for about five minutes, as the train moved slowly towards New Street, kids would be climbing up on luggage racks, and so on - making a real racket!"

There was an air raid shelter next to Monument Road railway station. Although Pat and Peter Berrington often train-spotted as a pair, they would sometimes join the three other boys. According to Pat, they eventually learnt the timetables by heart, and could predict which particular train was about to arrive. They'd watch from the station platform, on some occasions; at other times, from behind the fence.

An entrance to another air raid shelter on Shakespeare Road, doubled as the group's goalpost. The boys played football and a simple form of cricket (with a proper bat) on the 'rec'; it didn't have a blade of grass, but was a good-sized, rectangular tarmac area, stretching from lower Anderton Street to Goodman Street. It was also a regular meeting place for rival gangs, including those from Shakespeare Road, St Mark's Street, and Garbett Street. They had no cricket stumps, so a lamp-post became their substitute target.

Johnny particularly remembers Yates's General Store, run by Bill Yates and his wife. Sandy and David were their sons. It was down the hill from Pat's, just before Anderton Street, four doors away from the Smiths' accumulator shop. Pete's grandfather, George Usher, told him that everything in the store cost half-a-crown: "I must have been about eleven or twelve then. I couldn't wait to get to work, to get half-a-crown, so that I could empty the shop!"

According to Pat's cousin, John Bevis: "Bill Yates told me that Pat rescued them, when the store was on fire. He said, luckily Pat was passing at the time. He bust down the front door, and went in. The Yates's moved to Quinton after that - either at the same time as us, or just afterwards."

Johnny 'Brough' Cloves got on well with Paddy, describing him as 'good-natured and friendly'. He recalls: "At one time Paddy kept white fantail pigeons in his gran's backyard. Mrs. Thomas, (whose low windowsill he sat on) lived in the house behind Amelia, at the back of the terrace, and used to shout at Paddy, because the pigeon droppings ruined her nice clean washing!"

Geoff recalls buying clothes from Sidney on the 'Never-never'. "You could go and get yourself a new shirt from there and pay it off weekly." One of Rose Collins' many jobs was collecting these payments. Ken explains: "My mother used to collect the monies, when people bought things 'on the strap'. They'd perhaps pay half-a-crown or five shillings a week for the goods. She had the same kind or arrangement, as a clothing agent, with a shop in Icknield Street called *The Mrs. Williams'*." Enterprising Rose found additional time to sell 'football tickets' to various people - promotional cards that newspapers would sell for 3d or 6d each, in order to boost sales. When the perforated top and sides were removed, if the numbers inside matched those published in the newspaper, the purchaser won a cash prize. Ken and his sister Jean would visit people's houses, helping Rose to run the scheme. She'd also come home for tea, from her factory job, then serve as a part-time barmaid at the *White Hart* public house, in Paradise Street, in Birmingham City Centre, until closing time.

Geoff Staley retains painful memories of the gratings outside Pat's house. "Shakespeare Road was a hill, as you know, and we used to run down, from Monument Road, and 'follow the leader'. I remember, we were doing that, and I went straight down Pat's granny's coal cellar and wor! - it hurt - because it took the skin of my knees and my legs! It had chains on it, so that no one got down to rob her meter. The coalman hadn't put it back right. His granny came out and bathed my leg. I was worried about getting a clip round the ear'ole for doing it!" Pat remembers that the gratings were quite fragile. Geoff adds: "They were cast iron, but they could break, with old age; some of the houses had been built in the 1800s."

Pat's cousin, John, recalls visiting Amelia, in Shakespeare Road. "Whenever I was up there, (it was usually the weekend), she'd give me gigantic jam sandwiches. She sliced the loaves up with a knife. She was very friendly, and she'd always got something cooking, on the old Triplex grate; they're collector's pieces now. Sometimes you'd get bits of ash that had come down the chimney, floating in whatever she was cooking. Where the coal fire was, in the middle, were old black grates. On either side of the fire were hotplates. The heat from the fire heated the metal hotplates, which were used to cook the food.

"She didn't have a proper kitchen. As you came through the front door, there was a section on the left, where Pat and Doreen ended up living. You'd go through the door this way; the Triplex grate was in that room. You'd go through a door at the side, towards the back, and that's where her sink would be. She had a main room, containing the grate and a living room area, with a table, and places to sit, and chickens out the back." On photographs, Amelia's house is double-fronted, so from the outside, it looks larger than the neighbouring houses, but, as Pat confirms, it had a fairly small interior. John recalls that when Amelia didn't have enough grit for the chickens, the eggs sometimes came out a peculiar shape!

Pat was too young to remember the VE Day celebrations, but Ken recalls that the heat from the party bonfire was so intense, it threatened to crack the windows, so wet sacking was placed over them for protection. A few 'merry' locals emerged from *The Commercial*. One of their number, Freddie Brookes, decided it would be great fun to walk through the dying embers of the fire. Sid Butts was collared, before he could do the same!

"We had Fancy Dress competitions," explains Geoff. "The yanks were there. I was a dumb blonde and my friend, Ray Whitehouse, was dressed up as 'Yank's Fancy'." Eight-year-old Shirley Smith, as 'Mrs. Mop', paraded the streets, carnival-style, with the other costumed residents. "All the Americans came to the party later, from the Ice Rink," continues Geoff. "They used to come to the Rink; we'd sit on the steps and ask them: 'Have you got any gum, chum?' "

In our first book, Pat asked an American the same question – very politely, outside the Ice Rink. "The other thing we used to say to them was: 'Can you change us a penny – for two halfpennies?' Well, they'd give you the penny," recalls Geoff, "but never take the halfpennies. So you'd sit on the steps all night and get yourself about five or six pennies. You could do a lot with that. With no disrespect to anybody, they were the first coloured people that we saw. There were quite a few GIs who were coloured men, and they were very nice people. You'd go back home and say: 'Have you seen that coloured man, up the road?' "

Geoff describes the Ladywood residents of the 1940s and 50s as, "very good, very friendly - doors open." Like many children during that era, his mum was a single parent: "My father died in the navy, having come out of an orphanage – believe-it-or-not! But then that's my story. He got killed in the navy; he was in, twelve-months-to-the-day. He was killed on HMS Neptune, in 1941- seven hundred and fifty died.

"The old Birmingham Mail boots started about then. I can remember having cardboard in my shoes. Monday morning, before I went to school, we used to go to the pawnbroker's. The lady who ran it, Mrs. Craddock, entrusted me with the takings from the shop, over the weekend. I used to take it up to the bank down Spring Hill.

"I knew Pat, as a boy, from playing in the street. He was obviously a big lad; it was particularly noticeable, as he was still wearing short trousers. Like Pat, I'd got holes in my trousers and all that sort of thing. We hadn't got anything. My mother was working on munitions. A lot of us had fathers who went to war and never came back."

Pat's been described as being 'tall and skinny', when he was a youth, before he started his weight training. "Oh yes – he wasn't muscular," recalls Geoff. "As you came round the corner from Pat's house, into the top end of Anderton Street, on the right-hand side – which would be the last house in Anderton Street, a man named Mr. Blakemore used to do us lantern slides, until the end of the 40s. You couldn't afford the pictures – if there were any on at the time. But he had this 'Magic Lantern'. We all used to crowd into his one room, downstairs, and he'd put these slides across - it was a halfpenny." Pat moved from his Nan's, back to his mom's house in Balsall Heath, from time to time. "I remember that, as a lad, he'd disappear, every now and again," comments Geoff.

He has similar post-magic lantern cinema experiences to Pat, Brian and other local children. "You all came out, on the horse, slapping your bum, along Spring Hill, on the Parade. We'd have a stick of liquorice root, or a bit of 'kali' – stick your finger in! I might have been a bit worse than Pat, because we used to run along, with a nail on a stick, push it into the apple, then run on! That was at Hickman's, the vegetable shop on the corner of Nelson Street. We'd get caught and slapped - in the days when anyone could slap you for doing something. We went to the *Lyric*, in Edward Street; the *Ledsam (New Regent)* in Ledsam Street, was called 'the Flea-pit', so we didn't go there very often, because we'd got enough fleas of our own! We went to the *Crown*, in Icknield Port Road, and we even went down to Hockley, to the *Palladium* – and the *Edgbaston Picture House* – at the top." Ken Collins recalls: "The curtains at the *New Regent* were raised manually, so we knew the film was about to start, when the curtain raiser came out on stage."

Geoff Staley used to be a racer at the Ice Rink, with the *Birmingham Mohawks*. "I'd be sixteen when I joined. We were speed skaters; that was from about 1952 to 54. The *Mohawks* came from all over; the trainer was from the Jewellery Quarter. There were about twenty-odd of us – all boys. I was doing quite well at the time, but then they whipped me into the army. Ray Harris, a lad in our entry, at 10 back of 64, was Area Midland Junior Champion, at figure skating and dancing. We wore tights and American jackets, raced at events all over the country, and did barrel jumping. The fancy work was done by the dancers. We were involved purely with speed racing: going round and round the ring, at high speed. They still do it – in the Olympics. I remember Shirley Smith. She lived just below Pat, on the corner, just before you come into Anderton Street. It didn't have a proper shop front. Her father sold accumulators in there and fiddled with radios."

I was brushing my teeth. I put plenty of toothpaste on the toothbrush – and I made a really big thing about it. I must have been cleaning my teeth for about four or five minutes. And after I thought I'd had enough of that, I spit the toothpaste out of my mouth – into the gutter. 'What a strange thing,' you might think. 'What was he doing?'

Well, the day before, at school, we'd received parcels from kids in America. There were all sorts of things in those parcels. We should have had one each, but of course, we didn't; we shared one between four of us. We were never that lucky: we always had bits and pieces. And what did I get? A toothbrush and toothpaste. I hadn't had one before.

So I was stood in Shakespeare Road, Ladywood, outside Sidney Butt's drapers shop – cleaning my teeth in the street. It's a thing I always remember. What an awful thing to do. But I thought it was great!

Peter Berrington went to a different school to me (he went to Osler Street School). I very quickly told him about my toothbrush. I think on more than one occasion, I lent it to him, provided that he didn't have too big a squeeze of my toothpaste tube… because we were great pals.

Norma and Carole explain that, unbelievably, soot was used before toothpaste was in common use; if you were very posh, you combined it with a bit of salt! They lived with their brother, Peter, and the family at 2 back 53 Shakespeare Road. "All my life I had asthma," Pete explains. "So much so, that when I was about ten or eleven, I couldn't even walk to the door. I remember going from our house up Shakespeare Road, to our doctor's, in Monument Road. It would be no more than a mile, with my mother: good as gold - well missed - I'll tell you! We used to say: 'I've been up the Mono' - that's what they called Monument Road. There was an outdoor shop up there, past the Bridge pub, and you could go in there and have a halfpenny or penny pop, called a Vantas. I remember Pat being in there with me; they used to do toffee apples as well." We return to the same shop, in Chapter 5, when Pat becomes involved in a street fight.

We used to walk up the road to the shop that Pete's referring to - the Parker's shop; a brother and sister ran it. As they sold penny pops, we'd walk in with our two-pence and say: "Two penny pops for Pete and Pat please 'Park'." (We thought it was funny because we used all the p's). He'd look at us. We'd say it faster and faster and faster; we used to think it was ever so funny. It wasn't really - but we thought it was!

Pete has a brother, Robert, in addition to his two sisters, Norma and Carole. He describes Pat as: "Big, tough: he was a forerunner, if you like, of the 'Gentle Giant'. From what I could gather, from our early days, he always seemed to be *working*. His dad was in scrap. I went over there, but I used to think his dad never really liked me.

"Paddy used to come over and sleep on our mom, Winnie's floor, when we'd had a night out. I think he'd be about twelve." Pete's Aunt Josie remembers the two boys sleeping in the attic, at her sister's: "They were always freezing cold, because there was no fire – no heating – only a gas mantle for a light." Peter continues: "We were that cold, we were heaping up blankets over us, and ended up with a big army coat chucked over us, to keep us warm. Pat used to yank the clothes off me! The coat was very damp." Winnie's husband was in the navy, during the war, so it may have been his coat, although they could also be bought from the Army and Navy Stores. "We'd have a good laugh!" recalls Pete. "We'd be up half the night talking – about what's going on and all that. I can remember we made jam sandwiches, and in the morning our dad had got no bread for his own."

Pete's sisters reckon that he and Pat were 'two-of-a-kind', because, as the shop episode illustrates, they shared a great sense of humour. They use the expression, 'joined-at-the-hip', to describe the close friendship that existed between Pat and Pete - ('two P's in a pod' would be considerably cornier!) Humour seems to have run in the Berrington family. Their father, Charles, Edward, Joseph, used to pretend that they were all on board ship. Pete recalls:

"We'd swing the lamp in our house – when we talked about the war. Dad would tell us about when he was up in the Atlantic Convoy, and my mother used to swing the lamp!"

Pete reinforces Josie's opinion of Pat: "Our mom used to think he was lovely: he was so kind to her; he used to pick her up and give her a 'smackeroo'. She loved it – she *always* liked him! We'd go down, Steward Street School when we were kids of about eleven." According to Brian, the playground and building remain, although nowadays it's used for training purposes.

"At dinnertime," continues Pete, "one of his relations, from way back, worked in the kitchens. Paddy used to say to me: 'You sit on the step there.' His relation would say to me: 'You come in here son and have something to eat!' I found out afterwards that Paddy told her I was an orphan – so she used to feed me better than she fed him!" He recalls coming out of the *Lyric Cinema*, in Edward Street, with Pat. As they turned the corner, near the Parade, they saw Mickey Mole, who'd been put in charge of the milkman's horse and cart. "Something sparked off and the horse bolted straight across the road and through the window of a shop!"

In those days, you could stand at the top of a road in Ladywood, and see one vehicle in the whole street. In Shakespeare Road, (which, from the top of the hill, right the way down, I bet, would be three-quarters of a mile), the only privately-owned vehicle you could see, apart from the Smith's, was parked on the right, and belonged to Billy Lowndes, the bookie. A little while later, somebody got an XWD Commer Van, and painted it silver; apparently, this was the only coating of paint that would cover the army colours properly.

You were happy because that's how you lived – that's what you did. That's why we sat outside the pubs, because people would come out smiling and laughing; they used to sing in there – and I suppose they danced as well. You were drawn to the pub. You'd never heard of the word 'stimulant', at the time, but that's what the attraction was; that's where people had a good time – that's where they laughed; that's where they enjoyed themselves. So this is why you were naturally drawn there. At on time, there was virtually a pub on every corner – and 'outdoors' – or whatever.

Josie Rudge, Norma and Carole give the following, combined description, of their section of Shakespeare Road: "Across the road, opposite Pat's, was Cutler's newsagents, Taylor's the sweetshop, Coleman's hardware shop - that sold paraffin. Then there was Sid Butt's. Leading up to Pat's, from Anderton Street, there was the tailor's, the accumulator shop, the butcher's – Redding's, the cobbler's shop and then Yates's. There were four houses before the entry where Pat's Nan lived, so Pat lived four houses past the shops. Going up from Pat's was the Outdoor, Lowndes the bookmakers, Mason's, and 'Wil' Smith's fish shop." (Wil was Shirley and Patricia's grandfather. When Shirley was three, he collapsed and died, in the shop). "Then a sweet shop where they had the old Vantas machine. From there, you'd got about six houses before you came to Monument Road, with a cigarette shop on the corner." So there was an abundance of pubs - and definitely no shortage of shops!

The general consensus seems to be that Pat was friendly, with no malice about him. Josie never saw him in a temper. Norma mentioned the softness of his voice. Josie added: "He's not broad Brummie like us!" Carole remembers: "Pat cracked our 'loo' seat, when he was about nine or ten, just by sitting on it! He must have been heavy."

Josie comments: "Considering where Pat started from, I think he's done very well. He started from nothing and he's done it all on his own, because there was nobody there to help him, was there?" Given a similar start in life, some people might have gone under, and taken a more cynical view of life. But with Pat, his disadvantages spurred him on. Josie adds: "I think it's about *determination*, with Ladywood people: we've all got this – if we put our mind to it and we say we'll do it – we'll do it!"

In the very early days, I wanted to be a guardsman, because I loved marching bands, and could see myself up there, with the Coldstream Guards - second-to-none. Then I went through a phase when I wanted to be a stoker. Can you imagine it? The imagination of the boy! I actually wanted to be on board a ship, stoking coal, in order to travel, of course. The nearest I came to that was when I became a coalman at Sheepcote Street Wharf, enabling me to get my driving license, at seventeen.

The picture of Pat that emerges, is of an industrious, affectionate and intelligent boy who, as a general rule, seemed unperturbed by the circumstances of his childhood, or that his backside might be out of his trousers; he seemed to take everything in his stride. He was courageous, particularly for his age, and would speak up for himself. He wouldn't let anyone 'clown' on him. If somebody challenged him, initially he would often walk away from the situation; not because he was frightened; he was simply being cautious. But if the same thing happened again, he'd fix them with a look – and that person would, by all accounts, back off.

Shirley Underhill concludes: "Looking at him as a child, you would never have thought that he would get on as well as he did. And he *has* made a really good name for himself: sport, films, television; he had the Fitness Club as well. We were a well-to-do family at the time, compared to him, but he's got *everything* now. He's by-passed us, because he's done so well."

Only two decades later, Pat had made the amazing transition from Ladywood to Hollywood! The boy from the backstreets had booked himself into the luxurious *Flamingo Hotel*, on Ocean Boulevard, in Los Angeles, following wrestling tournaments in Berlin. A few months before, he'd been playing the role of Toole, opposite Ryan O'Neal, in Stanley Kubrick's 1975 classic, *Barry Lyndon*. Stanley seems to have been impressed, and subsequently promised to help Pat establish further contacts in Hollywood – a place he was destined to visit several times.

Sure enough, all those months later, Stanley was true to his word. He was a very sensitive person, contrary to what some people might say. He'd made the phone call and put me in touch with the feature film casting director at Burbank Studios – Alan Shane - a prime example of the type of man he really was. He also put me in touch with the best agency in Los Angeles. That went pear-shaped because the guy he got in touch with was leaving the agency and setting up by himself, but is now the biggest agent in Hollywood. But Stanley still took the time to do that. I owe a lot to him.

In February 1988, an article in the Birmingham press announced that Pat had a key role in a Hollywood movie entitled *Willow*. It was described as 'an excellent film' and Pat was referred to as 'a Hollywood heavyweight'. George Lucas was the producer and the director was Ron Howard - Richie in *Happy Days*. It cost £30 million to produce. Pat also *wrestled* at the top venues in Hollywood.

Steven Spielberg once admitted to me, on and about the time I was wrestling at the Olympic Auditorium, on 15th and Grand in Hollywood, that he actually stood at the stage door, collecting autographs – having already directed his first film. I respect him very much for that.

At one stage, Pat's agent, Peter Charlesworth, suggested that Pat should actually *move* to Hollywood. At the time, his acting and wrestling career was very much in the ascendancy, taking him all over the world.

We'd hit the right note; Peter said we should go on to do bigger and better things. I got to the stage where we just never stopped: I just went from one thing to another; things were looking better and better.

However, the 'Hollywood Heavyweight' decided against the move, and to this day, is certain that he made the right decision.

The number one thing I've done in my career is, having done individually separately, all these things, I resorted back to no boots on my feet and my arse hanging out - and fish and chips. I was invited to go and live in Hollywood and never went. The most impressive thing to me, about my career, is to always be able to come back from London or abroad – and just return to normal each time.

Chapter Three –

A HORSE FOR BREAKFAST

While I was living in Belgrave Road, Balsall Heath, I attended Hope Street School, which backed onto St Luke's Road. The school went straight through the block. St Luke's Road, where the Jewish school was situated, was at the bottom of Varna Road. A large Jewish contingent lived around Balsall Heath, bordering on Edgbaston – by Cannon Hill Park and Bristol Street.

Dolly had been granted a legal separation from Frank; Lady Cadbury was the presiding magistrate. Dolly recalls that Frank was so angry about the situation, that she had to be taken surreptitiously out of court, by a back door and offered police protection: a policeman cycled round each evening to Garbett Street, to make sure that she was safe. "Then Pat 'mucked-in' with Aunt Hilda and his cousins," she explains. "I was going away, because I'd got to duck-and-dive from Frank Roach." This appears to tie in with the traumatic hat and coat burning incident, described by Pat in the previous chapter.

According to Dolly: "In 1944 I got together with my friend Gladys Scott, who was a widow, and we rented a house in Belgrave Road." Gladys' daughter, Jean Newbould, is able to give us a first-hand account of events. "When I came home from being evacuated, for five years, my mum was living in a bed-sitter down Summerhill Terrace, off the Parade, with my sister Eileen, and Dolly was living with her mother. We learned about this house, which was a pound a week – a tremendous amount. So Dolly asked mum if she'd go 'half-whacks'."

"Perry & Deakin advertised the house," recalls Dolly. "I was working at the 'Speedo Wilmott' at the time," (her nickname for Wilmot Breeden)! "I took all my pay-slips to the agents to show I had a regular wage coming in. We let a neighbour's daughter have the first house we were offered, because she was pregnant. So I thought I'd had the brush-off - that's probably the last I'd heard of that! The estate agent sent for me and told me he'd got *another* house for £1-00 a week. I couldn't afford a quid – I was separated from my husband."

Gladys and Dolly had been friends for some time, before the two families moved in together. Jean Newbould refers to Pat as 'Paddy' throughout: "He was always Paddy to me. There were five of us in the house altogether, when we first moved in. Paddy was about seven years old. Mum and Dolly went out to work, and I had to bring Paddy home from school with me - I'm five or six years older than him."

While Pat and Dolly were moving into Belgrave Road, Pat's cousin Walter, included on the Family Tree in *If*, was serving in Palestine. A caption on the reverse of an army photo reads: 'Trying to look smart, without cap!' A second photo featuring him on Cavalry Parade, was taken on 4 October 1944. Someone who appears to be a French army officer is escorting a dignitary, or possibly a high-ranking Civil Servant, on troop inspection. According to the family, the photograph was given to Walter, unofficially – probably sneaked out by the person who wrote the note!

The back row consists, ostensibly, of native cavalry soldiers. Walter's younger brother, Frank comments: "They look like Palestinian Cavalry soldiers. They *are* native, because Palestine didn't erupt until 1948, and in 1948, my brother was the last one to leave Palestine." Tom's wife, Glen, adds that by pure coincidence, "My brother-in-law was on the last ship to leave, and he probably took Walter off!"

"Walter told me that as they left Palestine, they put Arabs in charge, at each police station," explains Frank, "but that they stood no chance; they just had a few guns, and when the British went down the road, the Israelis took over. My brother has always said that he had friends amongst both the Arabs and the Jews, but his name came up, and he had to get out quickly. He was one of the last to leave."

Back in *relative* safety, Jean Newbould and her family continued to share the Balsall Heath house with Dolly and Pat, until 1949, when Paddy was twelve years old. Dolly gave him a special birthday party in the back garden, one year. "It was a large house, with a front room, middle room, kitchen and a long hall and was on three levels," recalls Jean. "There was a staircase going up to the first landing, which had a front and back bedroom. More stairs up to the attic: one big attic and one small attic – the type of house that people called 'attic-high'. It also had cellars. There was a cellar going underneath each of the rooms. You went down the cellar steps; we had coal down there and the gas meter. When we first moved in, there was only gas in the two downstairs rooms, that Dolly and mum used, and the hall and kitchen." Pat had the back bedroom, on the first landing.

"I had to collect Paddy from school and feed him. I used to make him pancakes, with flour and water. Can you imagine anything so horrible? He loved them, but I didn't!"

It's perhaps difficult to imagine, in our 21st Century, centrally heated world, but there was no heating whatsoever upstairs! Candlelight may *sound* quite romantic, but in those days, Pat and his fellow residents were *obliged* to light their way to bed with candles. It conjures up a graphic picture of spooky shadows on the wall!

Their home was about the third house down from Varna Road – an area notorious for its prostitutes. Dolly explains: " Not only had I got to duck-and-dive from my husband, but we had to run from the blokes on the street corners! It was opposite Alexandra Road and Princess Road. Going to work, I caught the bus round on Sherlock Street, to go to the Jewellery Quarter. Wilmot Breeden was by the fire station, in Albion Street.

"Harry Meakin was always at the bus stop. I thought, 'I wonder who that is?' Wasn't my style. Harry got on the same bus. I was blonde then, Mary Pickford curls - very smart - big lashes, big eyes: I've ruined them now - I haven't got any – they've all gone! Any road, he picked up his pluck while we were waiting for the bus back to Belgrave Road and told me he was one of the Meakins. 'Will you come and have a drink with me?' I said: 'Oh no!' Harry said: 'I can bring a friend for *your* friend – we know Gladys.' "

Unlike Pat's ex-army heavyweight boxing champion father, Frank Roach, Harry was of medium height. "He had beautiful eyes," explained Dolly, "but he'd got a slit down his nose. He was a polisher; a basket went round the mop, on a polishing lathe - and slit his nose. I'll never forget - we took our momma to see my new boyfriend." Dolly doesn't refer to her mother as 'Amelia'. "No – mommy! She never had a momma's love – no brothers or sisters; she'd got no aunties or uncles.

"My sister Freda lived in Monument Road, with our father, Bill Bevis. The three of us went into the Bridge pub, in Ladywood. I introduced Harry and he went up to get the drinks. Being deaf, momma shouted: 'Oh our Doris, what's he done to his nose?' Everybody looked – imagine it!"

Albert Townsend was the oldest of a family of ten children, who were well known in the Balsall Heath area, living in nearby Princess Road. His memories pre-date Pat and Dolly's by several years, and provide an interesting contrast. "In my formative years," he remembers, "the southern part – Princess Road, Belgrave Road, Varna Road, was primarily a Jewish family area. I used to have a paper round, but also did small jobs on Saturday mornings for the Jewish families, who observed Saturdays as their Sabbath. This included lighting fires in their houses, in Princess Road." The Townsends were a Christian family, living right in the middle of a Jewish community. As an adult, Pat was to meet many of what he calls the 'Liberal Jewish Crowd'.

Tony Green, a good friend of mine, who I trained with for many years, comes from a family of Lithuanian Jews. I also had a friend whose family name itself, Gurovitch, reminds me of the sheer strength of the race.

Roy O'Neill explains: "Tony had a place down town, originally, which he sold to Alan Solinger – who's got the coffee house opposite now: (he's noted for his breakfasts there). He had *Mister Egg* in Hurst Street, at one time. Tony sold, bedding, towels and sheets, and so on, in a big warehouse, in Tenby Street North, but he moved *years* ago from there - to that road that goes up to Dudley Road Hospital."

Following in his father's footsteps, Albert initially trained as a sheet metal worker when he left Hope Street School, later becoming a more skilled craftsman. Albert recalls: "We used to enjoy Balsall Heath. It was at the edge of Cannon Hill Park and you also had Calthorpe Park. As I remember, it was a very nice area to live in." Pat doesn't dispute the fact.

Shortly before we moved there, it was a well-kept area, with lovely big houses where maids were seen on the steps. Then we moved in - and brought the area down!

"When I first met him, Harry was living about seven houses up Belgrave Road, before you come to Bristol Road," Dolly explains. "His daddy, Mr. Meakin, was friends with Mr. Brown who lived next door but one. Mrs. Darling lived next to me. Me and Gladys dressed Mr. Brown and Mr. Meakin up with high heels, earrings, a turban and a dress and made them tuck their trousers up, for VE Day, in May 1945. They took a gang of kids all round, and gave them a treat.

"I lived with Harry (who I've got Pete Meakin and Rick Meakin by) for a lifetime - from when I was twenty-nine. He was a clever man, but violent – when he'd had a pint. Paddy was seven when I got with him - he was with us, on and off, 'til he was a teenager; he and Harry did some good scrap deals together." Frank Roach and Harry were both scrap dealers, each plying their trade by means of a horse and cart, the motor car being too much of a luxury for the average working class man.

Recalling Pat's childhood, Dolly makes the point that although he had many neighbourhood friends, he was more like an only child. Rickie was born the day before Pat's ninth birthday, on 18 May 1946, and Peter in December 1948, when Pat was eleven. "I had my two other sons in eighteen months and they were happier children than Pat, because they'd got one another."

Although, at times, life must have been very lonely for him, his mother remembers him as a very kind-natured boy. "Pat used to fetch me a loaf and run errands. He'd say: 'Shut your eyes mom, hold your hands out,' and put a loaf in, when he was a lad." Had she known that he was buying the loaf? "No. Very kind – loved animals – believed in God. His father, Frank Roach, thought the world of him." Pat's description of certain neighbourhood escapades sounds like a scene from *Porterhouse Blue*!

My mother, and next-door-neighbours - Mrs Doyle on the one side and Mrs Brown on the other side of Mrs Doyle, used to take it in turns every evening to go down the passageway at the back of the houses - with a stick. They were rather big old houses – six rooms – with big long gardens and a passageway – not a driveway – down the back. They had a paper bag and they used to pick up all the contraceptives, so that us kids wouldn't get hold of them and start playing with them – blowing them up as balloons, or whatever!

They used to take it in turns. My old mom tried putting them down the toilets – silly old sausage! And of course, they wouldn't go down. So eventually she had to get them all out again and bury them. I think they were scared to put them in the dustbins, in case the dustbin men thought badly of them – thought they were prostitutes! So they got their husbands to dig a hole and bury them.

"I lived with Harry Meakin," explains Dolly, "but his love was so great, he broke me spirit. I couldn't look left or right. He got drunk. The kids couldn't look at the telly – they had a terrible life, when they were schoolchildren. 'Television-mad baskets', he called them. When he was drunk he used to say: 'I'll kick it in!' I'd put the big chair on him then, and we all had to run out – terrible!"

Understandably, I wasn't too happy about my stepfather. I moved back to my grandmother's again - when I was about ten. I just turned up at her house. I remember that she said, when I walked in through the door: "Go on, get off. I don't want you!" Somehow or other I smoothed things over between the two of us and moved back with her into Shakespeare Road, then went off to Steward Street School.

"She kept him, when I went back to the Wilmott," Dolly explains. "I paid fifteen bob a week to a woman over in the Scarlet Building, to look after him. Because there was no other children there I didn't want him abused or ill treated, or locked up. Momma loved him. She used to go down the market, after a full week's work in the factory – up until Friday. She loved the Market; she never failed going down the Rag Alley weekly, and brought plenty of food back. She'd bring all of us summat to wear – second-hand. Something happened to the market, in the late fifties, and lo and behold, they had to close it. That coincided with when momma was took ill. We *swear* she died with the market – when it closed. Golden – our mom."

In 1950, Dolly took her sons on holiday. She was thirty-five years of age. A photograph, taken on the beach, shows Dolly, pretending to play her 'stays', like an accordion! Her Belgrave Road address is written on the back. Dolly recollects: "Harry Meakin was jealous about us going with the kids on holiday, so I gave that particular holiday photograph to Mrs. Dale to hide; Freda was with me, because I didn't want Harry to see it.

"They used to sing 'Hello Dolly' in the *Grapes*, to tease Harry, or 'Good-bye Dolly I must leave you' (sings the first line). He was no fool: he'd sit me on a stool by the bar – away from the lads. They all knew how jealous he was. He played dominoes there with his friends. He'd say: 'Nice thing ain't it, when Ray Fine fancied you!' I'd say: 'What do you mean? Nothing of the sort!' Oh the language between us –always terribly jealous. But I was never unfaithful to him – never. As true as God's in heaven – and God knows I wouldn't tell a lie."

Jean recalls: "We used to have marvellous parties at the house – marvellous 'knees-ups' and get-togethers! They were on a Friday or Saturday night; they had them on the weekend, because of getting up for work during the week. We were supposed to go to bed, but my sister had a beautiful singing voice. So we'd creep down the stairs. Paddy was a good boy – he stayed in bed. One of the guests would see Eileen and say, 'Oh come and give us a song Eileen,' and of course, little Jean would follow in behind! My sister was nineteen months older than me." Coincidentally, almost sixty years later, in July 2002, two of Eileen's daughters visited us at a Northfield book signing.

Jean discovered that Dolly and her family had a very affectionate nickname for Amelia:

"They used to call her 'Feely', because she was only little, and she couldn't see the shelf, so she used to put her hands along, to see if there were any objects she wanted, or loose change!" Brian Webb recalls calling her 'Auntie Feely' - without understanding why!

Her son, Charlie, later included the name 'Feely' on Amelia's Handsworth tombstone.

Jean met Amelia occasionally, accompanying Paddy when he visited her. "I also went with him to his dad's scrap-yard in Handsworth. My father died when I was two, so all father figures were wonderful to me. I told Dolly recently that I remember Frank coming to Belgrave Road, and showing us how to balance a broom on our nose and forehead! He always made us welcome when we went to his shop. Paddy and I would go there on the bus, every now and again."

During the afternoons after school, when Jean had sole charge of Pat and gave him his tea, there would have been ample opportunity for them to have a chat, play games, and socialise. But it didn't quite work out that way! "I don't think I had much patience with him, to be honest. I was getting to be a teenager; you know what teenagers are like!

"The thing I *do* remember is that we had to go down to the cellar, to put a penny in the meter – if the gas ran out. I used to grab hold of Paddy and make him go down with me. I wouldn't go down on my own, because it was, as I say, two big cellars. I used to get a long piece of paper, light it, throw it to the bottom of the stairs, and then put the money in.

"One particular day we went down, I was trying to put the penny in the slot. The more I looked round for the slot, the more I couldn't find it. I realised that the front of it was missing, which meant that somebody had robbed the gas meter. I thought to myself, 'he might still be down there' – whoever had done it. So I just let go of Paddy and ran and left him! I ran up the stairs and he's running up behind me shouting: 'What's the matter? What's the matter!' I grabbed him, shut the door and bolted it. Then I ran out into the back garden and told one of the neighbours what had happened."

Jean's future husband, Bernard Newbould, lived with his family, in the same street. Pat attended school with Bernard's foster brother, Brian McDowell. Bernard confirms that "Paddy was a normal boy." "I don't think I've ever known him to be cheeky – he'd never cheek my mom anyway," explains

Jean. "Sharing the house together I would have been aware of any problems like that. I don't think I ever remember his mom having to shout and bawl at him." She and Bernard also recall that Pat had a good sense of humour.

Jean speaks highly of Dolly: "She used to tell me the most wonderful stories! Absolutely *wonderful*: they'd make you cry, some of them, and some you'd laugh at; some of them would make your hair stand on end! She used to make them up as she was going along. One of the stories she told us was that *she* was a gypsy princess. Frank rode in on his white charger, grabbed her up and carried her off. She fell in love with him, and all that. Paddy took that *very* seriously.

"I did for a while. Then I got to thinking about it. One day we were having a bit of an argument. Paddy upset me over something or other, and I said to him: 'Your mom *wasn't* a gypsy and your dad *didn't* ride into the camp.' It broke his heart, it did!" There's a portrait photograph of Dolly at the front of *If* – as the book is dedicated to her. Above the photograph is the word 'Ma'; underneath, Pat has added the caption: "Queen of the Gypsies?" It's a long-standing family joke, dating back to this time when Dolly used to tease Pat about being 'Queen of the Gypsies' herself - on the grounds that her mother really *was* a gypsy. Jean hadn't been aware of Amelia's background, but recalls: "Dolly used to read the cups – tea leaves. We'd sit there for ages – just listening to the tales. She taught us a couple of things about the way the tea leaves lay in the cup.

"There were so many people coming and going. It was Open House," explains Jean. "Everybody loved to come in, to be with Dolly, and talk to Dolly. There were all sorts of people. She was the one person in the road who everyone could turn to, if they needed help." Bernard recalls that Dolly used to "get night-runs up - in charabancs - trips out to places, for the whole street." "That's how Bernard and I got back together," Jean recalls. "We used to go out and then we separated. We went on a 'night-run' down to the *Old Dun Cow* I think it was, in Coventry. So I blame Dolly - she got us back together again!"

Harry Meakin arrived on the scene, some time after they moved in. "I remember him bringing a horse home once! He bought it from somebody. I got up first thing in the morning, to get ready for work, and there was a horse in the kitchen. Nobody would believe me! I tried to get to the sink – but I was screaming. My mom came down and said: 'What's the matter?' (We'd got electricity, then - by the way). Mom said: 'Oh don't be frightened of him!' She got the bowl and filled it with water for me to go and have my wash. The horse turned round, to drink the water, and mum threw it all up in the air. She was overcome - with the horse looking at her! It was just in the house for the one night, because there was nowhere to put him outside. My friend came to call for me, to go to work. She looked through the kitchen window, because she couldn't get any answer at the front door. Then she went running back to tell her mom that there was a horse in the kitchen." Not surprisingly, *her* mom didn't believe the story either!

"At one time, Paddy had a crush on my cousin, Brenda Marshall! I can remember Dolly washing his neck with a brillo pad - he used to have a tide mark – sorry Paddy!" Jean was in the house when both Rickie and Pete were born. "We went to live round the corner in Varna Road, just after Pete's birth, although I remember seeing him in his pram. Mom got another place to live. By that time she'd got a boyfriend, who later became my stepfather. She was looking after his son and there wasn't room for two children; there was only room for mom and Horace and Bobby. I went to live with my Auntie Gladys, down Ladywood, so I was out of the picture then."

Jean enjoyed living in Balsall Heath. "I got married from there, because Bernard lived at number 86. His mom was a taxi driver. It was a very friendly area. We used to sit out on the steps, having cups of tea, and talking with the neighbours - about twelve o'clock of a night, in the summer. It was a lovely area to sit out in.

"I was seventeen when I left Belgrave Road, so I didn't see much of Paddy as a teenager. We bump into each other occasionally – and he's still the same. He's got no side on him at all. I went down to his scrap-yard in Wellington Road. Bernard used to work in a garage, you see, and he called into Paddy's yard for his spare bits. I went down there a couple of times with him. And he'd come out, and - up in his arms, swing you round - give you a big hug. We've never met out socially, or things like that. But my husband, Bernard, knows him quite well."

Jean was treated to a 'Dolly Classic', on the corner of Varna Road and Belgrave Road. "She knelt down on the corner, to turn the tap off. Three fellas came round by the side of her. She turned round and shouted: 'I'm only down here to turn off the water!' " On a much later occasion, when Bernard and Jean were married, and living at number 86, Jean was ill with influenza, but had no one to look after her. True to form, Dolly came over, looked after Jean and her daughters, then went downstairs to help 'Mrs. Mac', Jean's mother-in-law, with a dying brother. "She came back upstairs," Jean recalls, "and said: 'He *is* dying – because he keeps slipping down the bed' – (I always remember that)."

During a 2003 Radio WM broadcast, with Ed Doolan, in *The Other Side of...* series, (in this case, *The Other Side of Pat Roach*), one of Pat's chosen records was for Frank:

This one's for my old dad. He loved 'Danny Boy', and I love Joe Longthorne singing it – it's just wonderful – it really is.

Paddy White met Frank on a couple of times when he was with Pat, and describes him as: "...very much an old-fashioned 'tatter': he was a scrap-man

– that's what he knew, that's what he did. He wasn't interested too much in Pat's life as a club owner, a drinker, a judo expert or a wrestler. He was quite *proud* of that, be he didn't seem to want to take any credit for the fact. The conversation always came back round to how much light iron is, how much lead is; what 'Hookie Thomas', Billy Clarke, and the other scrap-dealers were doing. Those were the types of conversations that Pat and Frank seemed to finish up having. He was interested in what Pat was doing, to some degree, but it had no bearing upon Frank's life. Frank was a bit of a rough diamond anyway, who could look after himself. I think it was just a matter of – that's Pat's life, this is my life – 'I'm a tatter – that's what I do, that's what I know.' He struck me as a nice old guy, very self-sufficient. Pat can be very sociable, when he wants to be, but he's also very private. With Frank, it was simply a case of 'this is my business, and if we want to talk about it, we'll talk about it.' He was a strong personality-sort of old guy, who wouldn't suffer fools gladly, and wouldn't be behind the door in telling you. He wasn't rude in any way, but he wouldn't hesitate to tell you, if you were 'out-of-line'; an old-fashioned 'tatter', who knew his business, knew his game, kept himself very much to himself." Dolly seems to have a warmer, outgoing personality; as one might expect, Pat seems to be a mixture of both parents.

Ken Collins relates the following true story, which happened shortly after Jean and her family had left Belgrave Road, and Pat had returned to Shakespeare Road to live with his gran. "Pat knew me by sight, before I joined the Royal Navy, but he noticed me particularly when I used to walk up Shakespeare Road, in my best 'Tiddly' outfit (the tailor-made version of a sailor's uniform as opposed to a 'work-a-day' one). I got the impression that he admired what he saw, as I did, when I saw Norman Pearce, Bernard Pearsall, and Jimmy Foxall; we were all in the Royal Navy. Charlie Lillington was a tall young man, about 6-foot one, or two, much taller than me, and I always admired *him*, when I saw him in his uniform. I knew that I was going into National Service at some point, so I decided to volunteer, in June 1948, so that I could be sure of being in the right branch of the service." Pat remembers that the Lillington family ran a second-hand furniture shop, but didn't know Charlie personally. Ken's cousin, Brian Webb, later joined the Merchant Navy.

"I'd overstayed my leave," explains Ken, "and the police were after me. Coming up to 2 back of 19 Shakespeare Road, hammering on the door – with what we call a 'copper's knock'– usually with the heel of the hand. The first time they came to see me, they warned me I'd got to return to my naval station, because they'd had a report from there, asking them to chase me up, to get me back from my leave. They were giving me this chance to come back 'of my own free will', instead of being escorted back in handcuffs!

"So after that scare, I decided that I needed to stay somewhere else, in case they arrested me the following day, or the day after that. My mother, Rose who, as you know, was a good friend of Dolly's, recommended that I call on her to see if she *could* put me up for a couple of nights, until I decided to go back to my naval station.

"I turned up at Dolly's house in Belgrave Road. I knocked on the door, she received me; she knew who I was. While I was talking to Dolly, explaining the circumstances, her huge dog, about the size of a Labrador, was lying on the hearth. Every time I spoke to Dolly, the dog growled, and each growl got nastier than the one preceding it! In the end, Dolly said to me: 'Take no notice Ken, he'll shut up in a minute.' But of course, the dog did *not* shut up, but continued growling. So finally, Dolly lifted her foot and said: 'Shut up you bastard!' It was very funny.

"As it turned out, Dolly couldn't put me up was because, had the police arrived, they would have caught me. They were after Harry for some reason; I never asked what it was. She didn't want to be caught with two of us in the house, but she *did* take me to the scullery, where the big caste iron gas stove was. She opened the oven door. I looked inside and a pit had been dug specially, on a level with the stove. Harry used to step into that pit, when the coppers were chasing him. Dolly would close the oven door, and of course, it was the last place that they would look – inside the stove – for an individual. It was very, very funny: I couldn't believe what I was seeing!"

Shirley and Patricia (Smith) remember visiting Balsall Heath, on one occasion. Shirley recalls: "There was a crowd of us went over to Pat's house with him. It was during the night time – dark. We just went there for a walk, and waited on a corner for him, because he wanted to go and see his mom. I think he wanted to ask her for some money. He was living with Amelia at the time, but just visiting Dolly."

Pat eventually returned to live with his mother, and immediate family, in Balsall Heath, completing his schooling at Hope Street, by which time his height problems were even more accentuated! Peter Berrington explained that by the age of fifteen, he and Pat were both over 6 feet tall. Ken recalls: "The time when I noticed that Pat had sprung up about a foot, maybe a foot-and-a-half, was when I came out of the *Tower Ballroom* early one evening, and he was outside the ballroom, with a gang of his friends. He spotted me and said: 'What-oh Ken!' I turned round and I could not *believe* it was Pat Roach, because he'd shot up and he seemed absolutely enormous: tall and thin." Pat's height was sometimes a disadvantage:

There is a message here for tall young lads out there – and girls too – and for all sorts of teachers. It's very unfair to expect too much of a young, tall person, because it undermines you so much, when you are expected to be the best high jumper, a good cricketer and a good footballer. I was expected to be a good runner. I played cricket and football for the school, but only at a secondary modern. Having said that, I would imagine that there were some good cricketers who came out of Hope Street School, in Balsall Heath. But certainly not me.

John Bevis, Pat's cousin, and Dolly's nephew, explains: "Harry Meakin and Dolly later moved from Belgrave Road, to Poplar Road, Sparkbrook, where Harry used to keep his horse in the back garden! My father, Charlie, always said that Harry was 'coffee house reared' – which means no proper food at home, just living on food from coffee houses; because there were no Fast Food places in those days, just a corner coffee house. Harry was a down-to-earth character. He never actually used to say a lot. He'd just sit there, probably thinking about how he was going to make his next 'crust'. I'd go down to Poplar Road, with Charlie, for Sunday dinner, sometimes. Dolly would always cook something for us.

"The continuation of Poplar Road runs into Roderick Road, so she and Freda moved further down the road, later," continues John. "When Dolly and Harry lived in Poplar Road, Peter, her son, lived there for a while, with the horse round the back. I don't know whose name the rent book was in though – probably the horse! Their house was near the top end (the Stratford Road end) of it. There was a cinema the one side, and the *Mermaid* was just along from there."

'Colonial' Walter, Pat's cousin, was married in Hong Kong. Frank explains: "When Ruth went across, to marry my brother Wal, in Hong Kong, the *Express* ran an article about the way of life she would be leading over there." Ruth was a Police Superintendent's daughter. "Walter was in Hong Kong in 1954 and 55, then he moved to Somaliland," continues Frank. Glen adds: "He was Police Commissioner in Somaliland.

"He was in charge of the prisons, and used to catch them, try them, judge them and hang them!" Helen explains: "If you'd have met him, he was a gentleman. He could speak Arabic and Chinese – he used to say a bit of that, when he was in the car. He retired when he came back from Somaliland." This coincided with Somaliland wanting its freedom. Also, they wanted the three children to be educated in Britain. "The Mau-Mau were very active in Africa at that time," explains Glen. "Their bungalow was surrounded by a big wire fence and guards. He was worried for his wife and children, while he was away on duty. So they came back to England, and he stayed there, until he retired. Their children are Michael, Lindsay and Frances - so we get the Michael and Frances names repeated again." Frank adds: "Michael was born in Hong Kong, Lindsay was born in Somaliland, and Frances, the youngest, was also born in Africa." Ruth and Walter ran a post office, in Litton, Somerset, when they first retired, then moved to Compton Martin, in Devon. Walter's final years were spent in Barton Close, Kingsbridge. He didn't return to Birmingham during this period, so his brothers and sisters would sometimes visit him in Devon. Walter died at the age of seventy-six, in 1996.

Pat describes Dolly and her sister, his Aunt Freda, as being like a music hall act! He has a hilarious video of them 'performing' together. Brian comments: "Freda was very much the same as her sister Dolly, and still is - one of those big, bluff-speaking people – with a heart of gold. I had lots of girlfriends when I was young – Pat will probably tell you. I took this one particular girlfriend up to Auntie Amelia's, to say hello to Pat. His mother Doris was there; they were all having a bit of a 'get-together'. I said: 'Auntie Doris, this is my girlfriend.' She said: 'Ah, ain't she lovely?' I said: 'For God's sake Doris, I'm grown-up now!' 'She's a lovely little girl Brian.' (I'd been in the navy about five years)! 'Ain't you two lovely little people?' Of course, Pat was trying not to laugh – obviously, - he was sort of sniggering!

"Even in the 1980s, when my mother lived in a flat with my brother, down by the old *Bristol Cinema*, the back of the *Trees* public house, on the Bristol Road, Aunt Doris used to keep in touch. She'd send her a letter every so often, with a lot of jokes in it – 'ha-ha' and all this - and a pound coin or a pound note. 'I doesn't *mean* anything,' she wrote in one letter. 'It's just a token.' I've got some letters from her somewhere – packed away in my mother's belongings."

Josie recalls: "Peter went and picked Pat up on his motorbike, from Balsall Heath. He said Pat had no crash helmet, but all he wanted Peter to do was let him have a go at driving it. He was bringing him back home to Shakespeare Road." Peter adds: "When he lived down Belgrave Road, that was a bloody laugh in itself. Sunday morning – (I'm not supposed to tell you this really, you know), he used to say to me: 'Can I have a go?' He hadn't got a crash helmet - well it never mattered to him, did it? If it was a cold morning, there he was, going round in his vest. He'd have gone round in his underpants, I'll tell you!"

Pat was enthusiastic about vehicles in general, from an early age; he also developed an interest in 'plant' and the scrap metal business, from helping Frank and Harry with various deals. "Pat didn't know his father really," explains Dolly, "but being a kid, he liked to go and sort things out; he felt grown up being amongst them. The dealers' time was any time – 11 o'clock. They'd please themselves when they went to work. They didn't have to clock in at a factory or anything. Pat got to know his dad better, when he went in the coffee houses, when he was about fourteen."

Ronnie Callow, Pat's friend and fellow businessman, recalls Frank's visits to his yard. "He'd get his glasses out, sit in my caravan, and have a cup of tea. He used to dabble in stocks and shares; the first man I met who did. Before he married Dolly, he'd been a lumberjack in Canada, for ten years. He was a very intelligent man – a lovely man to talk to. I was probably early thirties and he must have been about sixty-five, at the time.

"He'd say: 'Can I have a look at your paper? Are you going to put the kettle on?' Then he'd just sit there - make himself comfortable in the corner of the caravan. He wasn't as tall as Pat: he might have been about six-foot, about 1½ inches taller than me. Always wore a dark overcoat, had silver-grey hair, with sharpish features."

Dolly explains: "Paddy went to live with momma, 'cause she was deaf, when he left school at the age of fifteen and worked for Frank. Then when he was seventeen he started on the coal, and passed his driving test."

When I left school, my mother really didn't want me to go with my dad, because of my dad's lifestyle, which, of course, is why they parted company. She said to me: "Oh son, don't go and work with your further." (Laughing) - I'll never forget! "Marry yourself a nice local wench, go and get yourself a job in a factory, get yourself a nice little local house." Those were her very words – I've never forgotten. I couldn't quite see myself living in a local house for eight bob, or working in a factory. Not that there's anything wrong with working in a factory – it wasn't for me.

When I worked for my father I used to get about £4-10s. a week. Dennis Sullivan was one of the dealers; there was quite a little mob – not a firm – of dealers: a scrap-dealing mob.

Roy O'Neill and Frank Roach first met at Tommy O'Neill's yard. They later became friends, through meetings at *Shay's Café*, which eventually changed location. "We all used to go down there after we finished a job." They didn't have regular breaks and lunchtimes. "We'd just see what jobs came in. Frank had what he used to call his 'pensions'. Now Frank's driver was Harold Harris, who lived opposite *Mist's Garage*, on Hockley Hill. Harold had thirteen kids, and he'd never pay his rates." (Pat said later that he thought it was seventeen!).

"He used to buy potatoes in hundred-weights, and cook them in a boiler, down the back of the house," Roy continues. "He wouldn't pay his rates, so the police used to come round to his house and say: 'We'll give you the first fiver towards them.' And he used to say: 'No, the country ought to keep me.' He used to go away for a month or two. While Harold was away I did jobs for Frank – his 'pensions' – which were of a Friday and a Saturday. He used to go round to little factories and 'blag' a tea chest of brass, or a couple of bags of brass swarf off them. They could be worth anything between 12 or 25 quid. He used to just give them a couple of quid for it. So he'd say, 'I'm just going to do me pensions today' - if he wanted a few quid.

"Frank was a *terrific* storyteller: he'd have us listening for hours, in the café - about when he was a hobo in Canada – and on the trains and that." Pat's cousin, Joyce Taylor, recalls a story about when the police were chasing Frank on a train, and he escaped through a window. I've heard another about when he climbed a lamppost to escape them!

According to Roy, "We used to have another fella who came in there – Jimmy Jones; he was shell-shocked, so we could only get him half a cup of tea!

But Jimmy was into a firm at *Stancrofts*. Frank used to sell him hand presses. Jimmy would stick them into *Stancrofts* and we'd get so much a number for them: £10 a number - £20 for two – and so on.

"Jimmy Jones used a red phone box as his office, outside one of the openings in a factory, at the top end of Great Hampton Street," Roy continues. "His cards had the telephone number of the box on them! Where the pub is, on the corner of Great Hampton Street, there used to be a Brass Founders, just down from there, before they knocked it down. There was Harry Edwards, a machine dealer kid, and then some little workshops – and one of the little entries was their office! The entry went up, and the doors went off it. They used to sit in there, until the phone rang!"

Such practices bring to mind the 'hookie gear' and 'Direct' antics of the Summer Lane Mob, previously described by Pat. "We used to go to *Leek's*, on the corner of Northwood Street and Livery Street," continues Roy. "They'd got an opening in Northwood Street. They used to look in the opening, (because there were sometimes brass coils in there). If there were any coils in there, they'd order a taxi. As it drew up, they'd load about four or five coils into it, and then bugger off down to Clarkie's. Then they'd 'live it up', down at *Shays*. There's loads of strokes they used to pull!"

In Barr Street, there was a firm with a double gateway entrance. "The boiler ashes used to be put onto the one side. The maintenance man over there had to get rid of the ashes. There was a fella who used to come into the café, named 'Blackie'. Only a little fella: always in a pair of all-in-one overalls – scruffy." According to Pat, 'Blackie' was also known as 'Darkie Cruise'. "His friend, or brother-in-law, was the maintenance man," Roy explains. "Blackie used to be able to go in, get a load of ashes, and give the maintenance man a pound for them – Frank used to draw £3. Frank had a motor, but Blackie didn't. So Frank used to collect the rubbish, but instead of making it one load, he'd make it into two; but he'd still only give Blackie a pound for it. If Frank was short, he used to say: 'I'll go and get Blackie, and we'll do a couple of loads of rubbish.'

"They were fine ash, so we used to sell them to these 'fly' car pitches, to put on the ground, to run over. We'd sell things to anyone we could – (for footpaths, and so on)."

So Frank, Roy and the other 'coffee house merchants' were into all *sorts* of deals. Frank moved from his shop in Hamstead Road, to Hunters Road, in Handsworth. "He sold it to a guy named Plotnik. The old guy was young Harold Plotnik's father. Harold was the director of *Allied Carpets*. Hunters Road was a combination of house and yard." Roy agrees that Frank's house and yard was, (as Pat explained on the Ed Doolan's radio programme, mentioned earlier), "Just like the one in *Steptoe & Son*."

He placed sticks at intervals, to whack would-be intruders! My dad was so-called 'King of the Castle' – 'Stick of Troche'. They all looked up to him – very much so. Later in my life, I put together a few words: "If it moves, buy it, if it doesn't, sell the damn thing!" And that was my policy, when I used to buy and sell and 'wheel-and-deal' – just as my dad did before me. Frank would buy ferrous and non-ferrous metals, and little job lots off companies; he'd go to sales with his old pal, Tommy O'Neill – Roy's father. There was a fight between our two fathers, Frank and Tommy. Roy and I kept walking past them – not getting involved.

"Yes, the fight didn't take very long," confirms Roy. "It was an argument over a half crown lot. They said: 'We'll go outside and sort it out.' Pat and I followed them out. As they walked out of the door, in Camden Street, by Spring Hill, there was a lamppost. Frank took the first swing, missed, fell against the lamppost and blacked his eye. My dad took the next swing, missed and hit the door-jam on the door – and *he* had a black eye. They both walked off, and when we went down to *Shay's Café*, they were in there together, having a cup of tea; they must both have been about sixty at the time! I don't think Pat was as tall or as broad as Frank, but they may have been of similar height. Frank's brothers were even bigger than he was." As Frank only had two brothers, Roy must mean Walter and Peter.

Frank and Tommy would walk into an auction house, probably a factory closing down, which would have a 'lot' up for sale, of various, miscellaneous items. I'll never forget, my father's opening bid was always: "Half-a-crown sir!"

Chapter Four –

GYPSY IN MY SOUL

Over the years, I'd look at places and think: 'Oh, you could live there - you'd get a good night's shelter there; it would be a good place to be.' Before I sold my yard, I even considered staying in the caravan that was on site there - (I've always got one somewhere). It's struck me now, as I'm speaking about it - it's the first time I've realised the significance of it! At the time of writing, I've got two living wagons, two caravanettes. It's really strange - probably some kind of genetic inheritance or memory, from my gypsy ancestors.

This instinctive, Romany side of Pat has been singled out by various people, and is best exemplified by the 'ducking-and-diving' aspect of his nature. His 'eye for a bargain', and finely tuned, quick-fire ability to sum up situations and individuals, combine with an acute sense of timing, and a strong instinct for self-preservation. Added to this is a wanderlust, which has taken him to the 'four corners of the earth'. His nomadic ancestors, (without benefit of jet engine), at the tiller of their barges, or guiding a horse along some muddy towpath, would have been green with envy!

In the previous chapter we described his mother Dolly's bohemian characteristics, inherited from Amelia, and possibly her father, Bill Bevis; the romantic 'campfire' tales she enjoyed telling, such as Frank riding in on his charger to carry her off. All of this, the reading of tea-leaves, and fortune telling, were guaranteed to capture the imagination of a young boy, who *already* had a natural gift for story-telling, as witnessed by contemporaries, such as Pat and Shirley Smith.

During the course of a conversation, Dolly explained: "Freda's very jealous of people thinking that I look like momma. I have to say to her: 'You've got momma's brown eyes – I haven't.' But when we were shopping up Acocks Green, we sat on the bench and this woman, who we'd met before, said to me: 'Will you tell my fortune?' I said: 'You must be joking love!' The neighbours in Garbett Street, Ladywood, would say to momma: 'Bevis, read our cards!' She was beautiful – bluey-black hair. Sad life – she worked all her life. I said to this woman, 'No, my sister's like my mom, she's got her brown eyes. I haven't got brown eyes.' She said, 'You've got a different face – you've got high cheekbones. You can't tell me you don't read fortunes!' "

The gypsies had their own verbal shorthand, or code, which was particularly handy when arranging secret deals. Amelia used a form of 'backslang', or 'half-chat', (as it's sometimes known), which was in common usage among Birmingham traders. Pat reminds me that, originally, it was spoken by butchers. Having learned backslang 'at his grandma's knee', he can switch into it at a moment's notice. To an untrained ear, it sounds like a bizarre foreign language, involving the splitting of syllables to confuse people, then reversing words. Billy Sutton, a former market trader-turned entrepreneur, is one of its leading exponents; he slips into half-chat in a later chapter. Gordon Fewtrell, whom we meet in a later chapter, also speaks it in expert fashion. Billy and Pat met originally in 1961, when Billy was a 'street grafter', selling goods out of a suitcase, on an illegal pitch, at the back of *C&A*. The following are a few examples of backslang:

Amelia would describe herself as "dlo" – (pronounced 'deelo') which is old, spelt backwards. "TFEL at the renoc", would mean "Turn left at the corner." The Birmingham dialect would sometimes distort this even further, so that 'renoc' sounded like 'renic', obscuring the fact that 'renoc', if an 'r' is added, is simply 'corner' spelt backwards! If someone suggested that you "Pipe the Drib," he would mean "Look at the bird" (woman or girl); 'drib' is 'bird', spelt backwards. When a friend wanted inside information about a situation, a fellow backslanger might reply: "I'll mark your drac," meaning "I'll mark your card," – (tell you what's going on!)

While Billy was being, "chased all day, by about twenty coppers," Pat and Jim White sold carpets and various other goods, as yet another sideline. Billy explains: "Pat and Jim worked a bit of the 'swag' game, but they never worked the streets. They used to do a bit of wholesaling and retailing, but they didn't do 'fly-pitching', like me."

During the Second World War, Pat's friend, Pete Berrington, had a memorable gypsy experience of his own. It must be said that many water gypsies were perfectly respectable people, like Amelia, but there are always exceptions to any rule. Pete recalls: "My granddad on my mum's side, George Usher, took me down to the canal. I was very small, but even so, I can still see all the boobs, of the women! They wore gypsy looking things on their heads, earrings, and everything. It was the part of the canal going down from *The Bridge* public house, on Monument Road, along toward Sheepcote Street - in Ladywood. Me granddad only had one arm and one leg."

The 'Bridge' didn't have a ladies' loo, so female patrons were obliged to walk down by the canal, and form a protective screen around each other!

George Usher's daughter was Josie Rudge, featured in our opening Ladywood chapters. She explained that her father lost two limbs when he was hit by a train, but nevertheless continued working on the railway, for a total of fifty years.

Pete continues: "Even though I was young then, I used to help George put his leg on and strap it. He'd go along with his stick and he'd say: 'This is going to be an education for ya!' They were 'big-made' women, with black hair, and they just pulled their tops off. They were hitting each other like men. They weren't twenty-five or twenty-six; some of them were fifty looking. Their bodies had aged – and to a little kid of four or five... They were standing on the towpath, next to a barge. But the fight was arranged, as though it was a normal Sunday morning event. There were thirty or forty people watching!

"Without a doubt, I must have been the very youngest. But the look on the faces of the people who were fighting!" When asked if he could remember if there were any other boats moored there, Pete quipped: "No - I'm trying to remember the *faces* of the women who were fighting - I used to have a few nightmares about that!"

This vicious tournament finally ended when one of the women reached back against the barge. "There was a lot of sacking," explained Pete. "She reached back and got a boat hook - ready to do whatever she was going to do to this other one. This gypsy bloke who was with her, banged her and laid her right out, or threw her into the canal – to cool her off!

"But I fell in there, you know. With the best will in the world, I wasn't strong: I always had asthma from an early age. I had a job to get out. I'd been doing something stupid, walking on a wall or something. The water was in me trousers. I'd got little thin arms and I was trying to lift the rest of my body! My legs could reach the bottom and it was all rough. And there was like a little rail track. You had to get one foot up onto that. Climbing up to the top was like climbing Mount Everest for me. How I got out, I don't know." Incidents of children drowning in the canal weren't uncommon. In *The Treacle Stick*, Helen Butcher describes how her younger brother was drowned in a nearby Ladywood canal.

Pat's father, Frank, also narrowly escaped death, somewhere between 1945-1948. Helen Roach recalls: "He was living on his own at the time, when his ulcers burst, and he dragged himself, on his hands and knees, (because he was a big strong man), from his house in Camden Street, to get help at the Albion Fire Station. It was a 'touch and go' situation. He'd had Paddy, but it was before he had 'Frankie'. My father, Walter, had to run up to the General Hospital; and yet Frank was a man who didn't drink. They don't know how he managed to drag himself; it must have been his sheer strength. Paddy wouldn't have known about it, but I remember that, because it was so horrific - to think that his ulcer had burst – he was dying – and he dragged himself all the way to the fire station!" Frank adds: "I remember him coming to the house, afterwards, to show us the scar – down here – and he had the dressing on."

Contrary to information given previously by others, Pat's Uncle Peter (Walter and Frank's brother), didn't make a career of the army, lived into his late 50s, and *did* have a family. "He was a toolmaker who worked at *Fisher and*

Ludlow," explains Frank. "I first came into contact with him in my teens, when I came out of the army. I was in hospital, and Peter was in the bed opposite me – in 1950. Straight away, we knew who each other was. I started visiting him, from that point onwards. He had two daughters, and a wife named Daisy. His two daughters were Myra, who was living at home, and Daisy, who was living in Canada. Daisy came back from Canada, with her husband and two children. Their surname was Brown. Her husband was invalided out of the war; he was limping, with a bad leg. Uncle Peter died in the late 1950s."

Meanwhile, in 1952, when Pat began work at the age of fifteen, and returned to live with his former water gypsy grandmother, he and Pete Berrington continued their friendship. "We always had a laugh," recalls Pete. "We used to go down the 'Rec.' – at the bottom of Anderton Street and Alexandra Street. I knew someone down there on the end. His name was Norman Watson. He was a bit of a 'dude'. Pat used to organise – well we were all into it – we had coaches and we used to go to Halesowen." Pat has also mentioned these outings, when he and a group of friends, including Pete, and Georgie James, would visit Halesowen Town Hall, and make a nuisance of themselves!

"I'll tell you a story," recalls Georgie. "We were at Kyrle Hall, in Halesowen – and I always had a 'mouth'. I was seven-stone twelve at eighteen, but I'd always got Pat behind me when we were out, you see? I let it all go one day – and I did it all wrong. And the guy had a chip at me. And Pat's gone: 'No more son. I *keep* getting you out of trouble, you can do it yourself this time,' – and I had a good hiding! When I got home, the old man said: 'What's happened?' Pat said: 'He opened his mouth again, didn't he? And I left him to it.' That was the first good hiding that I ever had – and the last! Pat sorts things out properly. I've never known him do anybody any harm. Pat was always very *genuine* – pretty honest," adds Georgie. "He was a big man, but he never ever caused any trouble."

Pete Berrington recalls that the coaches they used for such outings, belonged to a company called *Nash's*. "We used to charge them a dollar – an 'Oxford Scholar' – 25p now." Like Dolly, Pat was the main organiser of the trips. "But we used to have a laugh," continues Pete. "I always remember the bandleader, at a Birmingham night-club - Sonny Rose. We were given free tickets to get people there. We'd go for a dance and a drink. It was Saturday night out – you've got to, haven't you?" Pat explains that Sonny was the bandleader at *The Casino*, a Mecca Dance Hall, opposite where Lewis's Department Store used to be, on the Steelhouse Lane side of the Minories.

We used to go to the Casino. We'd got a few quid, so we'd 'do the flash' – flash our money around. I'd have a little dance - in the early days this was, when I was seventeen. Very often when we were in town, we'd go to 'Yates' Wine Bar' and drink Yates' 'giggle water'- (as we called it). This was a schooner of wine for 1/6d /1/9d. Three glasses of that and it used to drive you barmy! Ronnie Callow sometimes had a drink with us there.

Pete recalls going to a 'Blues' (Birmingham City Football Club) match with Pat. "We were on the bus, and I was hanging on the bar. We used to drop off the bus – on the corner. When I went to drop off, Pat held my hand; the bus dragged me a bit, but I landed back on. Between you and me, I always used to think I could beat him you know! I hit Pat, for dragging me, and he said – I knew then – 'Don't do that again mate!' That was enough – despite being well over six-foot himself, Pete didn't need telling twice. "We never got to fight – or anything like that."

Without hesitation Pete describes Pat as: "Giant, gentleman – absolute gentleman, – and I mean that!" Regarding the days when he and Pat first became friends (he was eleven, and Pat was nine), he comments, 'tongue-in-cheek', "Nobody seemed to pick on you!" Why did they become such firm friends? "We could always talk about *anything*." Had they used to confide in each other? "Oh yes – but we're men – so we don't tell you!"

His sisters, Norma and Carole, recall a trip that he and Pat made to Blackpool, when Pete was eighteen. "It's where we left all our shoes outside, to be cleaned," explains Pete – "Pat suggested it. There were about five or six of us, and all of our shoes got stolen. I had to go out in the morning, with some money, and buy five or six pairs of pumps. We never got the shoes back." Pete's aunt, Josie Rudge, explains: "Pat cut his face with an old razor; he ended up with half a newspaper stuck to his face, because of the number of cuts he'd got." According to Pete: "Pat seemed to shave a couple of years before us – oh his face! He was a good mate of mine. I remember a copper stopping us on the motorbike, and saying: 'Do you know there's a bit of cotton sticking out of your back wheel?' We were a bit lucky there!

"Did Norma tell you about taking all the furniture up to Wales?" The two friends drove a truckload of furniture, all the way to Norma's Welsh cottage, in Bodedern, but got stuck on a bridge, only a mile or two from their destination. Luckily, a local farmer came to the rescue. "But from the main road," explains Pete, "when we turned in, the snow had to be four-foot deep, or something like that! We stopped at a café. My next brother down, Robert, was with us. I ain't gonna say what Robert's reaction was, but Pat was going round those bends a bit sharp! The truck was open at the back, it was snowing; we hadn't got the furniture covered up. Pat gave the farmer a dollar. He took us a mile-and-a-half up this little country road, to where my sister lived."

Poor Norma's furniture was wringing wet, by the time they delivered it! Pat recalls being exhausted and frozen. "When they got to Norma's," explains Josie, "Pat said: 'I'm going over to the pub for a drink.' " "He had *more* than one glass of Drambuie brandy," recalls Pete. "It was only ten pence a glass." Pat didn't ask Norma for any payment for the trip: she still has a conscience about it!

Pat was the proud owner of a pink Buick, which he parked outside his gran's house in Shakespeare Road. "It was camouflaged: you could hide it amongst trees and not see it," recalls Pete. "But he said, because it was in the *Birmingham Mail* – a picture of the car – 'I'll tell you what, that's worth two hundred pounds worth of publicity.' So everyone knew it was Pat Roach's car. He was forever swapping them! I remember him saying, one day: 'If you've got twenty quid, I'll pay twenty, and I know where there's about five or six cars. We'll get a runner. We can sell it and build upon that.' I wish I'd have gone halves with him on it, but I never. He always seemed to come back with a motor – hard-working bloke. Always tried."

Patricia Smith remembers Pat courting. "He had a car– it was all the colours of the rainbow."

It was a Hudson Terraplane – an American car purchased from a local dealer named Sid, who used to run a car pitch in Saltley.

Pat and Peter were friends for about thirteen years. "When I was courting my missus, Cynthia, I used to see him up the *Tower Ballroom*, Edgbaston - and after. I got married when I was twenty-four." According to Norma, Pete knew Pat so well - "he could write the book for you!"

Pat first met Roy O'Neill, when he was about fifteen: "He'd get me up of a morning, because I used to be out all night, until four o'clock, at clubs and casinos, and I could never get up," explains Roy. "In my house, the kitchen window was very low. Pat used to open it, step through, put the kettle on – and give us a shout." This was the house in Brougham Street, from which Pat and Doreen would later be married. "I bought a little Alsatian puppy. Pat wouldn't come in, because it used to bark at him," recalls Roy. "Pat was very shy – well, very calm: he wasn't aggressive." Dolly recalls Pat visiting the café's, as he got older, and meeting the dealers like Roy.

"But he got involved with a fella who I didn't like," Roy adds, confirming that this was Georgie Cullen. "I threw him out. I had a yard with my friend, Teddy Skett, in Church Street, Lozells, which used to be open most of the time, because I'd let cars park in there. We were together from when we were lads at school. (We used to do Black Market stuff, when we were at school) That's how I met Joan – my wife, she was working in a café at Farm Street. Eggs were rationed, and Lucas's used to come up for half-egg sandwiches, because they'd only got so many eggs. I used to drop her a gross of eggs down, at the end of the war, when rationing was still with us, (I'm seventy-three now). We'd supply school dances with butter, eggs, sugar, and tea – anything; caster sugar to the houses at Christmas. We took them around the streets, in old leather hatboxes. You couldn't get combs at the end of the war, so we used to do those too. We were thirteen, when we did the hatboxes."

Roy saw Pat at the cafes, sometimes with his father Frank. "He was on and off with his dad," recalls Roy. "The trouble at the auction, between me and Tommy Barrett, was that he was 'slagging' Pat's dad off, and Pat never said a word. So I stepped in and said, 'You can't talk to him about that' - which caused trouble. But Pat wouldn't fight at all then."

Pat and Georgie James also continued to keep in touch. "Whilst we didn't move around together, we used to *see* each other quite a lot. We've always been pals," explains Georgie. "When we were sixteen, seventeen, we all used to go out together – to Kyrle Hall, in Halesowen, at the weekends – dancing and such. Norman Watson used to dress us. He worked at a tailor's shop, on the Soho Road. When we bought our clothes, we all used to have *exactly* the same coats and trousers. So, as a group, when we walked into the dance – we were all dressed the same!"

Having completed his National Service, Geoff Staley, (from Pat's Shakespeare Road days), met him again, when Pat came to his workplace – the *Walker and Woodward* factory in the Jewellery Quarter, Legge Lane, around the corner from Albion Street Fire Station. "He was our local scrap man," explains Geoff. "We were in the brass trade, making door handles and hinges – that sort of thing. He used to come for what I would call, in those days, the 'rough scrap'. His dad used to come, of course. Pat probably didn't come every time, but sometimes they'd come together. Frank used to bring an old van.

"The two of them came, this one particular day. My boss, Mr. Woodward, said: 'Go down Geoff and see what's going – tell him what's there for him to have.' It used to be up the side of the factory. I left them to carry on – which I would. He came running down the yard – literally - with his dad in his arms. Frank had had an accident of some kind. The thing that stuck in my mind is that, in later years, having seen Pat wrestle, how strong he was, to have picked his dad up! I think it may have been something really bad with Frank's leg." Strangely enough, Pat doesn't recall this incident. As his father weighed nineteen-stone, it's not the sort of thing he'd be likely to forget!

Undaunted, Geoff elaborates: "They used to break up 'lacquer' tins, which were made of metal. Today we'd call them petrol cans. They were full of lacquer, to go onto the press, to keep it dry. They used to smash those up and use them as scrap – and I think that's how he did it."

Throughout his cosmopolitan career, Pat has met a host of tremendously varied, frequently very attractive individuals. However, what has become abundantly clear, during wide-ranging conversations, is that the woman who has had the most profound and long-lasting effect upon him, is his wife, Doreen, whom he met years ago in Birmingham, as a relatively inexperienced teenager. A regular meeting place for Pat, at eighteen years of age, was Laura Dixon's, above *Chetwynd's* the tailors, at the bottom of Hill Street in Town.

We were a bloody nuisance: Alfie Evans, Harold Evans, Tommy used to come sometimes, a couple of other guys. Little Vince Turner – always turned out smart little Vincie Turner. I was always a scruff – but there we are! We met a few girls from time to time, I suppose. One particular time, in the nicest possible way, between us we met a couple of sisters named Pat and Doreen Harris, who lived out South Yardley way. Pat and Doreen were both very beautiful girls. I think Alfie fancied both – so did Harold - everybody did. To cut a very long story short, I finished up courting Doreen, who I later married, when I was nineteen years of age. The day we went to put our banns in, I used the same big red V8 Tipper truck, which I'd already passed my test in, with a load of rubbish in the back. I got Doreen up into the seat somehow, and we went to put our banns in, in the big old red truck.

Roy O'Neill was their 'best man'. Doreen and Pat married in February 1957. According to Pat, this was at Broad Street Registry Office, Birmingham. Shortly afterwards, they moved in with Pat's grandmother, Amelia, in Shakespeare Road, Ladywood. Amelia died unexpectedly, just a few months later, so unfortunately was never able to see her grandson. According to Georgie: "Roy gave them the money to get the marriage certificate!" Like two or three other contributors, he remembers Doreen as "… very quiet. She was a 'lady', if you like. She never got involved in the conversations; she was just there."

Roy explained that Pat tried to contact Frank, to sign the consent forms: "As far as I know, this went on for about three days. My wife, Joan, kept on to Pat about getting it signed. Eventually I signed it for him, in the house, and Joan signed for his wife."

Possibly, consent forms were required in those days, for people under twenty-one years of age, although we haven't verified this.

"There were four of us at the Registry Office," explains Roy. "I stood next to Doreen. Pat stood the other side of me, and my wife was the other side of Doreen. They had the ceremony, then the registrar congratulated me! I said: 'No – It's not me – it's him!' " Money was in scarce supply for them, in those days. "The registrar said: 'That will be 7/6d,' " recalls Roy. "Pat said to Doreen: 'Have you got 7/6d?' Doreen said, 'No', so *I* paid the 7/6d. Then we walked down the stairs, and the fella on the stairs said: 'Thank you very much.' He swept the confetti up; (there was only one little bit of confetti that Joan had bought). So I had to give him half a crown an' all! We got down to the bottom of the steps. Pat said, 'Well, I've got somewhere to go. I'll meet you at your house.' So I took Doreen back to my house, and Pat met us back there." Pat said recently, that although his wedding day was a bit of a blur, he had no problem remembering the anniversaries that followed.

The four of them had a celebratory meal in Stratford-on-Avon, after the wedding. "We'd met a retired man from Plymouth – his surname was Miles," explains Roy. "I bought some fire salvage, including some Valor heaters. I

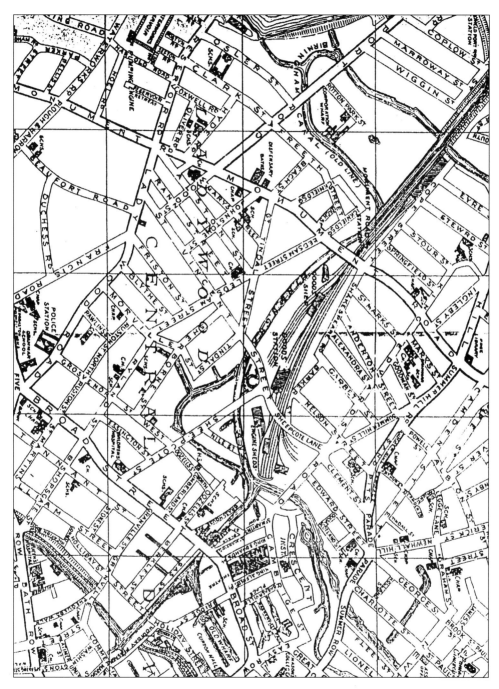

Map of Ladywood, 1907, shows the area as it would have been when Amelia and Bill Bevis moved there. Pat's mother, Dolly Bevis, was born in Garbett Street, in 1915.
By permission of Norman Bartlam

I

In the mid-to-late 1950s, Pat had breakfast at Foxall's café, Sheepcote Street, whilst working at nearby coal wharves. He later discovered that his grandmother, Amelia, had been born in the canal cottage next door, (between the café and the Albion public house).
By permission of Brian Webb - (Private Collection).

Local residents at an Anderton Street Party, May 1937, celebrate the Coronation /inauguration of King George VI and Queen Elizabeth, the Queen Mother - just a week before Pat was born.
By permission of Norman Bartlam.

Shakespeare Road – Alexandra Street, 1948. Pat and Amelia's house, at 68 Shakespeare Road, was on the left hand side, and just a few houses up the hill, (off the picture and to the left).
By permission of John Landon.

Ron 'Smudger' Smith, brings the previous photo to life, in his own, inimitable style. It was originally drawn as an anniversary present for Ted and Maureen Rudge.
By permission of Ron 'Smudger' Smith.

Sid Butt's draper's shop, Shakespeare Road, a name that 'crops up' frequently in our Ladywood chapters. Pat lived almost opposite the store. Ken Collins and family lived down the bottom of the hill, on the right-hand side. The Moles lived to the left of Sid's store. Ray Green and Johnny Cloves' houses were in the first entry down from the shop.
By permission of Brian Webb (Private Collection).

The Sandpits, 1953. On Saturdays, Pat often visited the Lyric Cinema, with Brian and Terry Webb. Afterwards, they'd start playing at the Sandpits. The car on the right marks the spot where their games began.
By permission of Brian Webb - (Private Collection).

The Crown Cinema, Icknield Port Road, Ladywood, now the premises of Landon & Sons, the bathroom specialists. According to Pat and his friends, this cinema was 'upmarket', compared with the Lyric or the Ledsam.
By permission of John Landon.

During the Second World War, Peter Berrington's grandfather, George Usher, took him down to the canal, by the Bridge Public House, Monument Road, to watch a fight between two gypsy women.
By permission of Brian Webb - (Private Collection).

'The Parkeston Five', playing at the Dover Court Hotel, 1957. Pat used to manage this 'rockabilly' group, which included Brian, (centre front row). The guitarist on the left is Al Wiles (London). Rocky Rodriguez, on the right, was originally from Barcelona.
By permission of Brian Webb.

A day out at the Lickey Hills: from left to right, Pat's former judo instructor, Frank Ryder, Pat Knowles (née Smith) and Wilf Ryder.
By permission of Pat Bowen, (formerly Knowles).

Cynthia Berrington (née Carter), Peter's wife, in the back yard of 2 back 53, his home in Shakespeare Road. Like Ray Green's, the whole house trembled, when trains shot by – so she only stayed the once! By permission of Pete and Cynthia Berrington.

Pat's good friends, Peter Berrington and Ray Green, plus a 'mystery man', on the right, (perhaps he will enlighten us?) The celebrations were at the Tower Ballroom, Edgbaston, c. 1952.
By permission of Jean Newbould.

'Dressed-to-the-Nines': Lily Webb and Dolly Roach, on holiday in Spain, 1975.
By permission of Brian Webb.

Holiday photograph of Lily Webb and Doreen Roach, Pat's wife, 1975.
By permission of Brian Webb.

The Allensmore Development Project: Pat, hammer in hand, prepares to strike the first blow, in the demolition of Allensmore House. Residents were re-housed, as the flats had developed major faults. By permission of Norman Bartlam.

Two schoolboy pupils of Norman Bartlam's, (former Head of Geography at Ladywood School), interview Pat outside the flats, in 1987. Stuart Bevan holds the camera, while Christopher Heard tapes the interview. Stuart's subsequent article appeared in the April 1987 Edition of the award-winning school magazine, the Ladywood Bugle. By permission of Norman Bartlam.

Josie Rudge and Pat, re-united after many years, at an Ottakars book signing in Bromsgrove, for our first book - 'If – The Pat Roach Story'. The co-writer is seated on the right.
By permission of Ottakars Bookshop, Bromsgrove.

Seated from left to right, Norma Knewport, her aunt, Josie Rudge and Norma's sister, Carole Bailey, recall Pat's Ladywood childhood. Photograph by Shirley Thompson.

advertised them, and he bought them. My dad's old friend named Tommy Barrett had an argument over these bits of scrap, from a previous auction. It was all about ten shillings difference, between what we'd got to give Tommy, and what we'd got to draw. It caused a bit of a fight. They stopped the auction, and sorted us out. Then me and Pat started to load our scrap on.

"This old fella, Miles, who had come from Plymouth, saw me there. I'd got a leather coat, and I'd hung it on the mirror of the truck. He came round and said: 'What was all the trouble about?' I said: 'Oh – about half a quid!' He said: 'Well ten shillings is nothing.' So I said: 'Well we're skint – we're just trying to earn a few quid.' So he said: 'OK.' He turned around, came back and said: 'I've left you summat in your jacket.' We loaded up the scrap. I walked round, looked in my jacket, and there was a bundle of notes - £500. I said: 'That silly old sod's put this in me coat!' So we went over to the café and he was in there. I said to him: 'You can't go around doing this – you don't know me from Adam!' He says, 'Well, I'll see you again. I've asked the auctioneers about you (which was *Stevens, Champion and Slater*), and they've given you a good name. You can give it me back when you like.' I gave it back to him. He said: 'Well, here's my address.' He lived in Great Alne. So when we went to Stratford for this meal, at *The Silver Grill,* after Pat's wedding, we called in at his bungalow, for tea, on the way back."

While they were there, they discussed business. "He said to his wife: 'Go on!' She went into the bedroom and came back with two attaché cases," continues Roy. "He said: 'There's ten thousand quid in there!' (You remember the plastic tablecloths they used to have? It was pieces of that, stitched up in bags). He says: 'Open up a place – and give it back when you like.' I thought: 'This man's mad!' What he'd done was, during the war, when petrol was short, he'd bought all the cars off people, who had put them in their garages, and put them on contract to the army, for the duration of the war – at so much a time. Also, he'd designed a tubular steel gate. He took out a contract for it, for the Queen's Cornish estates. But I wouldn't take the money off him."

When my poor old gran died, they moved us into a back-to-back house in Stoke Street, in Ladywood - within a stone's throw of the canal. Stoke Street was off the back of Broad Street, a hundred and fifty yards from Gas Street Basin. We lived there for a while and after about a year, our son, Mark, was born.

Helen Roach recalls: "Frank moved me into my house, fifty-three years ago this September. Because I moved to Shard End in 1951. He used his van to move me and my husband and my child, to our new home." Luckily, he no longer had his horse and cart! "I didn't know Frank did that," comments her brother, Frank. "Uncle Frank, with his scrap business, had a horse and cart, and you could often see them outside Jones's Café, at the corner of Buckingham Street and Hospital Street. He used to put it outside our house, as well."

Was Jones's anywhere near Shay's Café – because that was in New John Street West? I had always assumed that was Frank's favourite café. "It's not far away – probably a quarter of a mile up the road," comments Helen. "The only one I know in Summer Lane was a coffee shop down the bottom end, by Loveday Street," adds her brother Frank. "It was called *Wragg's*. They made lovely bread pudding – but I don't remember seeing him in that one." Pat said recently that he remembers Alfie Wragg's Café too – he used to go in there himself. Helen explains: "When Pat's father, Frank moved me to Shard End, that was the last time I remember seeing him." That must have been some move!

Although she never met Doreen's mother, Dolly explained that Mrs. Harris worked stoically through a debilitating illness. Doreen inherited her mother's determination, and hard-working disposition, and later ran her own farm, independently of Pat. With some assistance from Mark, and an ex-wrestling friend of Pat's, she fed 300 pigs, and looked after 60 calves and 30,000 chickens.

Doreen's always been very been fond of my mother – very close to her. She's a hard worker, a good provider and tremendously loyal over all these years. As the book progresses, you'll see that I was a hardworking person too. But if you're in a marriage, or any sort of relationship, it always requires a partnership. Doreen has given me total support all the way through my life. Without her, in the early days, nothing could ever have happened.

"I've met Doreen once," explains Brian. "I came home on leave and I brought a girl home from Harwich, who I was with then. We were sailing from Harwich to the Hook of Holland and back. We had a weekend at home and I went to see Doreen. I'd got my girl with me and we went to visit at their home in Shakespeare Road. Pat introduced us to her. That was when he took us down to the *Casino*. He said: 'Are you playing in the finals?' I said: 'Yes we played in the heats two nights ago.' "

Brian was lead singer with a group called The *Parkeston Five* – named after a ship the *Empire Parkeston*. Parkeston Quay is a quay in Harwich. They were known as a 'Rockabilly' group, because they played a mixture of skiffle, rock and pop music.

Pat became the group's manager. "He said: 'I'll take you down and I'll provide the transport,' " recalls Brian. "I said: 'Ok – great!' So we got all the gear together, outside my house in Anderton Street, guitars and everything – whatever we'd got. He came round in a coal lorry and said: 'Put everything on the back and I'll take you down to the *Casino* in Corporation Street!' Oh dear, oh dear! There were no sides on this lorry. We had to hang on for dear life! He took us down there and we won the talent contest. But we had to borrow one of the preceding group's snare drums because we had a snare drum that I think got damaged on the way down there. Perhaps it was Pat's driving?!"

During that era, guitars were mainly acoustic. Brian began playing when he was seventeen - in 1955. "I was working out in South America then. Our ship was half West Indian and half white. There was a West Indian lad on there - he was a good kid. He was playing the guitar the one day, and he taught me. He said: 'If you can play better than me, by the time we get back home, I'll give you that guitar.' And I could – in the end. I sang all the calypsos and everything – and he gave me the guitar.

"I only knew one group with electric guitars and that was the *Gators*. They were quite famous; they were in the finals with us, and we beat them. I think it was called the *Midlands or Warwickshire Championship for Pop Groups*. We took a crowd of Ladywood people down with us to make sure that we won it - Pat had a hand in that as well.

"Two or three days after we won the competition, he came round and told me that he'd got us a booking at the *Tower Ballroom*. I thought he was joking, because no group had ever played there before. This was in 1956/57. He took us up to the *Tower*. They'd got a residential band, Cliff Deely, but it was all ballroom dancing - no rock'n roll or anything like that. He got us half an hour up there. How he did that I don't know. Anyhow, we got on the stage, and started playing and it was amazing really. It was like a scene out of the *Glen Miller Story*. All the kids stopped dancing and crowded around the front of the stage! There were so many of them. My cousins were there, and I think the Berringtons were."

Pat continued to arrange bookings at different venues. "We used to make a few bob here and there," recalls Brian. "But the two lads from the ship were getting a bit restless, because we weren't allowed to stay ashore for more than three months in those days; otherwise we'd be liable for National Service. So in the end we decided to go back to Harwich and sign on another ship."

Brian later became lead singer with a second group called *The Teen Scene*. They specialised in melodies and some rock'n roll. "We didn't do Elvis. Trevor Greaves sang the ballads - he was quite good. Gary Mellor was an excellent solo guitarist. You can see from the photo that all of those are electric guitars: we'd progressed by then." Johnny Turton, from Smethwick, was their drummer. Brian was joined by another singer - Heather Boxall. "She was a beautiful girl, a hairdresser's model, and much taller than me - about five foot nine, five foot ten. She lived up Edgbaston. Her mother was a doctor; her father was a ship's captain. She was a lovely singer.

"She came up one night; we were rehearsing somewhere in Spring Hill. There was the old *College Arms* pub, where the boxers used to play sometimes. Billy Middleton was licensee. He would let us have the clubroom for rehearsals, in exchange for one or two gigs we'd do for him. Heather said: 'Can I have a go?' She started singing. I said, 'Pretty good! Let's have a go, if you want to come up.' She used to sing *Dream Lover*." There were five of the group members, including Heather. "She'd just come in – do a couple of numbers – and then sit down - like a guest singer. Trevor used to do one or two. Then both of us would do the Everlys – and numbers like that. Gary would do his guitar solos: *Fickle Chicken* – he used to play; that was a good one. I was still playing in 1962 – so I was in groups for about seven years altogether. Even when I got married I was still playing."

Sadly, Pat and Doreen's son, Mark was handicapped by deafness. The family moved from Stoke Street to a house in Melbourne Avenue. Shortly afterwards they moved again, to Middlemore Road, Smethwick. In true entrepreneurial spirit, they turned this third home into a coffee house and later a fish-and-chip shop.

When we did it up, we were scraping all the bits and pieces off the doors: it turned out to be some woman's brains! The guy who lived there had killed two of the women in his life. When we were scraping the door down, there were bits of bone and stuff on it!

During this period, Jimmy White and Pat started a one-armed bandit business, and ran a chain of thirteen cafes. Jim occupied one of these, on the Hollyhead Road, with his wife Sylvia and the two children, while Pat, Doreen and Mark continued to live in a flat above the Middlemore Road café. Meanwhile, Pat had begun to travel around the country, on sports fixtures; some were judo demonstrations or contests, in company with Jim.

We had cafés on Hockley Flyover, and one in Blackheath, next to the old Bingo Hall. A third was in John Street, on the corner of George Street. On the domestic side of my life, my wife put her time in, at home and waiting for me, while I was on the road, and being content that eventually, I came home. Her loving care within our relationship meant that it didn't matter how long I was away, I never had any worries or aggravation about my wife: I knew she would always be there, and that Mark had a stable home.

Doreen managed one of the cafés. Pat and Jimmy systematically acquired a string of them, and installed one-armed bandits. Meanwhile, Mark was attending the Deaf School at Bell Hill, in Northfield.

The poor little devil had to go miles and miles. As things got a little better for us, and as Mark used to have to get up at six o'clock every morning to get the coach, I said to Doreen: "Go out there and buy the nearest house, opposite the school." There was a house right opposite the main gate. I think we paid £2,760 or something; that's where we lived for quite some time. We moved from there and that's where she and I parted company. I signed the house over to her, I think; Mark would probably have been about five years old. So from 1962 onwards, we were separated.

It was always lovely to come home to my boy. I was away that much, my boy once said to his mother, when he was older: "Where was my dad when I was little? Where was my father?" He saw so little of me; he was out to school and I was up and gone and away.

To ease the problem, Mark would occasionally travel abroad to visit his father on film sets. Despite the fact that Doreen and Pat were separated, Doreen travelled with Mark on these occasions.

*Quite simply, we had a handicapped son, who couldn't travel by himself; he's deaf, he doesn't speak. Mark and I have always been in close contact, and we've always been a **sensible** separated family about things. So when Mark came to see me, his mother was the natural person to bring him.*

Ronnie Callow recalls seeing Pat around town, fairly often. "Pat was doing 'snatch-backs' for a car finance company, and he said: 'Ronnie, your car's on this list.' I said: 'You'd better have a cup of tea Pat – sit down.' I went upstairs and got out all the paperwork for the car. It was a white Zodiac that used to belong to Dennis Hamilton, who was Diana Dors' husband – the one who 'topped' himself in the early 60s. I bought it off Ronnie Frost. I showed the paperwork to Pat, and he said: 'What's that?' So I said, 'Well which part have you come for? Because I've 'dripped' the car to four or five different finance companies, to raise the money for the cafe!' He started laughing, and I pushed a tenner in his pocket, which is what he would have been paid by the finance company for snatching it back. And that was it – I kept the car. That was the first time we actually sat down and talked together. It was in 1960, and we 'palled up' from that moment."

Ronnie and Pat, following a schooner or two of 'giggle water', challenged each other to a race; the bet was – the winner takes the cars. Ronnie's car, an Opel Capitan was actually paid for, Pat's car was a Ford Zephyr. "So we were going to have this race," explains Ronnie. "We were walking out – like – three parts legless – and he said: 'By the way Ronnie, mine's on the drip!' "

Like Pat in his earlier days, Ronnie tried his hand at shovelling coal. "There was no work about so I went to work for Lawley's, near Salford Bridge, get some money in – 'cause I'd got the kiddie and the wife to keep. I lived in a little council house, 13 back of 54, Windsor Street, Winson Green. Then I got *Speedy Motor Spares* going, a scrap-yard, just down the road from where Pat was. When things improved, I bought a nice, four-bedroom detached house out at Tamworth. I sold that after about two years to a guy called Charlie Hines, one of the first men to get involved with 'cherished numbers'. I bought a cherished number – Ron 78, which became my racing number. When you race Hot Rods and Stock Cars you get allocated a number, you see." Ronnie won thirty-five cups and trophies, for Stock Car Racing, which he still treasures, together with a scrapbook of pictures.

Ronnie's car was part of the track - everyone recognised it. He had an Anglia, with a full race Cosworth engine in it. 1650 was the limit you could have at that time. He raced at several venues around the country - Aldershot, Southend, Hednesford, Wolverhampton, and so on.

The Law of the Jungle seems a rather apposite title for a potentially disastrous escapade involving the two of them. A group of men were looking for Ronnie. Pat offered to give him a hand, but it didn't turn out quite the way they'd planned!

Ronnie comments: "I think he nearly regretted it! I believe this started with a firm in Manchester selling a car to Ronnie Frost, who owned the *Jungle Coffee Bar*, which was opposite Snow Hill Station, at the time. It was like a café, but had three or four floors. Upstairs was a drinking club, and on the side of that you'd got a gambling club. Ronnie also had his office on one of the higher floors. I think Ronnie had a deal with a guy, and they'd changed a grille on a Bentley and sold him a Rolls Royce - I think that was the original grievance. Anyway, we got involved.

"I asked Pat to give me a hand. I said, 'When they come in Pat, just creep out of the shade and lock the door. We don't want anyone else involved, we want it contained.' They came in; Pat closes the door and starts coming up behind them. I'm at the top of the stairs, and I've got a 'double-barrelled'. And the look on Pat's face, because he was a foot bigger than anyone else. His eyes were like saucers, looking down the barrel of this shotgun!" Pat yelled something like "Whoa, whoa!" as Ronnie nearly shot his head off!

Have you heard that highly technical term "I nearly crapped myself?" It was the wrong mob wasn't it? They never turned up. It was just another crowd of people: a lot of innocent people nearly got hurt.

Ronnie was the proprietor of *Paddy's Café*. "I think there were only two in Birmingham at the time, with what they called a 'Refreshment House Licence'. There was *Smokey Joe's* in Northfield, and the other one was mine. I was open twenty-four hours a day." Travelling along the Stratford Road from Solihull, just before the Bordesley railway-bridge, are some premises on the right-hand side, displaying a *Garrett's* sign - 'Anything Bought For Cash'. *Paddy's Café* was immediately next door. In the next chapter, we describe various illegal drinking clubs that Pat and George Cullen ran, together with stories about some of the dubious clientele. One of these, the *Oyster Bar*, was also on the Stratford Road, just a short walk away from *Paddy's Café*.

"The builders used to come in and have their dinners and their sweets like, at teatime, after they'd finished. 'Pay you Friday Ron?' 'Yes, no problem.' Never had any problems at all. It was just the drunkards. I opened a Tattoo Parlour down in the cellar. A guy called Mr. Chinn used to do tattoos. He died and his brother came down and sold me all this gear – the transfers and so forth. I thought, 'I can have a go at that.'

"This guy walked in one time, and he was drunk out of his brains. Benny his name was – Irish fella. 'I want a tattoo on me chest.' I said: 'Benny, go away, come back tomorrow when you've sobered up.' Anyway, he insisted, he put a knife under me chin! I said, 'OK Benny, we'll go down,' - because that was the sort of environment it was. I took him down, he was asleep on the couch. I got my tattoo machine. He wanted a crucifix and I tattooed on his chest 'Eat at Ron's Café' - honest-to-God. He came back the next day with a machete and chased me round the café with it. He still had it twenty years later, when I saw him!

At one stage, Ronnie had a few beds downstairs in the cellar of the café – can you imagine – beds in the cellar? He had a few fellas staying there. He went down there one day and there was this fella, lying on the bed in the afternoon. (I'll leave what he was doing, to your imagination). So Ronnie got his pellet gun and shot him in his - whatever you want to call it!

"I'd just bought a jukebox," recalls Ronnie, "and it was my pride-and-joy: six hundred quid - on the 'drip', obviously. Four guys walked in this one lunch-time - straight out the pub like. They had their dinners and sweets, but nobody wanted to pay. I'm getting agitated, they're getting agitated. A couple of them just chucked me across the counter. I ran into the back and got my shotgun. One's going like that with a chair – straight through me jukebox, me £600 pride-and-joy. Smashed my jukebox and then legged it out of the door. I chased them outside, and they're behind a telephone box. I'm firing – I'm loading as I'm going. This is the God's-honest-truth; I swear it on my kids' lives. They're behind the telephone box and I'm firing, and the telephone box is just going everywhere - there's people with shopping bags, diving into the doorways! But the police came down.

"The café lasted about eighteen months, then it closed down. It wasn't 'cause I couldn't cope - I mean I was fit and lively in those days. I probably got my adrenaline going. I used to – not *enjoy* it…. I mean, the front of my window went two or three times. You're talking about a big plate glass window: it used to cost megabucks; nobody would insure me any more. It's been *Peters the Bookies* ever since – right next to *Garrett's Autos*. Next door to that was a pawnshop and then a Dry Cleaner's. Further down the road, by the telephone box, was a café where all the buses used to stop, so the bus conductors could fill their enamel tea jugs.

"Pat and I would meet each other now and again – I'd pop in and have a drink with him and George Cullen, or - 'We're meeting so-and-so tomorrow night, d'you want to join us?' One day, Pat came up to my yard and said: 'We've been invited down on Friday night to Eddie Fewtrell's place – the *Cedar Club*. 'Who's Tom Jones?' 'Oh, he's a very good singer – you've got to come down.' I didn't make it – for some reason or other. I heard that Pat had a row with Tom's Minder - a big Irish fella."

Roy O'Neill quips: "I've got another story about Pat, for you. One afternoon, we had been doing a job, at the bottom of Mucklow's Hill. Pat said to me: 'I've found a cracking 'pitch', a pub, where's there's a load of 'birds'. Tonight we'll go up there – and we'll 'pull'.' This was round about the mid-1950s. So we got in the car – an old Morris 12/4, and we went over there. We went in this bar – and there wasn't a bird to be seen. But there *were* a pile of big Irish navvies in there!

"We were up at the bar. One of the navvies was there, and he'd got about four pints in his hand; they were the glasses with the handles on. I ordered a Bacardi and Coke and Pat didn't drink, so he said: 'I'll have a shandy.' The Irishman said, 'A shandy - a lad of your size? You want a man's drink – a pint.' And he tipped it all over Pat. Pat went mad – 'Crack'! Before we ran out, they sent for the police. The policeman came, on a bike.

"I can't remember now, whether Pat hit the navvy or not. But we ran past the copper, who was holding the bike. As we ran out of the door, we knocked him over, and the copper fell over his bike –onto the deck! We got into the car, but we had to shove it – to 'jump start' it!" What was the policeman doing, while they were 'jump-starting' the car? "Trying to get up and onto his bike – across to the car park," explains Roy.

"We went home. The next day, we were finishing this place, at the bottom of Mucklow's Hill - clearing scrap out of an old plumber's yard. We'd just loaded the last lot on, to a Morris three-ton Tipper, and were about to put the lock on the place. Who should walk in, but the copper with the bike? He was coming in, to find out what we were doing. We told him, and he said: 'Don't I know you from somewhere?' We said 'No' - got in the truck, and went. Pat said: 'I'm sure that was the copper who we knocked over, the other night!' "

Working as Pat's biographer, on both books, has involved researching a vast network, because of the sheer amount of people that he's mixed with. His friend, Georgie James, likens it to his former club: "It's like a spider's web, trying to get into it. There was John Hunt involved with Billy Sutton. There was Peter Capener. John Hunt was a car trader from Birmingham – he was younger than us. He's another one who'd make a good story; made fortunes, but spent fortunes. I mean, some of the things *he* did. He knew Pat quite well." Ronnie Williams, who once rejoiced in the title, *Mr. Broad Street*, contacted us recently, through Georgie. He and Pat have known each another for over thirty years.

Pat had his head shaved, billiard ball style, for the role of German lieutenant, in *Raiders of the Lost Ark,* (and more recently, in aid of two charities). But despite some of his more grotesque screen roles, and the 'Big Bad Pat Roach' image, originally stage-managed to promote his wrestling career, the *real* Pat Roach is considerably more complex.

During discussion with Pat's fellow *Auf Wiedersehen Pet* actors, about the undoubted pressures of trying to combine family life with a showbusiness career, Chris Fairbank made a particularly apposite comment. "It's never right – that's the only constant thing about it – whatever the scenario - it's not right: there's something that causes a problem. Whether it's working away from home, not working, working on and off. It's not conducive to family life at all. But I don't think that there's a *blueprint* for a harmonious/conducive *anything* really." Nowadays, Pat tries to redress the balance with his young namesake.

I've got a little grandson, Patrick Mark Roach, whom I'm very proud of. I try to spend as much time as I can with him. I sometimes try to talk to him about serious things, which I think he'll need to know later, but he's probably a bit too young yet. He's ten now, and is very articulate for his age. I've taught him some German phrases and we enjoy having pseudo-wrestling bouts together. He's a special light in my life – and really rather wonderful.

I mentioned, in the 'Dedication', that it's probably every man's dream, to have someone follow in his footsteps, perhaps in certain ways - although Patrick's more than capable of achieving - in his own right - (I can see that my 'Big Grandson' already has qualities, beneath the surface). It would be lovely to think that I would be around long enough, to help them come to some sort of fruition.

Experience can play a useful part, in guiding a younger person – provided that he or she is receptive to it.

I try to explain to Patrick, at times, that it's quite a good thing to listen to someone who's made mistakes in his life, and has learned by them – and I hope that he'd listen to the advice given. I want him to aspire, even if I'm not there. I would hope that these qualities that I see, would win through.

Our gypsy theme comes full-circle. Pat was writer-historian Carl Chinn's special guest, on a *BBC Radio WM* broadcast in October 2002, in an hour-long programme, which included a phone-in. Carl mentioned the canal production, *So Far So Good*, in which both of this book's co-writers were due to perform - from 27 – 31 August 2002, together with the *Blue Spirit Productions* company of actors and musicians. It was ideally situated, as a 'moving venue production', where the audience would be taken, in stages, along a Jewellery Quarter section of canals, dramatically lit at night; close to where Pat was born, and where Amelia spent her water gypsy childhood, travelling by narrow boat with Grandpa Jackson.

Pat was playing a 'Big Ugly' part, once again, cast in the leading role of Hades, god of the Underworld. He gave full credit, on Carl's programme, to Jonathan Holmes, director of the company, for his excellent management of a young cast, brimming over with ideas, very democratic, and interacting particularly well. There were, for example, no 'prima donnas', nor any moodiness from individuals, if their ideas weren't adopted. A full cast and crew list is provided, in the *Acknowledgements* section, at the beginning of our book.

The production was to begin, ostensibly, as a wedding party at the *Tarnished Halo* restaurant. Disappointingly, after weeks of hard work, the performance was unable to proceed, due to an unforeseen legal complication. It has been put on hold for the time being. The intention was to go ahead, in the same evocative setting, during summer 2003. However, the show's director, Jonathan Holmes commented recently: "Both the cast and myself remain very keen to stage the production, in it's originally-planned setting, but at the present time, we have been unable to obtain additional funding for the project." This seems a great pity, as the co-writers can confirm, from first-hand experience, that the show would not only enhance the Jewellery Quarter's image, (which we are particularly keen to do), but would also promote Birmingham's reputation, as a city of culture.

Jonathan recalls: "Do you remember the anecdote of Katherine and the Willow mask? She'd been traumatised by it as a child, and had signed up to *So Far So Good* without knowing Pat had been in the film. Katherine turned up to rehearsal one day, only to be told, as stage manager, to repair the mask she'd been so scared of nearly twenty years before! What are the odds of that?" Pat planned to wear the mask - as Hades.

Actor-manager Ian Sandy, played Friar Tuck to Pat's Little John, in a *Babes in the Wood* pantomime. Without any prior knowledge of the family history, Ian, who began as a child actor, recalls this 'slightly sinister' side of Pat: "He's always got this aura around him – it's almost a mystery. It's a bit gypsy, isn't it? Almost Romany: I can see him in that guise." Tim Spall is of the same opinion. As he writes in the *Foreword*: 'He's got that gypsy thing about him which is quite interesting. Although he's a very personable, gentle, amiable man, there is something a bit *mysterious* about him.'

Chapter Five –

NIGHTCLUB TRAILBLAZERS

Mackenzie and Roachie are squaring up to each other; a few blows are exchanged. We're saying: "It's going to be a fair fight." After a few minutes I realised that my pal wasn't going to win, so I jumped on top of Roachie. It didn't turn out to be a great idea! But I thought: 'I can't let my pal get hurt.' Roachie immediately threw me to the ground: it was a scuffle - and nothing more. We became quite close friends, and grew to respect one another.

Paddy White

"The friend I'm referring to, a guy called Henry Mackenzie, now lives in Blackpool. We were fifteen or sixteen when the incident happened." Paddy White and I were seated in his Harborne home, as he recalled this first meeting with Pat, leading to a friendship that, unbeknown to both of them, would last a lifetime.

"We were in Monument Road, Ladywood," he continues. "There used to be a little shop there called *Mrs. Parker's*, where we could buy penny bottles of pop, and things like that. Somewhere along the line, Pat and Henry got into an argument. Pat was already a big guy, don't forget." Readers may recall, that by the time he'd reached only ten or eleven years of age, some of the Ladywood boys had christened Pat 'The Giant'.

"He was bigger than me when he was small!" quips Paddy. "So 'Mack' and Roachie decided to settle it outside - that was the thing to do at that time. I'm with Mack. Roachie and I just knew *of* each other, from being around Ladywood; we weren't close friends. We were living in Ryland Street, and Pat was in Shakespeare Road, just off King Edwards Road - with his grandmother. The lads down there were a different 'firm' to us. It didn't come into the conversation at that time, but after that first meeting, we got on with each other a little bit, recognised each other, and became quite friendly."

Paddy and Pat attended different schools. Two decades after George Smith, Paddy also went to St Peter's School, just off Broad Street, and from there, to Aston Commercial School. (George was the boatman, in our previous book, who'd befriended some of the canal boat children, when he attended St. Peter's).

On leaving school, Paddy worked with one of his older brothers, as a steel erector, and then with George Cullen, in the same trade. "Pat and I lost touch, things moved on. We didn't meet again until I'd come out of the army – I'd be around twenty-two." Twenty-one-year-old Pat, meanwhile, had just gained his judo White Belt, followed within a very short period, by a Black Belt. "After the army," explains Paddy, "I worked with George again, out of town, for a while; not only around Birmingham, but all over the country – on big steel girder jobs. We worked down in Wales a lot, on the towers and rope-ways, which took the slack out of the mines, into big buckets, then dropped it out to sea."

Due to their age difference, and because they were often together, people sometimes assumed that Paddy was George's older son. "George and I worked for a number of years, all over the country, then he opened a scrap yard, down by St Andrew's Football Ground – on the Coventry Road. As a fellow dealer, George also knew Frank.

"It was quite a surprise really, when Pat came back on the scene," explains Paddy. "George and I used to go out drinking together. He said: 'We're going to see a guy tonight – do a bit of business,' – and we went out to meet Roachie." However, Pat's relationship with George was of a different order: "Pat had more of a business relationship with him. I hadn't seen Pat for a *good* number of years, and was around twenty-four, when George introduced us. We looked at each other. It was not *unlike* our recent meeting at *Angels Café*: the little delay of recognition – and almost immediately, Roachie said to George: 'You know him? That bastard set about me, when we were young!' " One can only *imagine* George's reply! According to Paddy, that evening's meeting marked the beginning of Pat and George's business relationship.

The Birmingham's nightclub scene was 'trailblazed' by Eddie Fewtrell, assisted by his brothers, Frankie, Gordon, Don and Chrissie. "There was a Late Night petrol station," recalls Paddy, "down by Eddie Fewtrell's first club, *The Bermuda Club*, halfway down Navigation Street. I was out one night, with Jimmy Mackenzie, (no relation to my friend Henry), having a tot. Jimmy had a car –' POP 105'. We went into the Navigation Street garage, put some petrol in the car, £2-50, or whatever, and he's gone: 'Have one of these watches!' " According to Gordon, they were known as 'Mudus' – (Moodoos). "Jimmy always had about four or five watches on his arm," Paddy continues. "He'd probably got them from the 'Knockout Shops' for £1-00, or so. Or he might buy drinks, and he'd say: 'Ah – I've got no money – have one of these watches!' 'Jimmy the Watch' was one of his three nicknames. He was an older guy – about George's age, from the North of England, Darlington, I think. But he was around the Midlands for years."

Successful businessman and conservationist, Ken Schofield, who is also an antique dealer in the Jewellery Quarter, recalls, in his early teens, seeing Pat with a group of friends, somewhere in the vicinity of Hurst Street. Pat was smartly dressed in an expensive 'Crombie' coat and fedora hat, which strengthened Ken's resolve to achieve a comparable lifestyle. He describes Pat as, "… a very intelligent man who can switch very quickly between 'levels', according to the person he's talking to."

Ken and Pat have known each other, as friends and business colleagues, for over twenty years, although he's been 'aware' of Pat, for most of his life. "The first time I actually *knew* about Pat, was that his name kept cropping up. My two older brothers - Alan ('Schoey') and Ernie, used to talk about him, Johnny Prescott, and all these other people. He was really a 'name'. I saw and spoke to him for the first time, when I was in *The Tow Rope*, on Broad Street, opposite *The Rum Runner*, (where *Sting* made his first debut).

"Pat was in the *Rum Runner* that particular night. My friends and I tried to get into the club, but we couldn't. He didn't know who I was, until I told him that night. We were maybe fifteen or sixteen, so we weren't even allowed to drink. I tried to pretend I was with Pat, but he wasn't having any of it – and we're going – like: 'Bastard!' "

Ken eventually began trading with Pat, at his Winson Green scrapyard. Trying to get a deal out of him, Ken admits, was no easy matter: " 'Buy low and sell high' – that's his motto! Pat was into cigarettes and lighters, years ago - shipping them out to Ireland. He came to a house that I had in Bartley Green, although I wasn't there. I'd sold him a bookcase, containing a gold chain that hadn't been removed. My ex-wife, Susan, phoned up to tell Pat about the chain, and he returned it to her."

Both Ken and Pat share the view: "…as long as it's an *honest* deal, and nobody's been hit over the head for it. We have a saying: 'Can we put it in the shop window?' I've had this way of doing business, for many years," explains Ken. "Somebody brings merchandise to you to sell. So you say: 'The gaffer ain't here, and I'm dyslexic: I can't read or write, but I've got a Polaroid camera. You stand by the 'kit' (goods). I'll photograph you. You sign the back of the photograph, with your proof of ID, then I'll give you the cash,' (I'd show them a big bundle of 'dosh'). Sometimes they'd go: 'No – f*** you!' - and walk away. But the honest broker will say: 'Yeah – can I just brush my hair and straighten my jacket first?' It's the easy way out – it sorts out the 'schlock'. What people don't realise is that you've got a door saying 'open'. It's open to everybody – the policeman, the taxman, VAT man, Joe Public – whatever. So unless you want to hide it round the back…

"But as far as Pat and his friends were concerned, we were much younger, and these guys were revered. You didn't want to take the p*** out of them – you might end up in a cellar! All of the lads looked up to the likes of Billy Sutton, Bob Sayce, my brother 'Schoey', and Johnny Prescott. You'd think: 'That's where *we're* coming from.' They weren't drug dealers (as might be the case these days). Alright – a bit on the side here and there, but, generally-speaking, they were just looking for a straight deal."

Pat and his associates were always trying to keep 'one step ahead of the game' - living by their wits. Regarding the secret pockets they used, to conceal their money, Ken observes: "Yes – absolutely. Otherwise you might be 'turned over' - in the entry." He describes his early reaction to Pat as, "… a Big geezer, smart, 'proper order'. When you saw that crew together, you were afraid; or even if Pat was on his own, you'd just agree with everything they said!" There's an interesting contrast, between Pat's friends and associates, who realised that he was an approachable guy, and younger groups of lads, like Ken.

"You can imagine," he continues, "in the 1960s, we're all the 'Mods' – going round the clubs. We'd got to be careful with all these 'old hats' – because they're running the show, anyway." They'd frequent nightclubs such as *Midnight City, The Rainbow,* (in Erdington), *The Mexicano. The Dolce Vita*, and *The West End.* "*The Midnight City* was owned by the Prykes. It had another name before that – right opposite Digbeth; it was an illegal club. The Prykes earned a lot of money - the older one's now deceased. They put on acts such as *The Who*. Just illegal clubs, changing their names every so often, to suit their new clients!"

Billy Sutton knew them well: "Old man Pryke (Bobby) and his dear wife, Iris, had two sons – Chrissie and Robbie. They were great friends of mine. They lived in this big, beautiful house called Fulford Hall, in Earlswood - a palatial place in its own grounds. I think there were something like 400 acres of ground, with an *unbelievable* drive. I used to stay there virtually seven days a week. Chrissie, the youngest son, and me, went into partnership in the banana business, in the wholesale market in Birmingham.

"I used to drive the old man's Jensen registration 'ROB 1'. Bobby Pryke had all of Jamaica Row – it was his wholesale business. He used to wear a carnation and bowler hat – every morning at four o'clock – directing all the traffic (all the lorries) into his business. We had parties galore at Fulford Hall - they had three Spanish maids.

"When he had the famous *Moat House*, in Bradford Street, that was one of the first Society Clubs in Birmingham, in the early 1960s. That was another of my 'play up' places. The Big'un used to make guest appearances there, when he returned from wrestling abroad – or whatever; it was the real 'in-set'. But I have very fond memories of the Prykes.

"You see, when you had the *Cedar*, that was all the elite set of street-wise kids: bookmakers, steel stockholders. *The Moat House* was more up-market. That was the scene where they had one of the first early restaurants there. On the door, they used to have a long flight of stairs, going straight up. At the top, you'd be greeted by Jack Lemon.

"Now Jackie Lemon, (or Jackie Trevis as he was known), was one of the best street fighters ever in Birmingham. He used to work in the meat market. If anybody 'performed' at *The Moat House*, (unless they were part of the in-set, like Johnny Prescott, Roachie, me or Jimmy Sadler – the likes of those) – everybody was 'outed' very quickly – down the 'dancers': upstairs – down you went – if you started performing.

"But that, and *The Jewish Club*, in Moseley, where we used to go on a Sunday night, where all the 'heavy duty' Jews used to go – Jackie Freeman; the *Jewish Club*, Moseley Road -in Moseley Village itself. People like Dave Rubens – the very wealthy Jewish set; they were all play-up merchants. We used to congregate there, on Sunday night. Eli Davis's daughters were singers. According to Gordon Fewtrell: "Dave Rubens and Jack Woolf, both Jewish bookmakers, used to go to the club." He has a photo of the three of them, with himself in the centre.

"Shirley Bassey – I'm going back to the early 60s, when she was first starting," continues Billy. "When she was appearing in the Midlands, she used to stay with the Davis's, in their house in Moseley. Shirley used to be a regular visitor to *The Jewish Club*: proper 'play-up girl' of course – as they do! The classic clubs to me, were certainly *The Jewish Club* and *The Moat House*; the *Bermuda* and *Cedar* were the 'duckers-and-divers'."

Ken Schofield provides an alternative view: "So many people have been impressed – not only by Pat – because he was part of a whole *group* – but by the Fewtrells, and so on. You wouldn't want to argue with *any* of them. Eddie Fewtrell was a 'proper' geezer, and a very astute businessman. If you were in the Fewtrell's clubs, you never had bouncers of the kind that are sometimes on the door of *today's* clubs, where they just say: 'You're drunk, you've got to leave!' In the Fewtrell's clubs, if you got out of order, they took you out; but they didn't beat you up, they did it nicely."

Pat would sometimes help Eddie, with these situations. "They'd put you in a taxi, send you home, or whatever," comments Ken, "but if you wanted to come back, and start throwing bricks through the window - 'Sorry, you've made a mistake.' It's a much more intimidating approach nowadays. They knew how to *handle* customers in those days. They were the *guys* – in the city."

In addition to *The Cedar Club*, Paddy White was also a frequent visitor to *The Bermuda Club*. "It was an All-Night Café, before that, called *The Victory*, in Navigation Street, by where all the trams used to go to – from the Lickey Hills. A young lad was murdered on the premises, which were subsequently closed down, before Eddie bought it. He's a very nice guy." Patricia Bowen, (née Smith, from Shakespeare Road), confirms just how popular the *Bermuda Club* was. "It used to be absolutely *packed* in there – like sardines. My husband, Ken, used to go around, flicking the ladies' suspender belts!"

Gordon Fewtrell recalls: "Little Kenny Baker used to come down. He was appearing, at the time, in *Snow White and the Seven Dwarfs*. He drove a mini with blocks on the pedals, about nine inches high." Kenny, who is 3 foot 6 inches high, recalls first meeting Pat when he was touring the Birmingham clubs and Ice shows. "We were working around the Birmingham area, with *The Ambassador's Club, The Beverley Artists Club* at Yardley, by *The Swan. The Cavendish Club* in Hurst Street by the Hippodrome. *The Elbow Room*, Aston, was a first floor club, up some stairs. I didn't go there very often. It was an illegal drinking club. You had to ring a bell to get in. We did all the clubs – Wolverhampton – all over the place.

"I remember *The Flamingo Club*, near New Street Station; just off Hurst Street, and Eddie Fewtrell's *Cedar Club. The Castaways*, by the market, was about the best club in Birmingham." In 2003, Pat appeared at a Paris Convention, in connection with his roles in the recently revived *Indiana Jones* movies. Kenny Baker was also there, as R2D2, a character he made famous in *Star Wars*, accompanied by their mutual friend, Dave Prowse (Darth Vader).

"I happened to be working in London, with my partner, Jack Purvis, around the cabaret scene, when George Lucas came into London – at Elstree," recalls Kenny, whose showbusiness career now spans more than fifty years. "They'd already made the robot, but they couldn't find anybody small enough to fit into it, you see? I was just about the right size for it – that's all it was. It didn't have a voice, it just whistled. There were only two robots. I was the little one, the other one – C3PO, was the taller, yellow one. He was more like a human being, but I was supposed to be the *real* robot." The first *Star Wars* film involved twenty weeks' filming.

"Sometimes they just want Darth Vader and R2D2. At other times, Jeremy Bullock, or Peter Mayhew, who plays Chewbacca, will accompany us. We've been all over Europe: Germany, France, Belgium, Holland, Denmark and Sweden." Kenny started on the Convention Circuit in 1995 and has continued on a fairly regular basis since then: "Most weekends there's something on, somewhere; they're conventions rather than promotional stuff. It's called a *Sci-Fi Convention*. They've got all kinds of people: *Star Trek, Star Wars, Babylon 5*, and all the different American shows. Sometimes it's all four of us, sometimes you get the two of us, depending on how big the show is."

Returning to the subject of the *Cedar Club,* Paddy White continues: "Tony Johnson and I used to go out most weekends. Eddie and his brother Frank were running it, before Frank died. I used to see quite a bit of Chrissie too. Anyway, we were in the club, and Eddie told us he'd been away to America. I said: 'Brilliant!' 'Mind you,' he said, 'it frightened the life out of me. We were in the aeroplane, me and Frank - we've got ourselves a nice few quid. First time in our lives we're on top: pockets full of dough – and we're going to have a good time. Doing a proper 'number' on the plane: champagne – the works.

'We get to America and an announcement comes on the plane – "There'll be a delay in landing, due to a technical fault. But there's no need to worry, we'll be landing within twenty minutes or so." Now Eddie didn't like flying. 'I tell you what Paddy,' he said. 'I sat there, and I turned to our kid and said, 'F***ing lovely, isn't it? First time we've ever had any dough, we're in front, and this bastard's going to crash the plane!' I sat there and I sweated for fifteen minutes. I've never been so glad to get out of anything in my life!' I remember him telling me that story. It was really funny! You know the story about Roachie and Tom Jones' bodyguard?"

Back in the old Cedar Club days, Eddie, to help him out, had booked Tom Jones, weeks in advance. Tom then made it big. In the early days, we were all pals together. He used to come in to the Cedar Club. Eddie would say: "Oh Pat, do us a favour, just watch Tom on stage, would you?" There'd be about fifteen girls, trying to get to him – even in those days. I had a bit of a kerfuffle with his bodyguard (we're now friends) which I wrote about in my previous book. It's nice that Tom made it big – I'm sure he's still a lovely chap.

Don Fewtrell describes the fight, between Pat and 'Big Paddy' – (Paddy Hallett). "It was in about 1976 – I know – because Tom Jones won the Gold Disc Award, for *It's Not Unusual*. We had a party; we always used to have a party, for *Tom Jones and the Squires* and the other stars – *Lulu and the Lovers*, *Elke Brookes and The End* – they all played at the *Cedar Club*: it was very well known. Anyway, Pat phones me up. 'Don,' he says, 'I'm bringing Tom Jones' bodyguard in tonight. He's as big as me – if not bigger – and he's four-foot wide!' I was only joking at the time, but I said: ' If there's any trouble, you've got to get him out!' He said: 'OK!' Sure enough - what a business! I said to Roachie: 'Get him out, because if you don't, me and my brothers will!'

"Pat got hold of him and took him outside, and they went up the road – a little bit, to a place where they manufactured metal grilles and things; we used it as a bit of a car park." The outcome of the episode was typical of Pat: he took Paddy home, because he was in quite a state, put him to bed, and even made him a drink, the following morning!

On Ed Doolan's radio programme, *The Other Side of Pat Roach*, Pat requested Tom Jones' hit record, 'Sex Bomb', as a reminder of those days.

Pat knew all of the Fewtrell brothers. The youngest was Roger. "He's known as *Bomber*," explains his older brother, Don, "because his initials were RAF of Bomber Command, and he was born during the war. The name has stuck with him all of his life. Then there was Chrissie, who died of cancer, in August, 1999; he was the hardest man in Birmingham – bar none." Considering this description, I wondered why Pat has described Chrissie as a really nice man. "He *was* a very nice fella," observes Don. "You see, people get the wrong idea about the Fewtrell family – what villains they are. I literally had a girl come to me – when I took my young lady out – and she said: 'Oh, you're one of the Fewtrells are you? Is that right – you bury people in concrete postings?' She said that to my face. I couldn't believe it!"

The third youngest Fewtrell, Gordon, has run a second-hand dealership, on the Washwood Heath Road, for many years. "He bought Pat Roach's old place," confirms Don. "Gordon sells cars, 'made of a non-corrosive metal, of lasting durability, with a sparkling lustre' - and so forth - I should have been a salesman! After Gordon, there's Johnny, the fourth youngest, who recently sold the *Red Lion* pub, at Shirley, after years as the landlord." (What a small world – my uncle's garden backs on to it)!

Heading towards the eldest, Eddie's next, followed by Don, who's two years older than him, (both are in their early 70s). "Frankie came after me, then Kenny, the oldest brother. My two sisters, Violet and Phyllis are older. Phyllis is the oldest."

I interviewed Eddie for our first book, at his club – *XL's*, in Auchinleck Square. "I originally owned the club," explains Don. "I opened it as *Faces*." Don showed me two photographs, taken in 1973, at the opening night of his other club, *Pollyanna's*. "I didn't come on the scene until Edward had already opened the *Cedar Club*, at the end of '62."

As Pat has attended the opening of all of Eddie's nightclubs, I wondered if that was how Don had met him? "The first club that Edward opened was the *Bermuda Club*, where you couldn't get a two o'clock licence," he recalls. "The police used to smash the door down, at one time, or come through the roof! There was one occasion when the police came in, and this man was drunk. He had a glass of scotch in his hand. The police said: 'And what are you drinking?' He said: 'I'll have a double scotch if that's alright with you!' Everybody used to throw their glasses behind the bar, if the police came in - to destroy the evidence.

"I first met Pat Roach at the *Cedar Club*, in the early days. We became great friends, and I used to go out with him once a week, of a Tuesday night. We went to different clubs, including The *Rum Runner*. One evening, in that club, this fella, Teddy Major, a bookie, was with a man called Bryn Jones, from Coventry. Teddy said: 'I bet a thousand pounds that no one can out-drink Bryn.' Pat said: 'Don Fewtrell can.' I'd already had a bottle of vodka at the *Rum Runner* before we went to the *Tower Ballroom*, (which was being run by a pal of mine, Captain John Morgan). I said: 'No, I don't want to out-drink anybody.' Then one fella said: 'Fifty pounds on Don.' Another fella said: 'A hundred pounds on Bryn.' The bets kept going in. So I said: 'Oh, alright.' The final bet was, the first one to fall over, loses the bet – of a thousand pounds. This was held at the *Tower*, after the *Rum Runner* closed, at two o'clock in the morning!

"We had the drinks lined up – ten vodkas in a row. (I think we had tonic or lemonade in it). At one stage, he was ten in front of me! I drank those ten and another ten – in a matter of minutes. Cutting the story short, Bryn moved away from the bar, about ten to ten in the morning – and fell over backwards.

I said to Pat: 'Count how many drinks I've had'; he told me that I'd had ninety-three, (three bottles). But I'd never do it again – oh no! I didn't get paid either. Teddy Major died - not long ago. He still owes me a grand... *and* I had to pay for all the booze!

"I remember a Beauty Contest, at the *Tower Ballroom*, sponsored by *Energen Wheatbread*. Pat asked me to be one of the judges. I'll never forget. Pat and me were outside Dale End, and this fella comes out and he says: 'Do you think my bird could win?' He'd got a young bird there – and he was an old fella. 'We *can* be bent!' I said. Anyway, without any intervention, she came third. Bert Weedon, the guitarist, was on the panel too, plus other celebrities. They used to announce you as you came in the door and took your seat: 'Mr. Pat Roach, Mr. Don Fewtrell.' "

Pat recalls bringing Hawaiian wrestler 'Prince Ieuka', to the *Cedar Club*. They had to open both doors, to get him in! "Massive he was – sweating", confirms Don, "stood by the side there. I was *running* the *Cedar Club*. I used to get all the beer and things and get all the staff in – everything – the whole lot. Eddie would say, 'I want all you lads here tomorrow - our Johnny and Chrissie and Gordon.' But none of them ever turned up, so I had to do it all on my own." Gordon remembers it slightly differently!

I asked Don about Pat's Hockley café, the *Fly-over.* "He used to have a disco in there, with all the proper lights. He was quite a laugh – a lot of fun, Pat was. People took liberties with him, because of his size. They'd shout: 'I'll cut you down to size' - and all that crap. Pat had to back down, because if he hit them he'd kill them!"

Pat's cousin, John Bevis, recalls meeting Raymond Frogatt, the singer-songwriter, who had been at school with Pat. "I met Raymond at *Barbarella's*, the one night. He had lots of pints of bitter lined up, which people had bought him." He also remembers Don's club, *Pollyanna's,* just off Colmore Row. "It's called *The Lytton Tree* now. It's changed from being a club, into a pub." Gordon recalls that Raymond bought his old XJ6 off him.

According to Don: "I had another drinking match - with George Cullen. I've met his son – he's a 'different kettle of fish'. Georgie was in the *Cedar Club* once, and he thought he was a good drinker. Now I was the best drinker in town – bar none. I out-drank him and he got the raving needle! But we didn't care about that then." Pat and the co-writer met one of George's daughters at a book signing for *If – The Pat Roach Story*. She had a long chat with Pat, and seemed very likeable and level-headed.

"Georgie used to live up Kingstanding way,' continues Don, "on the right hand side. But his son's a very nice fella." Surprisingly, Don was unaware that Pat and George had run any clubs of their own (albeit, for a short period). "I used to go out with Chief Inspector John Rischmiller," explains Don. "He'd ring and say: 'Come round the town with me tonight Don, and have a drink.' We went into *The Speak-Easy Club*, on the Moseley Road: owned by Mick Riley and run by Desi. John must have accidentally bumped into this Irishman – about nine-foot tall, and four-and-a-half foot wide. I thought: 'Any minute now, there's going to be an absolute 'bang-up' – won't get your breath!' He'd got hands like shovels – you know? John said to him: 'Who are you shoving - you?' This Irishman said: (in brogue) 'I'm sorry there mate, I'm absolutely sorry!' I thought, 'Thank God for that!' There were 'long-lifers' in there – as canned as lampshades, and all the prostitutes – you'd never believe it!"

A few weeks later, I visited Don's brother, Gordon, the third youngest in the family. Like all of the Fewtrells, he didn't have an easy start in life: " My mother died when I was thirteen and I was fostered, first of all by Jack Rowan, my father's friend, who lived in Calshot Road, Great Barr. He took us to live in his house for a week, after my mum died. He came and rescued us, because they were going to take us into care – my brothers, Chrissie, Roger and myself." Their father had been a taxi driver, at one time.

"Chrissie lived with Jack and Edie Poynton first, in Saint Saviour's Road. Roger went to live with someone else. Then we swapped around and I went to live with the Poyntons." Gordon left school at fifteen, working as a projectionist at the *Plaza*, at the Co-op Dairy in Vauxhall Road, and then as a chauffeur. "My first business was in Icknield Street, with my brother-in-law, when I was about nineteen. When I was twenty, we moved to Camp Hill, buying and sell second-hand cars, by the 'Fly-over,' (as you went into town, it was on the left-hand side of the road).

"Eventually I left all that and went to work at the *Cedar Club*, as a croupier. I met a lot of people there, including the car dealer, Jack Evans, of *P.J.Evans*. I played him at 'Black Jack', and took thousands of pounds off him. He gave me a 50-dollar bill for my luck! I didn't spend it: it must be somewhere about still. I worked there for about two years, before Donald came on the scene. Then I became a painter and decorator, and eventually started up in business again. I had a smaller business, in the early 70s, just a bit further along Washwood Heath Road, before I bought this business off Pat. I used to come and talk to him here; he'd be drinking this milky stuff – for the wrestling. He said: 'I'm getting out of this bloody place!' So I bought it from him. While he was running it, I often used to come in and have a chat with him. Over the years he's phoned me up to ask advice about various things to do with cars; about the value of car parts, and so on."

I showed Gordon the photograph of Les Kellett holding Pat in a wrestling hold, the day *Pat Roach Cars* originally opened, on the exact site where our conversation was now taking place! "I didn't *buy* this property, because Pat didn't own it," he commented. "We just rented it. I gave him a thousand quid for goodwill – or whatever. I've been here for just over thirty years." As we enter 2004, Gordon has just purchased the site.

Pat and Gordon originally met at the *Bermuda Club*. "He used to come down with Billy Yukon, another Birmingham wrestler. I'm *sure* they were the best of pals. He died when he was in his late 30s - a stocky fella – about half the size of Pat. I'd also meet Pat at the *Cedar Club*. When I attended various functions, I'd see him in there occasionally."

Billy Yukon was a friend of mine. Later, however, when I broke my leg wrestling at the Victoria Club, Billy had a collection for me, but then shared the money out. We fell out over that.

Gordon explains: "Pat was often in the *Cedar Club*. I don't think he used to drink a lot, but women were always chatting him up. He was very friendly with people. I remember when 'Big Paddy' challenged him. Pat stood there for quite some time, taking all the 'flak'. Eventually he said: 'Hey you – outside!' I was sober, because I was working on the tables. The impression I got was that this fella was saying something very cheeky to him. Pat was very tolerant – because he's that sort of person. I followed them out, to a small yard, in front of the club. Pat was standing with his back to the yard. I think the fight only lasted a short while. I was never actually *involved*, because I was always on the tables." According to Pat, the fight lasted longer than either brother recalls.

"Chrissie had a bit of a 'do' at one time, at *The Last Drop*", (the pub which Jill and Paddy White were eventually involved with, as *The Actress and Bishop*). "He was trying to get things together," recalls Gordon. "It was a charity do – for cancer. I think some of the *Crossroads* cast was involved, including the chap who played Benny, Paul Henry. I was down there and had a drink with Pat. I've been to wrestling and talked to him there. I used to watch Pat wrestle at the *Digbeth Institute*, by the Irish club. At one time he was playing Little John, in pantomime, at the *Birmingham Hippodrome*. I'm sitting right in the front row, and he's come out, looked at me, looked down, then coloured up a bit. I said: 'You look like a right prat in those green tights!' "

Gordon met his wife, formerly Jane Lisle, in 1962, at the re-opening of the *Cedar Club*, following refurbishment. "Her brothers introduced me to her. I drove her barmy for a bit. She was only sixteen at the time. I asked her to give me a kiss. She said, 'I won't let you kiss me. I don't *like* you!' Anyway, she gave me a kiss and I said, 'I'm going to marry you,' and I did! We've been married now for almost forty years. We've got two grown-up daughters: one's a chiropodist and the other's a personal secretary.

"Johnny Prescott was a very good boxer. When he finished boxing, he started doing motor cars. He mixed with John Hunt and Duggie Nicholls, Bryn Jones, and they actually had a garage in Bloxwich, which is now a furniture shop. Bryn Jones was a magician with figures – he's dead now. If you had a list of figures, like that, he'd give you the total. That was his claim to fame – he was *brilliant* with figures. He liked the horses.

"Johnny was a nice bloke," recalls Georgie James, "and a very good boxer. He fought Billy Walker more than once didn't he? Johnny was another one who liked a drink in Eddie Fewtrell's club. The *Cedar Club*, in Constitution Hill, was Johnny Prescott's hangout. We all used to go there. It had one of the best poker games in the country. We'd go there in the mornings and afternoons and play." They had 'Black Jack' tables too. Gordon Fewtrell was the croupier. "We used to go into a private room, to play poker, with Eddie, Derek Baxter and a couple of the Directors of *Birmingham City Football Club* too," explains Georgie. "Pat used to go there for a drink, ever such a lot."

Don Fewtrell recalls that one particular poker game lasted three days. "There was a special signalling system which certain players had, to indicate which cards they were holding." Gordon elaborates: "There were a lot of foreign people in there, who used to speak in their native tongue - (I should imagine, telling their partners what they'd got). Rather than let them get away with it, my brothers and I spoke in our own English 'backslang'!" According to Don: "The club was haunted by a ghost - who I named 'Fred'. Quite a few staff left as a result! There was a secret room in the club, which *some* of my brothers knew about, which was accessed by moving a small wardrobe."

Georgie James explains: "I know all of the clubs in Birmingham. One of the Prykes' clubs was *The Castaways* – Rob Pryke's club, in Bradford Street." Pat happened to be at the club one evening, and was asked to resolve the situation because Georgie was his friend. (He's found himself in a similar kind of situation several times, over the years). "They fetched Pat Roach to me," recalls Georgie. "I went there with my first wife, June – having a drink – watching Tom Jones – and Tom knicked my pint! I had a chip at him. I said: 'Listen, you can afford to get your own!' But Pat was the one who had to come over to tell me to be quiet; and me and Pat, we're like brothers! They gave me a cheque for my wife's dress, which they ruined: they came by with a tray of gammon and chips, and caught her dress. We eventually sorted it out." Paddy White recalls artificial footprints, in the sand-coloured carpet, at *The Castaways*.

Whilst visiting Roy O'Neill at his Barr Street warehouse, he explained: "The *Cedar Club* didn't belong to Eddie. He was partners with the building king, Stanley Kay, whose wife, was murdered by her brother" - (a fact confirmed by Gordon Fewtrell). According to Don, Stan was a 'silent partner'. "Alan Manning put the first table in the *Bermuda Club* – upstairs," continues Roy. "You had to go up a funny staircase to it, like a trapdoor into it. He started a casino there. My girlfriend had a pub, *The Turf Tavern* in Spring Hill, a quartet used to play there. It was on the corner of Spring Hill – opposite the library. Kathy Tate was a friend of Vera Fewtrell's, (Frank's wife), and Tom

Jones, (before he *was* Tom Jones), used to come down there, and sing of a Sunday. We've had some times! We all used to meet in the *Cedar Club* in the Little Bar: there was a Little Bar and a Big Bar. Bernard Manning was in there, a couple of times."

Pat's café, *The Flyover*, was in the vicinity of Roy's premises. "You'd go down by the side of the Flyover, and the café would be opposite," he explains. "At the end of Barr Street are some shops. If you looked right across, from the shops, the café used to be there. There was a bus stop there and a copper used to be on point duty, right in the middle of the road. From my premises, if you turn right, and then right again, you'll come to the Flyover."

In the early 1960s, (before Pat grew a beard), he and George Cullen, established patrons of the Fewtrells, decided to experiment, by opening three clubs of their own. As they had no drinking licenses, their clubs were deemed 'illegal'. Nevertheless, they provided an alternative service to the public, at a time when Birmingham's nightlife was, relatively speaking, (not literally!) virgin territory. In this context, it seems reasonable to describe Pat and George as pioneers, in the nightclub scene; not simply by running their own clubs, but via experiences, (positive and negative), in a range of venues, right across the city. As Pat's career flourished, such experiences became international, involving *many* aspects of the entertainment industry.

Chapter Six –

IN SOME EXCLUSIVE RENDEZVOUS

The hill was sloping down, by that time, so it had a couple or three steep stone steps to it - well worn. It used to be a fruit and vegetable shop, but gradually transmogrified itself into a drinking den. It had a sort of Judas Grille, halfway up. The top step was rather narrow, so if you wanted to look through the grille, you often had to hang on to it, or you'd fall backwards off the step! There was a bell, but you had to know how to ring it - to a kind of Morse Code.

Ken Goodby

"The *Rendezvous*, was the first of the three clubs," explains Paddy White. "Then around that same time, we had this thing with *The Oyster Bar.* What a posh name – if ever there was the wrong name for the wrong place! But the *Rendezvous Club* was the predominant one." Visitors were expected to knock first, then a hatch was pulled back, so that they could be identified. "Most of the time I used to come and check," Paddy continues. "We learned a lesson. The first time we were raided by the police, we opened the hatch, but they broke the door down. So afterwards, we had a button fitted to the floor, by the door, that you could hit, and it would flash all the lights upstairs. Then everybody would just dump all the drinks. Our clients were often tough guys: car dealers, scrap merchants - 'wide boys' - so they 'knew the score'."

One of our photographs features Ronnie Callow and two of his sons, standing in front of *The Jeweller's Arms*, on the corner of Spencer Street and Hockley Street. Pat opened the club in the days before he grew a beard. En route to *The Rendezvous*, patrons would pass the *Jeweller's Arms*, on their left, then big double gates. There was a shop to the right of that, and then *The Rendezvous*, located at 31, Hockley Street, as Pat's business card confirms. Paddy explains: "They pulled the buildings down, a few years ago; it was vacant land for some time, but they've built big fancy flats there now, on the same site. There's Spencer Street, Branston Street and Great Hampton Street, which is the main road."

Engraver Ken Goodby, whose premises are in Spencer Street, just around the corner from the former *Rendezvous*, confirms that Paddy would open the hatch. "Check who it was – see if we wanted them," explains Paddy. "Yes, you're OK' – open the door – in. You walked past me, down a passageway, through what was the existing greengrocer's shop (it was a carpet shop too, at some time – I seem to recall).” According to Pat, the shop belonged to Tommy Richardson, whose son, Paul later ran the thriving company, *City Waste*.

Paddy continues: “After going through the shop, you’d turn left, onto a set of stairs, that went up *that* way. You came into the club at the far end of the room; it came back on itself, towards the front of the shop.” He drew a diagram of both floors. “*The Oyster Bar* was much rougher, but the *Rendezvous* was one of those places where you walked upstairs and thought: ‘Bloody hell – I didn’t know *this* was here!’ It was nicely furnished with red velvet velour seating, and was well lit. Even though it was an illegal-drinking club, it was posh – in its own little way, with proper fixed seating and tables.” The bar was quite smart, compared to the *Oyster Bar*, which had a plank for a counter, balanced on top of beer crates!

Ken Goodby recalls this particular section of Hockley Street, as it used to be in the late 1950s/early 1960s, when *The Rendezvous*, was in full swing. “In 1946, when I came to work at *Lancaster’s*, there were still quite a few families *living* in the Quarter, in and around Hockley Street, Branston Street, Vyse Street and Spencer Street. They lived mainly up entries, in back-to-back houses, but there was still a school - children running about and washing hanging from lines. Gradually they were moved out and re-housed, in the suburbs. I remember Hockley Street, in 1946, we were at Number 16.” The club was at number 31.

“From Vyse Street downwards,” continues Ken, “it had a large firm on the corner, which took that lot up.” Ken is describing his own side of Hockley Street – where the *Jeweller’s Arms* pub is located. His description begins at number 1 – on the corner of Hockley Street. “On the opposite side of the corner from Vyse Street downwards, to the beginning of Northampton Street, where it comes into Hockley Street and Spencer Street, starting at the top, on the corner, there was a firm that threaded beads and pearl necklaces. There was an entry next to that, with a family living at the back. Next door to that was another old house, that had been converted into a workshop, and that’s where *F. Goldsmith’s*, the jewellers were, (who are now a big firm, out in Henley-in-Arden).

“As you came past *Goldsmith’s*, the third building down, you’d got one or two more workshops, with the old stabling, up the back. You’d got the wall of the yard, and at the corner of Northampton Street/Hockley Street, opposite the *Jewellers’ Arms*, there was a place called *Payton’s Printers* – they printed cards and sold stationery and so on; a very old-fashioned place; they sold Christmas Tree baubles. Below the *Jeweller’s Arms* was another old stretch of houses, and shops. There was an old entryway below the *Arms*, which was part of the pub’s property, and led to the back of the houses. It was wide enough to take the old-fashioned handcart, I suppose.

Next door to that was a café, which I think was called *Harry's Café*. He was a nice chap but he *would* lick his fingers, every time he pulled off a piece of greaseproof paper, to wrap your sandwiches in! He made beautiful sandwiches, but it was this licking his thumb, every time he wrapped the sandwiches up. Next door to that there was another entry.

"Next to that there was an old antique shop of second, third and fourth-hand furniture. It was absolutely stuffed to the ceiling and windows, with pieces of furniture. You couldn't walk into the shop; the door would just about open – and that was it! A very ancient couple kept it: a Minnie Bannister/Harry Crumb type of couple. That was where local people bought and sold their furniture. It was full of old Victorian washstands and Edwardian knick-knacks. You couldn't walk across the shop: they had to thread their way through to you. And if you fancied something high up: 'Oh – could I have a look at that aspidistra stand?' (Mimics and elderly crone, replying!). You wondered who was the oldest – the proprietors or the furniture!

"Then there was another shop, which became a vegetable shop." That's where the club was. Ken confirms Paddy White's description of the entrance: the steps and so forth. Certain people's names had to be given, before customers could gain entry. "That was always the way," continues Ken. "You had to identify yourself, even to get someone to come to the grille. You had to know how many rings – and what pattern to ring it in. I dare say that was changed regularly, so only those 'in the know' could gain entry. Then they'd come and give you the 'once over'.

"To the left of the club, there was a barber's shop, with three blokes working there: the owner and two assistants, (the youngest, now in his 80s, has only just retired!). Down from that was a very old-fashioned grocer's shop, which sold 'á la mode' ham-on-the-bone, tinned vegetables and homemade sausages. Then there was a stretch of wall, and then we come to the corner of Branston Street. All those buildings have now gone. There were people living in the yards, at the back of all those buildings. It was still full of people, in back-to-back houses for some years, in Branston Street."

When Pat's club was there in 1959/1960 residents were already moving out. According to Ken: "One of the reasons was because, if we come down to the opposite side of the road, from the corner of Spencer Street and Hockley Street, on the opposite corner to that, going down the other side of Hockley Street, there was *Kileen and Bannister*, manufacturers of tissue paper and wrapping paper. Old Jimmy Grinter was the proprietor of that - a big moustache, Devonshire man – and never did he lose his Devonshire accent.

"That occupied the corner; the building's still there. But it's obviously been changed, since they built the *Prince Charles Business Centre*. Below that, the entire corner's different now, because that was *Moorhouse's*. Going round into Branston

Street, which is diametrically opposed to the corner of *Lucas's*, where the entrance is now, to those locks they've converted, there was a ramshackle café, which was called *The Commonwealth Café*. You went round the corner into Branston Street, and you'd got all the back-to-back houses along there – entries going off, and workshops in the front rooms of some of them.

"There was a disastrous fire in one of them, and because of the three storeys –(they were attic things) – two or three children were burned together, in the attic. It was happening all the time, in these back-to-back houses. It was always Christmas time, and it was shock-horror all round. But this time they decided that something would be done about it. So while they were getting ready to clear the properties out and move the people on, as a temporary measure, they put a 'kick panel' in the attics, through into the next room; it was a sheet of asbestos, over a hole in the wall, with a frame round it. You'd only got one double staircase, down two tiers of stairs, so you'd be trapped up there. You couldn't get down, nor jump out of the window, because you were on the third floor: little children wouldn't do that anyway; that's why there were so many terrible tragedies. So all of these places were equipped with kick-through panels of asbestos. There's still one in the pub – or there used to be, anyway! They were gradually cleared away, including the café. So far down the street, you can see where the new buildings finish and the old buildings start."

Jill White, Paddy's wife, was barmaid at *The Rendezvous*, (where the two of them met). "I can remember, a bottle of beer, *Newcastle Brown*, or something like that; all the bottles were 1/9d each, and all the spirits were either 3/6d or 3/9d. They were a little bit above pub prices," she recalls, "because we're going back forty years now. So it was *so* easy to work: you knew all your bottles were 1/9d and you knew how many six were, straight away; and the same with 'shorts'.

"I worked late hours – but I wasn't left to go home on my own. 'Popeye', (aka Mick), an Irishman, had an ice-cream vehicle. He'd drop me home, because neither Paddy nor I could drive; we'd sit on the fridges. I lived with my parents, in Bennett Street – just off Lozells Road. Mick used to put the ice-cream chimes on, at five or six o'clock in the morning! Sometimes I heard my dad get up, just as I got into my bedroom. I had a big black Persian coat. I'd throw it on the floor and dive into bed. Then the door would open – just to check that I was in. I worked from about eight o'clock at night, until about half five in the morning. Occasionally I used to help out at the *Pieces of Eight Café*, in Smethwick, during the day. I only worked at the *Rendezvous* – not the other two clubs."

Jill was twenty, when Pat hired her. "My dad used to say, 'They know you're naïve' - he used to tell me off." To prove that everything was 'above board', Jill's parents were invited to pay a visit to the *Rendezvous*; everyone put on a special performance!

"At the bottom of these stairs," continues Paddy, referring to his drawing, "as you came down, the toilet was there. You'd get raided periodically. Inspector Wanklyn, was the officer-in-charge, from Kenyon Street Police station - (I think Wanklyn was spelt without the 'r'!) Kenyon Street isn't there any more; it was a police station that used to be just around the corner – a stone's throw away from the club. Although I used to check who was at the door, on this *one* occasion, somebody presented himself. He looked like a proper punter – so-and-so sent him – and he said the right names. OK – opened the door – and in they came!

"Wanklyn was there and he said: 'Don't let them press that effing bell!' But I got me foot to the button – off went the lights. All the drinks were thrown to the floor, and these 'townie' lads are sitting there saying: 'We haven't had a drink all night guv'nor!' The place is *flooded* on the floor – but the whole idea is they're supposed to *catch* you drinking, or serving drinks and taking the money. Our simple idea was – throw the drink on the floor – how can you get 'knicked'?" Owners caught flouting the regulations were taken to court and fined. "Then you went back the same night, and ordered more drinks, as they'd been confiscated. We always used to *say* that the only time they ever raided us, was when the *Police Social Club* was short of supplies. Totally untrue, of course – we were just making that up!

"So the police crashed their way in, I managed to hit the button, and the lights flickered; drinks were on the floor." His wife, Jill, takes up the story: "What I was *supposed* to do – (although no one had really told me, the first time), was to empty the money out of the till. This policeman came behind the bar; there was only room for me really. The lager was on gas, and he asked me to disconnect it, so they could confiscate it. I was still a very naïve person – I hadn't got a clue; the lads normally used to do it. So the beer shot all over the policeman!" "There was beer and booze everywhere," adds Paddy. "Of course, we were all highly amused – *they* weren't!"

"Inspector Wanklyn told me, 'You should not be working here,' " continues Jill. " 'I'm going to let you off this time, but if you're here next time, I'm going to take you into court.' I said: 'OK.' I *was* there the next time. 'Look, I'm not *joking*,' he said, 'I'm *serious* about it!' I was there for a third time, by which time I knew the ropes. I knew I'd just got to keep my head together, get the stuff out, and just keep quiet."

Although customers weren't prosecuted, such raids sometimes served as a deterrent. Paddy explains, "It was also a case of casting your net, to see who's about; you never knew whom you might pick up! So I was standing at the bottom of the stairs, as people were coming down, and giving their names to a police officer, seated in the doorway of the downstairs toilet. I'd moved away to talk to someone. Inspector Wanklyn was going: 'Hang on – hang on a second –

just *hang on*! Paddy, come here, listen. You tell all these people (I'm going to swear now), the next f***ing John Wayne or effing Errol Flynn who comes down these stairs, is going to get well and truly knicked. Don't mess me about!' I said: 'You never know who's in the club guv'nor!' " Paddy describes Inspector Wanklyn as " ...a very *serious* guy. Didn't like us, didn't want us there – and went to great lengths to get us out."

In addition to *The Bermuda Club,* Pat Bowen, sometimes visited the *Rendezvous*, but never actually saw Pat there, as he was occupied with several projects, at that time. "We'd knock on the door and wait for somebody to come down," she confirms. "They'd see if there was anybody about before they'd let you in. Nobody knew the place existed. From the outside, it looked like a derelict building."

"The *Rendezvous* – oh dear!" remarks Pat's Anderton Street friend, Brian Webb. "I was in between ships, and saw Pat every time I came home. This one day he said, 'Get your togs on, we're going down the *Diamond Club* first,' (which is another little club in the Jewellery Quarter). Then we went on to his own club, the *Rendezvous*: he was very proud of it. We had a drink and Pat was showing me around.

"Suddenly, the coppers came in and I thought, 'Oh dear, oh dear! Every time I come home on leave, something happens!' I was sitting there with someone who *may* have been George's girlfriend, keeping her occupied. A policeman said: 'What's your name?' I gave them some name. 'And who's this young lady?' I said: 'This is my wife – we've just got married.' He said: 'Have you got any identification?' I said: 'Nothing at all.' He said: 'OK, on your way.'

"While they were going round to other people, Pat came over and pushed these car keys in my hand. He said: 'Get that car round the corner, and take her with you!' Then he added: 'The car's full of beer.' (And he wants me to drive it!) So I got in the car and *she* got in the car, and round the corner we went – out of the way. I was sitting there with this girl for about half an hour to an hour, and I suppose we got a bit amorous.

"Then all of a sudden she jumped up and said: 'Oh my God!' I said: 'What's the matter?' It was Pat: standing there - looking through the window. I thought, 'Oh I'm a gonner. I'm going to stay on me ship forever, I am!' He said, 'Come on - get out. Get in the back!' But he got his own back – with one of my girls. Heather, her name was – beautiful girl. She was a hairdresser's model; much taller than me: about five foot nine, five foot ten. Pat dropped me off to catch a coach back south, in the Bull Ring. He said 'I'll take care of her – take her home – make sure she's OK.' I was in the army then, doing the tail end of my National Service - I'd stayed ashore too long with the group. When I got back to the barracks about a week later I got a letter from her, saying that she didn't want to see me again. I thought, 'Thanks a lot Pat!' "

Brian also recalls that he and Pat used to visit a man nicknamed 'Gobi' (short for Göebels!), when he was on shore leave. "He had a massive house, with a partition - over in Hay Mills. There'd be a party at this chap's house every weekend - lovely parties. Pat and I used to go and have a drink first, before we went over there. Gobi had a big flash car – pink and blue it was. This was around the period 1959 to 1961 something like that. I met the wife in 1961 – and calmed everything down a bit!"

Around that time, Pat suggested that Paddy White should try his hand at judo. "It was Roachie's suggestion – typical of Pat. He was going to the gym, or the 'dojo', as he called it. 'Why don't you come? I'll show you a few moves. It's really interesting, and it will keep you fit.' And being the silly Paddy I am, I've gone: 'I'll have a bit of that.' To the best of my knowledge, the venue was *Nechells Community Centre.*

"So I've gone in, and it's the whole 'number', with the mats and the bowing and the suits. He showed me this move, called 'Harigoshi' – it's a hip throw. (He'll probably be laughing at me!) He flipped me on the floor, like a baby. And I've gone: 'That will do – I'm not having any more of that!' He tried to get me again. He showed me the same throw, and I said: 'Pat, if you can put me on the floor that easy, I don't want to play!' And I wouldn't do any more.

"I remember the early days, when Pat was trying to break into wrestling. He went to see a guy in Stratford, who Shirley tells me, was Jack Little. (I didn't know that at the time). I recall how *confident* he was, that he would be able to make the change – but then – that's Pat anyway. He *knew* he wanted to do the wrestling, and he did – he became *Judo Pat Roach.* I went to see him wrestle a few times, at places like Tamworth Town Hall." That was where Pat made his wrestling debut.

Paddy saw Pat fight *Lord Bertie Topham*, (on a different occasion from the one attended by Wally and Brian Webb, when *Lord Bertie* broke Pat's leg). "They were quite small venues, in and around Birmingham. It was the very early days for Pat," Paddy explains. "It's a technique – showmanship. But he persisted – and obviously, it took him on to better things – later on."

Paddy confirms that, during Pat's early wrestling days, his three clubs were well under way. "*The Oyster Bar* was the club where we started off with piles of crates, full of bottles of beer. As they became empty, we put them back into the crate, and then put a plank on top." Ken Schofield points out that *Wetherspoon's,* on Broad Street, has now changed its name to *Pieces of Eight.* So how did Pat and George's *Pieces of Eight* compare to the other two clubs?

"Oh, it was *very* rough," recalls Paddy. "The *Rendezvous* wasn't a rough club; we had trouble there because it was 'after-hours' drinking, so you're going to get some 'nob-heads' in there, at some time or other. *The Oyster Bar*, as we've said, was completely and utterly George Cullen's mother's backroom! Converted for the afternoon, on Saturday and Sunday. That's all it was – entirely!

"The *Pieces of Eight* was the room above a café in Rolfe Street, Smethwick - far less sophisticated than the *Rendezvous;* of the three, in terms of roughness, it was the 'middle-of-the-road' club. We put a bar in there – some tables and chairs; it was as simple as that." George Cullen's oldest son, 'Juno', ran the club. "The family was 'straight-down-the-line'. Juno was a bit more like his father, but not as aggressive. Juno and Joan ran it together," recalls Paddy. "Joan was a friend of George's: a lovely girl – and very 'street-wise'. Joan helped to 'look after' Juno - because she was older. George wanted to give Juno something to do.

"There was trouble, one Saturday night. Some rough young guys came in from Smethwick. They were drinking and behaving themselves, but somewhere along the line, it went wrong. They'd come in with the idea of making themselves 'busy': 'This is us – we're from Smethwick – who are you?' They saw a guy and a girl running the club – 'easy meat'! Or so they thought – and they were going to take over – threatened all kinds of violence. Juno ended up hitting some guy with a wooden mallet, during that first night. It went off quite badly; they broke a few tables. Later, somebody came back and put a firebomb through the window of the café – because we used that as well, in the day." Paddy confirms that there were fruit machines there too, as in Pat and Jim White's string of cafes.

"The club was upstairs. I can't recall whether they came back the *same* night, and firebombed the place. Pat, George, and myself were in the *Rendezvous,* when Joan or Juno rang, to tell us that the café was on fire." The café and the club shared the same name, (chosen by Pat), although the décor bore no resemblance to a pirate's ship! "It wasn't done out at all, just as the *Oyster Bar* wasn't," explains Paddy. "When we got the telephone call, the three of us jumped in the car and shot over there. The police and the fire engines were there when we arrived. Luckily, there was no major damage that couldn't be repaired, and it was just to the café itself.

"We spoke to Juno and Joan and decided that it had got to be the same 'firm' who'd caused trouble on the Saturday evening. So we said: 'OK, we'll go and have a hunt round.' George had very little respect for policemen. He spoke to the sergeant, who was on the scene of the fire, that evening. George was from Dublin – he'd still got a very strong accent: a very tough guy. He said: 'What are you going to do about this? We know who it is, I'm *telling* you who it is. I want you to go and arrest them.' The policeman said: 'We can't just go and do that sir.' George said: 'Well, we'll go and find them, and when we do, we won't be saying: "We can't do this or that." If you want to follow me, that's where we're going now!'

"So me, George and Roachie jumped into the car, and shot up into Smethwick. There were a couple of Late Night Cafes, and we hunted those places – looking for these guys. Luckily – or unluckily – I don't know which – we didn't find them that night. The copper was saying: 'If you do this, you'll get arrested, on an assault charge,' " continues Paddy. "George was saying (Dublin accent): 'What *about* assault? These are firebombs we're talking about, and these eedjuts are laughing at you. You'll send them to court, give them a ten-bob fine, and they'll come out boasting to their mates about it. You know what they need? They need a smack!'

"We decided, in the ensuing week, that the fire-bombers would be cheeky enough to come back. So the following weekend, we got together - myself, George, Pat, Jimmy Mackenzie, Jackie Jennings, and a couple of other friends. (Scotch Jackie was a tough guy - a nice, tidy little group). We decided to go back to *The Pieces of Eight* early, pretending to be punters. Let's see if anybody comes in – and if they get cheeky; they'd started a storm, so we'll just wait."

On cue, later on, a couple came in, followed by another two. "Juno gave us the 'wink' – there were about six of them altogether," recalls Paddy "There was no reason for anyone else to do it – we knew it was these 'merchants'. The plan was, when they're in, we'll sort it. So everyone's having a drink. We're all interspersed, around this room. Roachie or somebody had decided: 'OK – now's the time', went downstairs, locked the door. Because the entrance wasn't through the café, it was in a little tunnel/alleyway beside the café; you went in there, you came up the stairs. So we locked *that* door.

"Then we challenged them: 'OK, where are all the tough guys? Where are all the matches?' A little bit of this, a little bit of that; a bit of chit-chat, a couple of back-handers – and it was off! They obviously want to fight their way out – or try to get out. Maybe they thought that one or two of us were there; they hadn't realised that everybody in the club was the 'firm'. So we were prepared: we ambushed them – 'Crash, bang, bang,' it went off! All of a sudden there were people being bashed.

"The one thing that particularly sticks in my mind, is that Jimmy Mackenzie picked up a chair, to hit a guy with. He raised it above his head, to whack the guy, the legs of the chair stuck into the suspended ceiling. Instead of letting it go, to protect himself, he's more intent on trying to get the chair out of the ceiling. But in the meantime, he's got about six or seven smacks in the mouth, for all his trouble, before somebody's actually pulled the guy away. So Mackenzie's there with a bloody nose, hanging on with one hand to the chair, going – 'What?!'

"Something else happened that night, during the *Pieces of Eight* fight. I got knocked down the stairs, or fell down, fighting with a guy. Roachie had ensconced himself, at the bottom of the stairs. We were giving them a few whacks, a bit of 'verbal', then throwing them down. Roachie was getting them

Pat's grandfather, Walter Roach, was born in 1874 and died in 1930. He is pictured here, in the centre of the bench, in his later years. Photograph kindly given to Pat by his cousin, Peter Mulroy.

Pat's cousin, Walter, (Frank Roach's nephew), on horseback, second from the right, in Palestine, October 1944. He volunteered to join the Palestine Police Force. By permission of Tom Roach.

The wedding of Ken Lloyd and Frances Roach, St Chad's Cathedral, 1944. On the far left is Nora Mulroy, holding baby son, Peter. To the left of the groom is Harry Mulroy, Nora's husband. The bride's father, Pat's Uncle Walter, stands next to his son, Frank, with bridesmaid, Helen Roach, just in front. Young Tom Roach looks apprehensive about having his picture taken! Behind him is his mother, Hilda Roach, then Pat's Aunt Kate, (his father and Walter's younger sister) - in heart-shaped hat. By permission of Ken and Frances Roach.

The Next Generation of Roaches: At either end of the back row are David and Paul Roach, Frank's sons, with Tom and Glenys' son, Ian, in between. On the far left of the front row are Ken Lloyd, Helen, Tom, Glenys, Frances and Frank. The latter four, apart from Glenys, are Pat's cousins. By permission of Tom Roach.

Derek Hobson opens Don Fewtrell's Edgbaston night-club, Faces. The name derived from the fact that Derek was presenting the New Faces TV show, at that time. By permission of Don Fewtrell.

Pat and Don at Faces night-club, in the late 1960s. By permission of Don Fewtrell.

Nightclub Trailblazers, Don Fewtrell and his brother, Eddie, give it their best shot, in Gibraltar. By permission of Don Fewtrell.

Pat opened his Washwood Heath car business in the early 1970s. Fellow wrestler, Les Kellett, was there for the event, trying to persuade Pat to give him a better deal! Gordon Fewtrell bought the business from Pat, just over thirty years ago. By permission of Gordon Fewtrell.

A more recent photo of Ronnie and Pat, with Ronnie's son, Adam, in the centre. It was taken at Pat's Winson Green yard, c. 1999. Photograph by Mark Roach, Pat's son. By permission of Ronnie Callow.

Billy Sutton in 1986 receiving the Miami Police award for Outstanding Contributions to Communities and Children of Miami from City of Miami Chief of Police, Clarence Dickson. This was one of eighteen commendations awarded to Billy over a number of years, including the rank of Colonel.

Val Hastings was the original Spice Girl and Maureen Rivers was the cool blonde. Photograph by Mike Rawson. By permission of Val Hastings.

Kenny Baker, aka R2D2, in Star Wars. He and Pat were reunited, in 2003, at a Paris Film Convention. By permission of Kenny Baker.

Pat holds Mike Marino's head, in a figure four. Photograph by H.G. Stevens. By permission of Bill (Wayne) Bridges.

Sarah Bridges, (Wayne's wife), winning the 2004 Championship. Pat has been a source of inspiration for her, right from the start of her career. Her message to Pat, written on the photograph, speaks volumes. By permission of Sarah and Wayne Bridges.

Chris Millard's winning Porsche, passing the Start/Finish Point, Bristol Street, Birmingham. The car behind was driven by Barry Williams. Photo by 'JC Photo-Sport' By permission of Chris Millard.

'Roaches Three': pictured with Pat at a recent wedding, are his son Mark, and grandson, Patrick Junior, to whom this book is dedicated.

Pat at Howard Green's Retirement Ceremony. Howard was curator of the Avery Historical Museum, for many years. By permission of GEC Avery Ltd and Howard Green.

Pat and members of the press discuss his forthcoming role as Hades, in the subterranean, canalside setting, beneath Snow Hill Viaduct, intended to represent the Underworld. In the event, 'So Far So Good', had to be abandoned at the 'eleventh hour', due to regulations about a public entertainment license. Photograph by Shirley Thompson.

at the bottom of the stairs, giving them another whack, then throwing them out of the door – sending them on their way."

They'd got to come past me, to get out – (which was the idea). As they did so, I whacked them. I think I had the leg of a chair - or something. The funny thing was that as they ran past me, I must have disorientated them, so they ran the wrong way - into another room, instead of up the entry. They had to turn round, to come back, so I whacked them again – on the way out!

"They were just local Brummies," explains Paddy, "local 'tearaways' – who thought they were something. Black Country lads, they called themselves – from Smethwick. I tumbled down the stairs with this one guy, but got about three punches off Roachie, before I was able to signal to him who I was! Those guys didn't come back. I think they realised that we were in a different league; they hadn't realised there was 'back-up' there."

The period during which Paddy helped Pat and George with their clubs, was only a 'passing phase'. "From about 1960 – while we could keep our heads above water," explains Paddy. "It's like everything in life; it was just one of the segments – *people* moved on, *things* moved on. When George became more interested in his scrap metal business, I lost touch with him, for many years."

Jill referred to 'Big Pat' and 'Little Pat', in the *Rendezvous* days. " That was the joke," Paddy recalls. "I was six-foot something, about fifteen-stone, 'fit-as-a-flea' – and I was 'Little Pat'! It was a standing giggle between us all really. I could look after myself, and there was Roachie – another half size again: bigger and better. A comical incident that came out of that: the buzzer's gone. I looked out of the hatch and there was a little Irishman, on his own – 'drunk as a skunk'! 'I wanna come in,' he says. I said: 'No, you're too drunk.' 'I wanna come in!' I said: 'Sorry – are you a member?' (That was the usual first step). 'No, I'm not a member.'

"So I open the door. I'm standing on the step, talking to him – he's harmless enough. Now there are two steps up to this place. I'm standing on one, and I must look about ten foot four to this guy! He wasn't being aggressive; he just wanted a drink. He said: 'Now look, I was told that if I wanted a drink, I just come down here and ask for Pat. Who are you?' I said. 'I'm Pat – but there's *two* of us.' He said: 'Well it might be the other fella.' I said: 'But you don't know him.' 'I do!' I said: 'There's Big Pat and there's Little Pat. Now, who told you to come for a drink?' So he stood there; he put his head to one side – and he's thinking about it. He said: 'Well which one are you?' I said: 'I'm *Little* Pat.' He looked up at me – and – like I said – I was stood on this step – must have looked over ten feet. Then, with a little smile on his face, he said, 'Ah, f*** you and your club – who needs a drink?' – and went off into the darkness – just wandered back into the night. I was in bits, as I went back up the stairs – I just couldn't believe it!

"At that time Pat was doing the judo and also trying to break into wrestling. With most *other* things, we were involved with him. If there was a bit of 'tat' going on, a bit of business, we'd all be involved. But the judo was a *totally* separate thing – we knew nothing about it." Pat's life, at that time, must have seemed somewhat surreal: like existing in two totally different, but parallel worlds. "If you think about it, the club thing was about drinking and cavorting, and out late at night; going to bed – in the early morning," comments Paddy. One could reasonably describe it as the 'shadier' side of his existence: 'out on the razz' – in *Auf Wiedersehen Pet* terminology!

Paddy witnessed this phase, at first-hand: "If you look at his life on the other side of the coin, it was about strength and discipline, and whatever else goes with the judo. It was a completely separate side of him, which was quite *private*, in some ways. Pat was quite happy for you to come down the dojo and throw you on the floor, but he had his own friends from that sport – like Jim White, and later, those in the wrestling world. The discipline and fitness required of judo, was like a 'chalk-and-cheese' thing; I don't know *how* he balanced the two – personally."

The discipline of judo was such, that once it got into your blood, and you got the taste for it, nothing was ever going to stop you. Just about every Black Belt I knew was divorced from his wife; judo caused more marriage separations than any other sport you could ever imagine. It was this compulsion: 'by- hook-or-by-crook', you went to the dojo. I taught 'night in and night out'. Although I used to be out at the clubs 'til the early hours of the morning, I always found time for the Judo Club. It was something I just had to do. The esoterics describe it as 'a way of life' – and that's exactly what it was.

Pat has previously explained, on radio programmes, and in our first book, that fortunately, he has always been able to make swift transitions between two contrasting roles - referring to it as the ability 'to wear two hats'.

I could wear the hat of the nightclub proprietor, (albeit they were all illegal drinking clubs). At the same time, I would walk onto a mat, and all my students would either bow to me, or if I was teaching that particular night, I would 'rei' to them - a Japanese term meaning 'bow', and they would return the bow.

We would be on this journey of absolute discipline, which I extended when I taught kids – but it worked. Their parents used to say to me: "You know, Mr. Roach, (because it was always very formal), "since little Johnny has been doing judo, we threaten him that unless he behaves himself, he can't come to judo." When I allowed them to watch, (which I did now and again), they used to be in awe of the fact that the kids would respond to the short, very curt orders that we gave them, on the mat. In fact the discipline was, in its entirety, 'chalk-and-cheese', as described by Paddy White.

When I was in 'Clash of the Titans', with Laurence Olivier, Claire Bloom, Maggie Smith and Ursula Andress, amongst others, I was on that million-pound set: a hundred thousand pounds a day to keep it running. Jumped into my Bentley, drove up to

Birmingham, where I grabbed a broom and swept up a load of crap from my yard, because my guys wouldn't do it. Then I drove back to London again. I could wear those two hats: one day I was with Olivier, the next day I was sweeping up rubbish. I never had any problems changing over.

"I've seen him drink 'rum-and-blacks'," observes Paddy, "until it's coming out of his ears. Then getting up the following morning, going to the gym, and doing whatever he has to do. And I'm lying in bed thinking: 'I'll see you two o'clock Roachie … are you *mad* ?!' "

Chapter Seven –

BANDITS, 'TATTERS' AND WATER GYPSIES

Winson Green, is an area where I worked, for many years. Ronnie Callow had a yard, which was a hundred yards further down Wellington Street from mine. So although we'd previously had yards elsewhere, eventually we had businesses within walking distance of each other.

In Chapter Four, Ronnie described the rather bizarre experience of running *Paddy's Café*, and his success in Stock Car Racing, but his world and Pat's overlapped in several other ways, with quite a range of mutual acquaintances. Like Pat, he has also lived and worked abroad, sometimes in rather precarious circumstances, and is still very much the entrepreneur.

An *Evening Mail* article, written in the 1980s, refers to a mineral water factory, which Ron, who was then forty-seven, was building on the sunshine island of Malta, and describes him as a former fairground boxer, haulier, building contractor and entrepreneur. During that period, he was living on the island with his wife, Alison. His entrepreneurial activities included importing transport and engineering equipment to Malta, after striking a deal with Birmingham City Council. Business deals took him all over Europe, travelling nearly 50,000 miles a year by air sea and road. After a few years of the Mediterranean lifestyle, he returned to England. Like Pat, Ronnie has encountered several hair-raising situations in his time. This chapter contains just a brief selection. As he recalls, one particular return journey, via Naples, resulted in a life-and-death situation.

"It was 1983," recalls Ronnie, "and we were going back overland to the UK, but made part of the journey by ferry. The sea became very rough. We had the pick-up truck, packed with gear, and a caravan on the back. We got off at the first chance, in Sicily, but our timing couldn't have been worse. Believe it or not, as we drove, we could see the volcano erupting, in the background and red-hot lava running down the mountainside. We took photographs of it. The next morning we took a ferry across, then drove up, as far as Naples." They planned to sleep in the caravan, but as Ronnie was covering the pick-up with a sheet for the night, (it looked like rain), he was grabbed from behind, by a hooded robber.

"I felt a gun pressing into the right side of my neck, but eventually managed to hit this guy with my right fist, whilst keeping the gun pointing away from Alison and me. When I finally disarmed him, I suddenly realised that there were two of them with hoods on. The one I hurt got to his feet and both of them ran for cover. I pointed the gun at them, but it jammed. Cutting a long story short, soon afterwards, Alison and I were heading for the Italian-French border at about ninety miles an hour, still in shock - with the caravan jumping all over the place!"

Returning to the relative safety of Britain, Paddy White confirms: "Funnily enough, I knew Ronnie, prior to Pat having a yard up the road from him." Pat had a yard on the Queens Head Road, before moving his premises to Winson Green. He and Jimmy White subsequently opened *The Budokan*, on the same site. According to Ronnie: "The first time I saw Pat was on a mat, at the Budokan School of Judo. Pat and Jimmy White were both Black Belts, at that stage. At one time, Pat also had coal yard, down by Cuckoo Bridge."

Paddy White recalls visiting Ronnie, at his Winson Green scrapyard, before Pat moved into the area. "I've done some business with Ronnie – over the years – bits and pieces – and found him to be a really nice guy. Again, it's the breed of person he is. It's like Pat's old man – Ronnie's the same. It's a 'cash' business, and if you're dealing in that sort of business, you don't want to tell everyone about what cash you've got – so you tend to be private – and a 'loner'. That *makes* them private, secretive – a little bit 'dodgy': you know you're not being told everything! And you don't expect to be, because you, yourself, are probably doing something similar."

Ronnie recalls another mutual acquaintance: "George Cullen used to sit in the Jeweller's Arms, sucking on his pipe and drinking his pint. He'd always got a polythene bag in his pocket, containing various items of gold jewellery, such as gold rings, necklaces and bracelets. He was around five feet ten, and stocky - he weighed about thirteen stone. George had a beaky nose - and a typically Irish look about him."

During the 1960s, the other Georgie in our book, Georgie James, sometimes saw Pat in his nightclub, *The Spider's Web*, in Walsall. He recalls: "I was married at the time, and living in Walsall. Once or twice I saw Pat in the area. There was a couple, from London, hiding in Walsall, the Kray's henchmen – the Lambrianos. I got involved with them, because I had a nightclub in Walsall -The *Spider's Web*. They were going to *shoot* me. They were collecting protection money. I said: 'Forget about it. You get nothing!' Eddie Fewtrell stopped it all. He said: 'If you want to stop it, I'll come over with the boys.' I tell you what – he *did* stop them. He carried a lot of 'clout', Eddie did. It ended. I had a good hiding in there, they stuck a gun to my head, and all the doormen ran. I was stuck in the club, on my own. They finished up getting nothing, as it happened. They took a bag of silver, which was the 'float', for the next day."

It was a very close call for Georgie. "I had Regional Crime Squad following me around for two or three weeks afterwards, to protect me. A young lad who used to work for me, young Mickey '(The Animal'), palled up with one of the Regional Crime Squad."

I bought my Winson Green yard in 1986 and kept it for many years. A further coincidence is, the canal, running close by (shades of my grandmother, Amelia), and the fact that Ronnie Callow's got a water gypsy background too. He didn't realise that we both had, until he read a copy of 'If'.

Ronnie Callow's father, William, was one of eight children, born in 1906, to Romany parents. The family travelled the country in a Bow Top gypsy caravan, which William had been born in. His own father was also named William; they were both known as Billy. Ronnie's grandmother was Emily. In the late 1920s, Ronnie's grandparents abandoned the open road for the canals, becoming 'bargees', or 'boatees'. He explains: "They hauled anything from coal, grain, scrap metal and beer barrels, throughout the country, although the majority of their work, in the early years, was around the Black Country." His father narrowly survived a drowning in the canal. William's widowed mother's crippled suitor, Rubin, tried to hold him under the water with his wooden crutch. "Luckily for me, he did not succeed," continues Ronnie, "otherwise I would not be writing this." A few years later, William met Ronnie's mother, Florence, in Birmingham. When the children were born, the family settled down in Clay Lane, South Yardley. "My parents insisted that I went to school and got a proper education, as at this time, my father could not read or write."

Grandmother Emily lived to the ripe old age of eighty-five. "A photograph was taken of her, at the *Lea Hall Tavern* in Kitts Green, Birmingham, by the landlord, Mr. Keenan," recalls Ronnie. "Her black plaited hall went all the way down her back to the floor, touching her size nine shoes!"

In 1972, Ronnie went into haulage, working for Peter Taylor, in Aldridge. "Got my license when was I was in the navy, so that carried me through. After a couple of years I started thinking about getting my own truck. I got three trucks and five trailers and I had contracts with *British Steel*. That was running lovely until *British Steel* started selling off and closing down. Then you'd take a load up to Glasgow, but you couldn't get a load back, so you'd have to run back empty; you were running it for nothing. So I got out and went back into the scrap metal business." Ronnie was recalling these past memories, in conversation with Pat and myself.

"I had a place in Middleton Street, Winson Green. All of a sudden, a guy came up to me who worked for Pat, named Timmy. (To Pat) You'd got *Pat's Café* in Lodge Road – and across the road you'd got the breaker's yard. Timmy said: 'Ronnie, Pat wants to know if you'd mind if we went into breaking 'commercials'?' It's on my doorstep, you see. I thought, 'well that's nice of him to ask'. No objection whatsoever."

Ronnie broke cars, I broke commercial vehicles. If commercials came his way he'd phone me, if the cars came my way, I'd phone him up. We were working with each other, and things went well.

"How many years have you been in breaking Pat? Too many to talk about! The yard I started in, just across the road from Pat, was a vegetable patch when I moved into it - just allotments. I gave the guy £5-00 I think – a lot of money in those days. He was about seventy-odd and he gave me the key to the gate. British Rail property, about £2-00 a week rent."

Things were going well for Ronnie at these Wellington Street premises, and he was making a reasonable living. He recalls: " I'd got three lads working for me in the yard, dismantling cars and shelving most of the parts, ready for sale. We'd start about 8.30 a.m. and work until about 6pm, breaking and serving customers."

They took a daily lunchtime break, at a local café, where they would sometimes also play on the Pin Table. In those days, the Winson Green area was a reasonable place for Pat and Ronnie to run businesses, provided they kept their wits about them. But on this occasion, the situation changed drastically, when Ronnie, having won the game he was playing, asked the café proprietor for his winnings, but was refused payment.

"He was six foot three inches, and eighteen stone. He started to come round the counter, but not quite quickly enough. I grabbed a chair, and brought it down on the machine I'd be playing on. The owner was looking really evil and had a cleaver in his hand. All I could do was try to keep him at a distance. I started throwing sauce bottles, salt cellars, pepper pots, vinegar bottles, cups, saucers, anything I could lay my hands on, to keep this madman behind the counter.

"I eventually managed to make it to the door, but he came running after me with the cleaver, like a man demented, determined to bury it in my head! As I was running down Wellington Street, I could feel his breath on my neck and I swear, he was missing me by inches. Well, I was in better condition than he was, thank God! I made it, the last five hundred yards to my premises, totally knackered."

Ronnie bolted into his caravan, which served as an office and collapsed into a chair, trying to get his breath back. "One of my lads shouted a warning, not to go outside, because my assailant had pulled up outside in his red, 1100 saloon and he was holding a shotgun. I walked out to meet him and told him to put it down. We'd go over to Black Patch Park and sort it out like men. But all he was interested in was blowing my legs off. He was screaming and the hair on the back of my neck was standing up on end!

"All of a sudden, as calm as you like, one of my lads said: 'Do it – and I'll put one of these right through your head!' And there was this seventeen-year-old, with my .22 rifle – cocked and ready to fire – pointed at the café owner. Well, now it's a different ballgame. We talked him into putting the gun down. Then we began to walk towards the park, to settle it, once and for all."

As they walked, Ronnie began to think more clearly: "If I can't get him really quickly, I'm going to be spending time in Intensive Care. He was big, but slow. Anyway, we've passed Black Patch Garage and we're getting near to the park gates. My lads are walking about fifty yards behind, together with a couple of lads from the garage and a few others, who had heard what was happening. He stopped – and looked at me warily – and I looked at him.

"He said: 'Ronnie, I know I shouldn't have tried it on, but there was no need to smash my café up.' I told him it was only the machine, until I saw the cleaver. He said: 'Anyway, let's call it a day, before one of us really gets hurt!' I very nearly gave a big sigh of relief, as we turned and headed back towards the yard. I stuffed twenty pounds in fivers into his hand, for the damage. We became close friends after that, but he had a little more respect for me – and never pulled any more strokes."

Ronnie eventually returned to the relative safety of the Light Haulage business and has been running *Independent Courier Services*, for approximately twelve years, delivering mainly car parts. "I've got vans, flat-beds and I've got seven-and-a-half tons of curtain-siders, the sort you pull trailers with. We're contractors for the major companies and are based in Swadlincote, South Derbyshire. I've lived there for fifteen years. I like it out there. I don't think I'd ever come back to live in the city."

Like others in our book, Ron sometimes traded in the Birmingham markets: "Everybody used to want the hearthrugs – the half-circles. This was at the Birmingham Rag Market. The carpets were all rubber-backed. I used to get a piece of string and a Stanley knife and just cut them off. We got a load of these carpets and were putting them across the counter. The copper was walking around – they normally give you the eye. 'Come on lads – as advertised on *Police Five* next week!' Something like that – you know what I'm saying? He'd wink at me, I'd wink at him and I'd think: 'yeah, if you only knew!' As I'm knocking these out – taking the money. Needless-to-say, we only did it for two weeks, then got out!"

Ronnie was familiar with Pat's wrestling world. "I knew Lew Phillips, who started Pat wrestling, end of 62/63, I believe that was. The last time I saw Pat wrestle was at Walford Road – the old skating rink. He was a good 'crowd –puller' – he'd got a good following."

The same applied when Pat was the 'man on top' in Ronnie Taylor's wrestling booth. He used to take on all-comers. Gordon Corbett and Pat often earned the highest 'nobbins' (the money collected when the hat was passed around, following a fight). Ray Corbett, Gordon's brother, was a boxer. Ronnie knew both of them:

"We got Ray Corbett a yard, right opposite my garage, in Saint Peter's Place, just off Broad Street. That's when they opened the pub with the barge at the back." The pub in question was the *Longboat*. According to Pat, the pub is still there, but has been re-named. Ronnie tried his hand at fairground boxing, but soon changed his mind, deciding that the pain far exceeded the reward!

"The last time I saw Ray was in the *Jewellers' Arms*. I bought my meat off him on the Saturday, and I think the following Wednesday he died: he fell asleep on his stall while I was talking to him. He was grossly overweight – very, very tired. I think he was only forty-three when he went; he was the boxer."

Ronnie sums up Pat's personality, in one word: "Dynamic. He's got a very strong personality. He was a good thinker: he thought things out pretty well, before he acted on them. That was one of his strong points – a lot of people don't – they just act. You'd look at him and you'd think: he's put some thought into that."

How about weak points? "I haven't known any in Pat. OK, he'd like a drink, like we all do, but I can't name any weaknesses, because I've never seen that side of him."

As we explained in Chapter Three, Pat's father, Frank used to visit Ronnie's yard.

"After that I got to know Dolly. She had a café, just on the hill, as you came to the corner – by Soho Road. We used to send a fella down there to get half a dozen sandwiches for the rest of the crew, every morning. There were a couple of girls working with her."

The café was actually Pat's. Ethel Harris had been helping her son, Billy, to run it for Pat, but when she left, Dolly came to help, for a couple of years. Pat thinks that she may have had a shop around the corner, at one point.

Ron remembers the Budokan site well. "Jimmy White used to have a cottage at the back – there were two or three. If I remember right, Pat changed the one side of the Budokan. If you can imagine the one side of the wooden building: Pat changed that into a scrap yard. Right at the top were the cottages." There used to be three cottages, we'd previously researched the history of it. "Jimmy used to live there, in one of the cottages," continues Ronnie. "I visited Jimmy White and Sylvia at home a couple of times – by invitation."

Ron also tried his hand at judo: "In my navy days – on board ship, and I used to box for Lucas's, in Formans Road, in the days before I joined the navy – as a boy. Then I did a little bit of boxing in the navy. When I came out I was looking to earn a few quid, basically when I went onto the fairground, down at Tiger Bay, Cardiff. I stayed on there for about seventeen weeks, got my brains punched out, and packed up - found an easier way of earning a living!"

Fairground boxers had no advance knowledge of their likely opponents. "But it was a lot of fun – it gets the adrenaline going," observes Ronnie. "You were young, you were fit. You want to try your luck against anybody – do you know what I mean?"

Commenting on a photo of Pat's Washwood Heath car showroom, which the biographer happened to have handy, Ronnie comments: "I can't see any sign of Pat's guarantee: 'Six months or six miles – whichever comes first!' (Not true – a joke)!

"He got this car sales pitch. Just about that time, in the early 1970s, a guy came into my pitch and asked if I wanted any alternators or dynamos. I said: 'Whats' alternators?' 'It's taking the place of the dynamo.' I'd got a partner – Graham. He said: 'You can't have a few, you've got to have a 'whack' – a load.' I said: 'I'll make a phone call.' So I phoned a mate of mine who was in London – ex-navy, who was doing exporting. He said: 'Yeah, I'll have them.' He arranged for his export license. We arranged for a load, Monday, Tuesday, Wednesday, Thursday, Friday – finished. That was five lorry loads of Lucas stuff.

"You're talking about 25 ton, 147 thousand quid's worth in them days – it was a lot of money. It was dropped into Saint Peter's Place. I hired a forklift, bought a van. Trans-shipped it off a Lucas wagon, into a wagon. I dropped it off and took it down personally to my pal – so the link finished with me. Everything went nice – all paid – everything finished. Then the guy who dropped it off to me came back and said to me: 'Do you want some more of these dynamos?' I said: 'No, we've finished, we don't want no more.'" Unfortunately, that particular deal went pear-shaped.

After almost twenty years of trading, in Winson Green, Pat recently got rid of his yard, drawing to a close, a lifetime's experience, in a trade that had become something of a family tradition. For over four decades, a veritable cavalcade of humanity has crossed his various thresholds. Like Ronnie, Pat became an expert at adjusting his approach according to the client. From 'duckers and divers, nippers, nappers, tippers and tappers', searching for a quick buck, for very little outlay, to genuine clients and fellow dealers, with hopefully, a bargain or two. Friends who popped in for a quick chat, industrious employees, who would do an honest day's work for him, and stand by him - or unreliable, recalcitrant ones. Sadly, more recently, certain individuals who wished him harm, or wanted to steal, or put him out of business, (in one case, driving a car straight at him!) Only his stuntman's skills saved him on that particular occasion.

When a Shauman, (pronounced Showman), came into my yard, I could tell he was a Shauman, simply by looking at him; and certainly when he opened his mouth, I knew. I can also tell the difference between an Irish and an English gypsy; don't ask me how, but I know.

My grandmother, Amelia, was probably from a Romany family. She was always talking about renting a yard, particularly as I was a dealer, but she'd never pay more than a pound a week, and never think about paying rates. She'd worked out of yards herself, having grown up on the canals with the boats. They'd all worked out of yards, even though they worked off the canals, they'd have yard frontages.

Chapter Eight –

BRUMMAGEM BUMP

I get my opponent in a state of exhaustion and then lift him above my head and let him fall … it must be a nine foot drop. That's when the crowd goes really wild.

When Pat's co-writer asked Dolly whether she'd had an inkling, when Pat was a young boy, that he was going to be an actor or a wrestler, she hesitated: "He doesn't wish you to know - he doesn't want you to think he was rough and tough, because he wasn't. He was known as 'the Gentle Giant'."

Pat became a professional boxing protégé of Jack Solomon's during his teenage years, then a judo expert, but eventually realised that he preferred wrestling. Dolly comments: "I said, 'Oh don't - you'll spoil your looks!' He was *gorgeous* looking - like a big caveman."

I'd previously boxed for Mitchells and Butlers, for the Austin and into the semi-finals of the amateur championships. Meanwhile, I was a self-employed scrap dealer, but had forgotten to pay my National Insurance stamps. Old Tommy Richwood, who used to box for Birmingham City Police, became a court usher, in later days, before he retired. I was down in the toilets, which used to be opposite the old Casino, near to Lewis's. I looked up and there was Tommy Richwood, with two constables. They arrested me for not paying my stamps.

They walked me down, towards the Victoria Law Courts, and he said to me: "Here Roachie, I've got these warrants for you." I said: "Oh Tommy, can't you put them on the bottom?" He said: "I can't put them on the bottom – they're all yours!" He'd got a whole handful of these things, for various car offences – little things. Anyway, just before we got to the courts, he said: " 'ere Roachie, I'll have a deal with you." I said: "I'm always ready for a deal!" He said: "Warwickshire police are boxing Staffordshire police at the Tally Ho, in about a week's time." They wanted someone to box Terry McDermott, who was the Staffordshire Champion, at the time. "You come and box for us and we'll walk straight past the courtroom door." I said: "You're on!" Later, I boxed in the Jack Solomons Professional Championships.

We used to spar together, Big Albert and me, Ronnie Grey, and my brother Pete, at the Nechells Community Centre, in Minerva Road. We'd be all gloved-up, and all of a sudden, Ronnie Grey would throw a left over, and hit me right on the nose, and I'd say: "Oh, nice one Ron!" And we'd carry on like that. It was so funny!

Pat was first introduced to judo, by his friend, Jim White, and studied with him at Kyrle Hall in Sheep Street, under Frank Ryder. Pat and Jim later ran *The Budokan School of Judo* in Handsworth, after Pat became a First Dan in 1959.

There was no likelihood of Pat being influenced by American wrestlers, or those of any other nationality for that matter, because the opportunity to see foreign wrestlers in action during his youth, didn't exist. It was the ATV Controller who finally introduced them to British screens.

Greg Dyke decided to throw British wrestling off television and bring in American tapes.

For thirty-five years, wrestling was on television and actually had good figures on 'Grandstand', except for one year - and it went out to thirty-seven countries.

Pat's friend, Pete Berrington remembers him courting, (around 1955/56) "He had a car – it was all the colours of the rainbow." Pat confirms that the vehicle was an old Standard – an American car purchased from a local dealer. Others have described it as having some kind of camouflage over it. In the early 1960s, they lost touch for two or three years, Pete ran into Pat again, in 1962/63, while working in Liverpool. "I went up to do a roof job at the YMCA, in Mount Pleasant, and there he was – having his breakfast!" Pat was in Liverpool for a wrestling match. "He said: 'I've just finished a couple of things on the telly,' " continues Pete. "I said: 'It's bloody fixed all that, isn't it?' He said, 'Oh-ah. Of course it is!' He pulled his jersey up and his body was black and blue!"

Pat grew his beard, just after 1961. He was disqualified from the final stages of a boxing contest, in case he rubbed his beard in an opponent's wound; it was against boxing regulations, to grow one. Georgie James recalls: "The first match he promoted *himself*, was in Temple Street, Wolverhampton, early in 1962. I paid for the hall, a Rollering, so that Pat and Gordon Corbett could promote the match, (wrestling other opponents, not each other). Pat explained that he self-promoted one or two matches, initially, and was billed as *Judo Pat Roach*.

Bernard Newbould, (Jean's husband), recalls: "When Pat first started wrestling, I remember him driving around in a mini van, working for *Swift Fire Extinguishers*. He sold them when he was going round wrestling. It was a bit of a laugh – a big man like that getting into a mini van!"

Roy O'Neill explains: "Pat was down Walford Road, wrestling. We used to go to the *Masked Ballroom* afterwards, and have a drink, with whoever he was fighting." He recalls Pat's wrestling friend, Billy Yukon, who died at an early age. "Billy used to do some driving for an LF firm – (Long-term Fraud). He came here with some stuff that I'd bought - he'd got the forms and everything. It was late, and I asked whoever was driving, to unload it. He'd backed in, and got up onto the back of the motor, so I couldn't see him properly. He said: 'I ain't unloading this on my own!' I said: 'Unload it, or I'll come and bleedin' *throw* you off that motor!' As he turned I realised: 'Oh – it's you Billy!' He said: 'We'll unload it then!' "

Two 'Jacks' are featured in this chapter, which *could* prove confusing, as they're both linked to the wrestling world! They are, (in order of appearance), former British Lightweight, Middleweight and Cruiserweight Wrestling Champion and entrepreneur, Jack Taylor, whom the co-writer interviewed at his Leicester home, in October 2002, and also wrestler Jack Little (aka Jack Perkins). Following our meeting, Jack Taylor wrote an article, for the *Fanzine* magazine, which is Middlesborough based: he contributes to it on a regular, monthly basis. The article summarises Pat's wrestling career very concisely. He has kindly granted us permission to reproduce it here, *almost* verbatim, in our UK wrestling chapter:

The Good Old Days, by Jack Taylor

'A little while ago I received a letter from Shirley Thompson of Solihull, West Midlands. Shirley did the research and co-authored the biography, *If – The Pat Roach Story*. It covers the early days when life was not too rosy for young Pat. Right up to him entering the Judo field and, of course, coming into professional wrestling, Pat's giant build and wrestling prowess brought him to the attention of various film producers, and his career in movies went from strength to strength. I purchased a copy of *If* and thoroughly enjoyed the ups and downs of Pat's younger days in Birmingham. In the initial stages of his career, he was often billed as an 'Irishman'. He was actually born and bred in Birmingham, but his paternal grandfather's family originated from the old Emerald Isle.

What pleased me no end was the fact that in the book, Pat gives credit to the man who launched him into the pro wrestling whirligig! Pat says: "That Leicester fellow and entrepreneur, Jack Taylor, first sized me up. And got me to go along for a Saturday afternoon private preamble, in the ring of the famous Granby Halls. Jack ran Saturday night tournaments in Leicester's premier fight arena, for nearly twelve years, drawing astonishingly packed houses."

Pat was already the *Midlands Counties Judo Champion*, when Alf Kent contacted Jack Taylor, who recalls: "On that particular occasion, I had asked another would-be wrestler, Jack Little, from Stratford-upon-Avon, to come along. He was a six-foot tall ex-Guardsman, in the ilk of Shirley Crabtree. Naturally, Jack pulling along in the ring with Pat, would test the Judo lad and initiate him into the business. As a Judo champion, Pat, like most amateurs turning pro, was as stiff as a board. I recall saying: 'For Christ's sake Pat, ease yourself up, relax and perform. If you don't you will damage yourself, as you hit the deck.' But Pat was a fast learner; he really wanted to get into the wrestling.

In the book, Pat also says: 'Jack Taylor gave me my start, but he did not really teach me anything.' Quite true. Remember, in those early days of the

1960s, many athletes, from all sports, craved to become wrestlers and achieve fame on TV. Every town I visited, I would be approached by several people - all anxious to know the easy way to become a pro wrestler. I used to assure them: 'There is no easy way to get into wrestling. You have to have guts, ambition and determination, and a certain degree of luck, to make wrestling a career.' I would invite many wannabe wrestlers for a trial at our Leicester Gym, which in those days was a spit and a stride down Granby Street, near the YMCA, at the back of a public house. It was fully equipped, with a ring, floor mats and weights. The number of people who came through the doors was astronomical, but sadly, only a handful really made the grade. Then you would have to train solidly for two or three months, before getting your first trial bout. Quite often a rookie, on his test contest in the ring, before a very critical live audience, would be un-nerved, and fail miserably. Promoters were very wary of giving outsiders a chance in the ring, for that very reason. But Pat romped on with Jack Little and had his first bout against the ex-Guardsman. I believe it was on Little's home ground, at the Stratford-upon-Avon *Hippodrome*. The six-rounder proved a sizzler, from start to finish. With both men getting one fall apiece, the resulting draw pleased both participants. Pat's career took off. He became in great demand for promoters everywhere. Jack Little established himself as a popular wrestler, appearing on the independent circuit. At that time *Joint Promotions* had a tight grip on the TV output. The Independent Promoters were as big and powerful as *Joint Promotions*, but a little hamstrung, simply because their wrestlers were not regular TV faces. Many TV wrestlers fell out with the so-called big promoters, and went to work for the Independents. People such as – wait for it – Judo Al Hayes, Don Mendoza, 'Gentleman' Jim Lewis, Bobo Matu, Bob Sherry, Les Kellett, Ron Harrison, Big Benny, Chic Knight, Ray Appollon, Ray Hunter, Ken Joyce, George Kidd, Joe D'Orazio and Eddie Capelli. The list could go on and on. Often a wrestler would conclude that being on TV was being exploited. Jim Lewis thought so, and actually formed a wrestlers' union, trying to break the monopoly – of course – to no avail. He *did* call the wrestlers out on strike, on one occasion. But there was an abundance of quality performers anyway; some, who would have appeared on TV for nothing - just to get the exposure. So the Union just died out. But it did create another side to the Joint Organisation. If a star became unhappy with the way he was being used, he knew that approaching the Opposition would not only guarantee regular work, but also, in a lot of cases, an increased purse too.'

*   *   *   *   *

The legendary Randolph Turpin had a manager in Birmingham, Alf Kent, who happened to be very friendly with Boxing Promoter Lew Phillips. All three men became good friends of Pat's. (There is a photograph of Lew in one of Jack's programmes).

Jack Taylor explains: "Lew Phillips rang me up one particular day – would I go and see him? He used to run the Sportsdrome, Tipton Baths, all over the place, you know? I popped in to see him at his office and he was still doing boxing. Lew's office was close to the Victoria Law Courts, in Birmingham. He said: 'I'm revoking my boxing license because there's not the quality of boxers that there used to be, but I'm fascinated by this wrestling. I've got several places lined up, where I already present boxing. Will you match-make for me?' I agreed to do so.

"So beside our own promotions, I was drawing up lists of names. Right out of the blue I got this phone call from Pat saying that he was interested in wrestling. I didn't take any notice, because at that time there were *dozens* of lads interested in wrestling. I said: 'Well, you'd better come and see me then.' We were at one of Lew Phillip's shows and we were introduced at the back of the ring, if I remember rightly."

Pat subsequently visited Granby Halls one Saturday afternoon, to see if he had any potential, which is where our *second* Jack, former wrestler Jack Little, (aka Jack Perkins), takes up the story, with his first-hand account of Pat's transition, from judo to wrestling:

"I was talking to a friend of mine, who promoted wrestling in Stratford - Rab Barker, who also ran Stratford United football team. He introduced me to Jack Taylor, who invited me over to his gym at Kirby Bellars, in Leicester. I went over there every Sunday morning, for about twelve months, until I got my first bout, which was in Northampton. I had a phone call from Jack Taylor, asking me to go to Leicester one Saturday afternoon, to try out a wrestler who'd been recommended to him by Alf Kent." (Sadly, Alf died later, of a heart attack). "I went over there and got into the ring, to warm up. I looked around and saw a giant walking towards me. I thought: 'What the hell am I going to do with him?!'

"Jack Taylor was stood over by the door, looking at me," Jack Little continues. "I think he'd been afraid to tell me about the size of the fella, because he looked *really* big. Pat got me in the ring. I looked at him and said: 'How much do you know Pat?' He said: 'Well, not a lot.' I said: 'Well OK then, let's see what we can do.' I went to grab hold of him and it was just like holding a brick - he was so tight and hard. So I immediately said 'Slacken off Pat, and relax. We're not trying to fight each other, we're just trying to see what we can do.'

"Then we started. I said: 'OK, what we'll do, we'll go into the 'wrestler's hold', in the first place.' The 'wrestler's hold' is when you put your arms around each other's neck, and pull at each other, without hurting. Pat was very, very tight and I had to pat him on the back and say: 'Slacken off. If you don't slacken off, you can't wrestle. It's alright in judo to be aggressive, but you can't be tight in wrestling – that's the difference.' Pat wanted to be aggressive, but that's no good; you've got to get into holds – you've got to use each other."

Pat received no formal or systematic training for wrestling; it was more a case of getting in there, trying out various moves and practising - doing the best you could, in the circumstances. He was to visit the Halls on six occasions. "I had to try to persuade him, without letting on," explains Jack Little, "that there is a certain amount of entertainment in this business. With judo, you're being aggressive from the start; you're out to win as quickly as possible. With wrestling you have *got* to entertain the public, otherwise they're not going to come to see you again. You won't get any work if you're no good. It's an entertainment before it's a sport. So once you've got that, then you've got to pit your skill against each other. I had to help Pat understand that you've got to give and take in wrestling. It was very difficult at first, because he was so *sincere*. He wanted to wrestle me. I said, 'I don't *want* you to wrestle me Pat. I've got to wrestle someone else tonight. I don't want you to break my neck *now* you see!' "

In view of Pat's size, Jack had to make doubly sure that Pat understood that vital difference between the two sports; a very daunting task, in the circumstances! "What I did was to stop him and say: 'Let's just have a chat for a minute or two.' So we talked and I actually (demonstrating) – give me your hand please Shirley." (Readers won't be surprised to learn that I was rather reluctant - to say the least: "Don't break it!"). Fortunately, as he had all those years ago with Pat, Jack used the lightest of touches to demonstrate - using minimal contact only.

"I said, 'This is how I want you to hold me,' continues Jack. 'I just want you to touch me like that, and vice versa. I don't want you to *grab* me and be hard on me. Once you can do that, you can go into holds, you can move around, you can get me into a lock; but there's no pain; it's all *holding*, you see? So if you get into an arm-lock, or they're in an arm-lock, there's no pressure.' Obviously, if Pat put any pressure on me, he'd break my arm – straight away. So you've *got* to have faith in each other, and you've got to entertain the public. I keep saying this, because it's a fact." Described in these terms, wrestling begins to resemble more of an 'art-form' than a sport. "That's right," agrees Jack. "You're an actor: tell a part, act a part. Let's tell them a story – and the story's going to be – two people wrestling each other."

In a similar vein, Jack recalls taking Pat to different shows for Lew Phillips, in the Birmingham area. "He'd have a 'ding-dong' battle with somebody, and afterwards in the dressing room, the fellow was infuriated: 'What the hell's the matter with you Pat? Look at the bruises on my shoulder!' " What emerged from the Jack Little interview was that it takes a while to learn to put the correct techniques into practice. Jack Taylor adds: "To be a good 'professional' doesn't mean that you go into that ring to 'see off' your opponent!"

Pat had travelled to that first meeting at the Halls, with another Judo Black Belt, from Milton Keynes. Jack Little gave them a lift home, as far as Coventry. "Coming back, I was thinking: 'He's going to be good, this fellow.' I'd formed an opinion of him, straight away. 'He's going to go places and if I play my cards right, he's going to drag me along with him!' So I was a wrestler with experience, but I realised that one day, Pat was going to be far better than I was, because of his ability."

Manchester is generally acknowledged as the birthplace of wrestling. Jack Taylor summarises the heyday and decline of the sport:

"Originally, before television started, and television was active for thirty-two years, there was an abundance of international wrestlers, like Jack Pye, Bill Beny, Jim Hussey, and Vic Hessle, who was the father of the famous Royal Brothers. Bert Assinati, Bill McDonald, Tony Baer, Dave Armstrong, Pat O'Reilly, etc. The shows were in 'Baths' halls, Drill Halls, and so on. In September they stopped the swimming and put boards over, to convert it into an all-purpose hall. They'd have sports like badminton too. (Smethwick Baths, Tipton Baths and Willenhall Baths, Leicester's Cossington Street and Vestry Street, are typical examples). They'd put the boards across and have boxing and wrestling – wrestling every week, for that matter."

A familiar local venue of this kind, for Pat, was the *Tower Ballroom* in Edgbaston, which had sports matches as well as dancing. "But the important thing," continues Jack Taylor, "is that wrestling predominated during the winter months, in baths and drill halls all over the country. I wasn't in it then, by the way. But the point is that they'd already created a cheap entertainment for the working man. This started immediately after the war finished, in 1945, and for ten years after that, the wrestling thrived; it was a cheap night out. Although everybody used to say at that time: 'Oh, it's bent,' nobody could prove it, because, besides being first-rate wrestlers, they were good actors and good performers too. People would say the same thing to me later, but I'd say: 'Come in the ring with me and I'll show you whether it's bent!' "

The decade between 1945 and 1955 established the sport as a popular entertainment, and therefore a natural for television, prompting promoters to seize the opportunity to make a lot of money. Wrestling was first televised, on a fairly regular basis, in Britain, in the late 1950s. By the mid-60s it had become increasingly popular. Jack Taylor explains: "By the time it started on television, there was an abundance of wrestlers. So the fans had a wide variety to choose from – 'The Wild Man of Borneo', 'Giant Anaconda', there were always some different personalities: Francis St Claire Gregory, Ray St Bernard, Alf Rawlins, Bert Mansfield, Bob Silcock, Billy

Riley, etc. Then later on, the likes of Jackie TV Pallo, Les Kellett, Mike Marino, and so on."

So what *precisely* determined whether one wrestler was awarded a television contract, as opposed to another? Jack Little makes the point that there were perfectly good wrestlers who were never given the chance. Did it perhaps revolve around having a unique image, which made them stand out from the crowd – as in Pat's case? According to Jack Taylor it was more complicated than that: "No, the thing was, there were two organisations: there was *Joint Promotions*, which had the television contract, and there were the opposition promoters, which was the *British Wrestling Federation*: they had equally as many wrestlers as *Joint Promotions*. What *Joint Promotions* were doing, (it's like what's happening in America), they'd have a wrestler who got a bit too cocky – he'd want more money; so eventually they'd dispense with his services, not realising that he automatically went to the Opposition and got more work and money."

Jack Taylor's organisation was *International Promotions*. "But beside myself, there were five or six other major promoters, all through the country. There was Norman Berry, Shirley Crabtree and his brother Max – *20th Century Promotions*. There was a fella in Manchester, Jack Jefferson – *Northwestern Promotions*; a fella in London, he's dead now, Frank Price, he had *Premiere Promotions;* there was Paul Lincoln, who was *Doctor Death*, Eddie Capelli, Joe D'Orazio. Several of them left *Joint Promotions*, which was a syndicate. Had they not been well positioned, of course, they wouldn't have had any work."

Jack confirms that the heyday of wrestling was probably the mid-60s to the 80s. "It went through a transitional period of about fifteen years, then began to decline about '1974 or '75." Jack Little recalls it reaching the stage where wrestlers were saying: "If we're not on telly, it's no good." So they left because they couldn't get television coverage, which in turn hastened its demise as a high-profile sport. Because they lost interest, it became a kind of 'self-fulfilling prophesy'.

Jack Taylor views this from a different perspective: "My honest estimation of that remains that television did us good, because over a period of time, gradually people began to think: 'What a load of rubbish! Let's go and see the *real* wrestling, on the independent side' - which was a bit more savage. Gradually one or two of our wrestlers were poached by *Joint Promotions* – like Pat was – eventually." One of Pat's first television bouts was against the then *British Heavyweight Champion*, Billy Joyce. Jack wrote: 'Billy is full of praise for Pat, who has also had a go at the present *British and European Champion*, Billy Robinson – so in no uncertain terms he can now consider himself fully initiated.'

Television coverage had proved extremely useful, in promoting the careers of several wrestlers. Pat describes it as a 'latch-lifter'. It launched him into the film world, because Stanley Kubrick, (or possibly one of his agents), saw Pat in the wrestling ring and offered him a part in *A Clockwork Orange* on the strength of it. The same thing happened over in India, to Dara Singh, the Asian World Heavyweight Champion. Although Pat makes it clear that, in his case, a film career wasn't something he'd *planned*, when the opportunity came, he made full use of it.

There were numerous memorable occasions in Pat's sports career, but his performance in a Benefit Match for one of the Belshaw Brothers must surely rank as one of his most spectacular. During the bout, he performed an almost impossible manoeuvre for a Heavyweight, which exemplified World Heavyweight Wrestling Champion Dara Singh's subsequent description of Pat as a very 'flexible' wrestler. Furthermore, the two Jacks' account of Pat's *initial* approach is particularly interesting, when one considers the type of wrestler he eventually became. This earlier, aggressive stance is also the total opposite of the 'gentleman wrestler' label, which several wrestlers awarded him – (not least Dara and Randhawa Singh) - once he'd had the opportunity to hone his skills.

Jack Little still recalls the Belshaw Benefit Match vividly: "Pat wanted to use his own techniques; he didn't want to just be a 'run-of-the-mill' wrestler. Like the 'snowball': I'd never seen that done before! We had to decide, as we went along in the car. I said: 'Well, that's alright Pat, but you'll be counted out on the floor - and that's not good, because then, the bout's over. We've got to do it so that at the end, you'll be able to get out of it, before you're counted out to ten.' "

The match was staged because one of the three Belshaw brothers had recently died. All three worked for *Joint Promotions*. Jack Taylor asked Jack Little and Pat to stage a special exhibition fight. "Incidentally, we finished the bout in the 5th round, because we thought we weren't going down very well," Jack Little explains. "The promoter came to us and said: 'What did you pack in for?' We said: 'It didn't seem to be going very well.' They said: 'It's been the best bout of the night!' "

Geographically speaking, Jack and Pat were conveniently located: with Jack in Stratford and Pat in Birmingham. Jack's daughter, Lynn Perkins, recalls being quite overawed, as a young child, by Pat's massive frame, when he visited the family home. He and her father often travelled together by car, to a range of venues. The Belshaw Fight was fought fairly conventionally, for the first round or two. "We started off by coming over strong against each other. Obviously, being big men, we could work with 'strength'," explains Jack. "What you did was to use the strength *against* each other, so you did falls and rolls. He would throw me across the ring and I would rebound back up and grab him – get him in an armlock.

"It was quite a large club, so I should think there were five or six hundred people there. The disappointing thing about it was that they weren't sat there watching us, they were sitting there, at their tables, drinking; it seemed to be what they *did* up there."

There may have been some big names on the bill that particular evening, although Pat and Jack would have been unaware of it; they simply got changed, went in the ring, did their bout, came out, got changed and went home! They went approximately three rounds, before Pat went into the snowball. "Pat said: 'Do you think it will go down?' I said: 'Well, let's try it, we can't do any more than that.' Having talked about it in the car, we'd made sure that he wouldn't be counted out – so there'd be no 'foul'. At the end, simply by going over and hitting him on one particular part of the body, he would just spring out - like a jack-in-the-box.

"He had to practise it in the dressing room first, to make sure that he could get into it. What he did was to put both of his legs went round his neck," (semi-demonstrates)! He would need to have been almost double-jointed. "Honestly, I'm not joking," insists Jack. "His two arms went under his legs. So you can imagine, he was just like a ball. His head was between his legs."

His vision would have been practically zero, while he was rolling around. "But you don't need to see much, do you?" observes Jack. "You're in a ring – you're not going to fall out of it. And I was there to make sure he was OK." With his head pointing downwards, Pat had to rely totally upon Jack, to manoeuvre him in the right direction. Fortunately, by this stage, a relationship of mutual trust had developed between the two men, in much the same way that Pat and Harrison Ford learned to trust one another, while making the three *Indiana Jones* movies, twenty years later.

"Pat knew just what to do, to spring out of it," explains Jack. "For a man of his size to be able to do that was just *unbelievable*; lightweights could do it. I noticed that he actually tucked his stomach right into his chest! He was in the ball for no longer than a minute – if that." The muscle strain must have been tremendous – for a Heavyweight, and, one would have thought, impossible to maintain for very long. "The pre-arranged cue for coming out of it was when I gave up – because I couldn't do anything with him, like that." Pat couldn't *see* Jack do that, simply trusting that, eventually, he would do so. "The referee came over and he was trying to get him free then, because – were we going to leave him like that all night? He appeals to me: 'Well what are we going to do?' I said, 'Hang on, hang on,' and just rolled him over one way and then went (slaps his hand) like that and Pat sprang out."

Jack Taylor, who had commissioned the fight, recalls that, in the event, the snowball was more difficult for Pat to escape from than Jack Little's description implies. "If you keep a hold like that on, for some considerable time, your muscles consolidate with it. Even though the referee would sometimes come and *try*, it would take two people to manoeuvre and lever that leg over. Pat *definitely* had problems because he had quite a bit of bulk. His muscles weren't really relaxed like they should have been. I remember it took about two or three people to virtually *tear* the leg back over the top." Although he didn't spring out of it immediately, he was able to do so, once they'd released his legs. It remains, nevertheless, a remarkable feat.

"The amazing part about it," Jack Little adds, "was that at the end of the bout – I couldn't say it was a *standing* ovation, because I wasn't looking at people. But there's no doubt about it, we did go down *very* well and they gave us quite an ovation! Those people watched it elsewhere, day after day - wrestlers like Tibor Zakash and Billy Robinson."

Jack Taylor observes: "With *Joint Promotions*, of course, they had the prerogative of *World of Sport*; they had the television rights. Nobody else could get in, although we tried several times, we were a new organisation, although we had more wrestlers than *Joint Promotions.*"

He recalls a particular bout, which Pat had later on in his career. It was at Digbeth Civic Hall, Birmingham, next door to a large police station. "Pat Roach was on with *The Monster*- listen to this! The police station was two doors down and when the wrestling was on, the coppers made it their business to walk in – just to have a 'look-see'. Something happened that night - a bit of a disturbance; the crowd was absolutely packed solid. The fire people came in and Lew Phillips thought we might get 'done' - because of the Regulations regarding Hall capacity; people were standing everywhere."

Jack regrets the fact that British wrestling these days seems to lack any real *characters*. "Nobody like Les Kellett, Jackie Pallo, or Pat Roach, is available these days. That's why wrestling will never really make a comeback – simply because there aren't any more 'personalities' like there used to be. In our day, every bill was different. You'd put on a wrestling show and you could guarantee that the next one would be entirely different. Today, there's a shortage of 'would-be' wrestlers anyway, who know how to perform like they should do. Today's young 'wanabee' wrestlers fail to comprehend that in *every* bout, there must be a 'beginning', a 'middle' and a conclusive end. Today's lads go through the same stuff endlessly."

So it's the showmanship that's missing? "Exactly, and they all want to work in jog-suit bottoms or vest tops. One of the attractions of the old-style wrestling – and this applied to men *and* women – was that you went along to the diversity of physiques in the ring. You got thin men, but with good physiques, and fat men – but with solid physiques. Pat Roach looked like a bloody giant – you know! Shirley Crabtree, in his prime, before he became *Big Daddy*, he was 6 foot 2 and sixteen stone, an ex-guardsman like Jack Little – he *looked* an athlete."

Jack Taylor writes and publishes a bi-monthly magazine, called *Wrestling Whirl*, which he started a couple of years ago, and also *Wrestling Review*, which he has been successfully publishing for many years. "We include all sorts of the old time stuff – and modern stuff in *Wrestling Whirl*; there are even some old time wrestling bills –which you see there. I reduce things, to fit the space available. Every copy of is different from the last, to cater for what I think people want."

Pat and Jack Taylor continue to meet at the annual wrestlers' meetings, in Kent, held at Bill (aka Wayne) and Sarah Bridges' public house – *The Bridges*. "Pat's quite imposing: in wrestling, you can typecast people into types. If Jackie Pallo walks into a room, straight away, he's got this brash attitude. If Pat walks into a room, he's not quite the same, but he's equally imposing," continues Jack Taylor. "Because Pat is the opposite: he doesn't push himself or anything like that. He's always very pleasant with people. I've never seen him rebuff anybody – even fans. A lot of people will walk away from fans – not give them autographs: I've never seen Pat do that, neither did I, when I was wrestling. He's not really difficult to define: he's a really thoroughly reliable type of family man, as far as I'm concerned. And he deserves everything he's got.

"We set a price for his initial 'purse' and, unlike some wrestlers, he never varied from it; we gave him increases as the time went on. Whereas other wrestlers would be back for an increase every year, wanting a lot more money. I can't say that for Pat. He was a contented type, like me: he was interested in doing the business. Unlike the normal 'villain'-type, Pat has a very likeable kind of personality; he'd a smile for everybody. We deliberately cultivated the 'Big Bad Pat Roach' image, because that was the character he played."

Pat made the point in our previous book, that people quite often accuse him of being arrogant. "It's not necessarily that he's arrogant," comments Jack. "He's forceful and he believes in himself. That's why he's got where he is, really. Whereas a lot of us take the negative view sometimes - we get down – it's just the luck of the draw really. In Pat's case, I think he's got every confidence in himself and that's what's made him successful. I've never actually seen him in an arrogant mood, but there again, you've virtually got to live with a man, or be his next-door-neighbour, to witness this sort of thing. Apart from that, you show a different face. If you meet someone that you're working for, and you're earning money, your personality changes." Neither of the two Jacks has ever heard Pat say a bad word about his fellow wrestlers, whereas they sometimes heard comments from others, about opponents, as they came out of the ring.

"The best bout I've ever seen – Lou Thez versus Dara Singh - was at *Bingley Hall*. I match-made that for Lew Phillips, whilst Lou Thez was on tour," Jack

Taylor explains. "Dara was expecting to be paid about five hundred pounds. Bear in mind that he'd come over from India, and they were used to large crowds. I got him down to the same price as Lou Thez and I thought it would be a washout because there was haggling over the money. But the match was absolutely beautiful – poetry in motion. It was the year before *Bingley Hall* was knocked down."

According to former *World Heavyweight Champion* Wayne Bridges: "We were all there at *Bingley Hall*, wrestling, and Pat came into the dressing room, saying, 'How are you all?' – and so on. I said, 'Oh God – I'm not on with you, am I? I've not come a hundred miles to be on with you!' Then he said: 'Oh no, I'm here to earn money tonight.' I said: 'Who are you on with?' He said: 'I'm just going to show you my money – and I don't even have to take my clothes off for this!' He'd come in and emptied all the fruit machines, and put this pile of money on the dressing room table. He said: 'If there's anyone here who can match this, they can have it!' "

"Dara Singh also came to *Granby Halls* and had a marvellous bout," continues Jack Taylor. "Packed the place out – it was full of Asians; there were more Asians than whites there. In the end, Pat did gain and achieve the *British Heavyweight Championship*, but I think he only defended it twice. Because promoters had put him in print, which they do (without his knowledge) and he just couldn't do it."

Kent Walton, probably the most celebrated British television wrestling commentator of all time, died in August 2003, at the age of eighty-four. Wayne Bridges sometimes joined him in the commentary box, during the popular Saturday afternoon's television programme, *World of Sport*.

Three-and-a-half years down the road from when we started our first book, we've completely omitted, I think, to mention the fact that I was Chairman of Equity for eight years, from about 1975, until 1983. It was quite unusual for a wrestler to be Chairman. The meetings were held once a month in Broad Street, in the Ex-Servicemen's Club, directly opposite Bingley Hall, on the present site of the Hyatt Hotel."

It was during that era that Pat had his first TV role, a walk-on part in *Crossroads*. Then he became chairman of *Equity*, for eight years.

It was an eventful time while I was Chairman. I used to upset them all the time! I'd say things like: "You know, the reason Equity struggles so much, in getting things right, is because all the people who do the voting are people like us, who haven't got any jobs. The people who are working haven't got time to attend the meetings and do the voting." And that used to upset everybody - the fact that we were always available, and yet were bringing our influence to bear, by voting for policies that working actors then had to adhere to. I can remember having letters from people such as Jane Fonda, saying something like:

'Dear Comrades, please picket the corner wine-shop, because the people who pick the grapes are being exploited.'

Then someone would jump up and say: "I propose a motion…" and someone else would shout: "I'll second that motion." I'd say: "Hang on a minute, just a second. Before we do this. We are a fair-minded bunch of people here, aren't we?" They'd say: "Of course we are, of course we are!" I'd say: "Well, do you think we should picket the other corner shops, where they sell cocoa, coffee or tea? Because they're all exploited!" At that point they used to sit down, cursing me blind, mumbling under their breath, because they hated me. We used to get all sorts of very 'left-wing' stuff. By and large, I think a lot of actors, (without saying they're 'lefties'), favour the Labour type of movement. I think there's no secret about that. Certainly a lot of people in our group, at the time, used to support causes that were to the left – there's no doubt about that.

I did a lot of bookings for the Gangsters series, in 1974/75 when they wanted various types of people. I found a Chinese guy, with an HGV licence, for example, and a black girl, with the same kind of licence too. I got little Bhingi Lal an acting job in Gangsters, as a doorman. He now lives in Belgium. He was a Lightweight wrestler, about five-foot three. The other one was big Khalsa Singh. Bhingi, Khalsa, Paul Rajpal and myself used to all train together at the Nechells Community Centre: we were quite a little unit down there.

Pat's cousin, John Bevis, also recalls training with them, and with Maurice Colbourne, who later played the lead in *Howard's Way* - (theme tune, *Always There*). "Pat was stunt coordinator on *Gangsters*. Chaman Bhingi Lal was involved in the fight scene between a load of them, filmed on the derelict Snow Hill Station. Maurice Colbourne played an ex-SAS man, who refused to go to Northern Ireland."

I'll never forget, I arrived one day, and there was a kerfuffle going on. I asked Paul Rajpal (a Sikh lad, but westernised – born here), what was going on. He said: "It's Khalsa and Bhingi!" Khalsa was about twenty-three stone and six foot five and Bhingi was about five foot three and nine stone, and there they were – squaring up! It's the funniest thing you've ever seen! Everyone was terrified.

So I walked in and said: "Hey you two. What are you doing?" They stopped straight away. Khalsa said: "Ah – Mr. Pat!" He started to explain. I said: "Hey Khalsa, never mind what's going on. You don't fight like that! We all train together here." Paul said: "It's Khalsa. He just won't let Bhingi train." He was being a bit overly aggressive; it wasn't really Bhingi's fault. This is why, among the tribes in India and Africa, it used to work when the Brits were there. I only said: "Hey, what's going on?" and they both stopped. Anybody else, they would have killed them. They finished up as the two doormen in Gangsters, wearing big white jackets.

Pat involved *real* club owners in the club scenes – Pat Mannion, and so on.

I used to do things like that all the time. If they wanted a barrow boy – I'd get an authentic, real-life barrow boy to do it. That way, you see, they didn't have to have Equity Cards, because they were playing themselves. That's how they used to get round it.

While Pat worked on the *Gangsters* series, a visiting studio executive voiced his concern that Asians, West Indians and Greeks were being portrayed as gangsters.

The director, Alistair, was quite worried about it, so I said to him: "The next time he comes down, I'll talk to him, if you like." During his next visit, I said: "I understand that you're worried about the ethnics being depicted in this way?" He said: "Yes." I said: "Well look, over there is Joe, who is taking the part of a drug pusher in this series. Well, he's just done some 'porridge'. In fact, he's had more porridge than the Three Bears, for pushing drugs – so he's pretty real! Over there – those couple of Asian guys – they've been doing some kind of credit card fraud: they've both been 'knicked' for it. Then there's that West Indian fella over there – that coloured fella, he's just been knicked for sticking an electric drill up somebody's throat, with another guy named Bennett. And they're both on bail for extortion." So we cleared that up – he went away. We had Asian gangsters, West Indian gangsters and Greek gangsters. Before that stage, nobody ever thought that people who weren't white were gangsters – and of course, they were; there were one or two around. There were other white gangsters in the programme too, of course. So that was quite interesting.

Frank's last scrap business was in Hunter's Road. He died in his early 70s: around 1976/77. According to Pat's cousin, John Bevis: "He was doing some cutting, or work of some kind, for Pat, in his scrapyard on the Queen's Head Road. He finished his work, walked out to go home, because it wasn't far to Hunters Road, from Pat's yard. I don't know how far he'd walked, but he just dropped down dead! It was just before the Queen's Silver Jubilee." His nephew and namesake, Frank Roach, explains: "They took him to St Chad's Hospital, on the Hagley Road, suffering from a heart attack. So I presume, that's where he died."

In what ways did he resemble Pat? "I can't remember any similarities really, except that he was a big man. The mannerism was sort of the same," continues Frank. "Pat's father Frank never shouted: I never heard him raise his voice. Frank had a lot of consideration for other people, in spite of his rough exterior." Brian Webb confirms: "Pat was the same, in that respect. He had deep feelings, especially when he was growing up. If someone said anything stupid, and it hurt Pat's feelings, he wouldn't react in a bullying way, or anything like that, he'd just stand there, look at them, and then just turn away. Perhaps later on he'd get a bit angrier. As I remember him, he was a very sensitive person. Likewise, I remember Frank as a very respectful man."

The problem during research for our previous book, was that Dolly's description of Frank was inevitably 'coloured' by their past history, and the fact that she and Frank had separated. The intention is to redress the balance, in this book, because several people have since remarked that Pat's father was generally more even-tempered than previously described. Brian continues: "I could have a nice conversation with Pat's dad, in later years. We used to talk about Pat: he was *very* proud of him. Last time I saw him, in Hunters Road, by the scrap metal place, we were talking about things in general. He said: 'Pat's doing great for himself.' By this time, Pat had reached his celebrity status, or was near to it. Frank was proud of Pat's wrestling, and he'd been dabbling about on the edges of showbusiness too, by that time."

At one stage, they wanted to close *Birmingham Hippodrome* down. Pat and fellow *Equity* members picketed the building for quite some time.

I would like to think that we had some influence in it not being pulled down. They've spent millions on it since. Look at it today. It has the biggest pantomimes in the country today, and I would have thought, is very much a paying proposition.

Val Hastings, who was Secretary of the Birmingham branch, between 1976 and 1981, recalls: "I remember the day Pat opened the *Pat Roach Health Club*, in the Piccadilly Arcade. I went along with my husband Brian and daughter, Karen, my cabaret partner, Maureen Rivers and Variety artiste Pauline Millman, to generally help out, showing guests round and serving drinks etc. At the end of the day, Pat gave us all a bottle of champagne. Pat also gave me free membership and Brian one at half price. If you did Pat a favour, he always showed his appreciation." Val and Maureen formed a cabaret artiste/singing duo, called *Ice and Spice*. Maureen was blonde (the 'Ice') and Val was the brunette ('Spice').

Bear in mind that we were very much involved with the Variety Artistes side of things, because the VA joined Equity. So many thousands of variety artistes – live stage performers: stand-up comedians, singers and so on, all joined Equity. So they were very much a part of the union too.

Val Hastings played an active part in recruiting Variety Artists into *Equity*. "The reason I think we picketed the *Night Out* was because they employed about ten to twelve resident dancers," she explains, "and only half were members. When we tried to recruit the rest, the Management were not happy, because that meant they would have to start paying the *Equity* minimum wage, (which was more than the dancers were getting)."

The 'Night Out' is now 'The Dome', of course. The guy who ran it brought people in by bus, from all over the place – Coventry, Leicester, Nuneaton; he really worked, to keep the place going. Like all Birmingham venues, it suffered because of the lack of support from Birmingham people. Birmingham's always had a bad name with venues, and being a hard audience.

When Val resigned in November 1981, to become an agent, the actor, comedian (and eventually after dinner speaker), Len Edwards, volunteered to fill the post, on a temporary basis: "Here I am, over twenty-two years later, still doing it, because you make so many friends. You try to give it up, but people won't let you," explains Len. "As Chairman, Pat always dealt with things in a very straightforward fashion. He would think of things, but more or less instantly come to a decision, because what struck him as being straight and fair - that's the way he would go. At a first meeting with Pat, you might see him as someone who wasn't really 'on the ball'. That could be the biggest mistake you'd make - because invariably, he was way ahead of you! Pat is very thoughtful: he considers many aspects of the question or problem, and then comes out with a very straightforward way of tackling it.

"He's got a very wide and knowledgeable range. Very often, I've asked Pat for advice, on certain questions, and I value what he has to say. More recently, he's been to a number of our meetings, and when we have an issue, Pat sits there, very quietly, waiting for everyone else to have *their* say. Then he'll say: 'Mr. Secretary, fellow members, ladies and gentlemen,'-whatever – and put his point of view.' " Len makes some additional observations about Pat, in our closing chapter.

After our Equity meetings, we'd go for a drink, to the Wine Bar at Five Ways (which is still called 'Hort's'). They sold wine that quickly, they couldn't keep it cool – (they hadn't got any room to do so!).

Eventually, Pat resigned as Chairman because he was away filming, ironically proving his point, by becoming one of the people who couldn't vote. He was too busy working!

Chapter Nine –

A WALK ROUND THE
JEWELLERY QUARTER

(Centre of Excellence... or a Disappearing World?)

As I walked out by the James Watt house,
Close by the churchyard, early,
I did a-spy a craftsman, skilled,
A-weepin' for a memory...

(Extract from **Fool's Gold**, Traditional, Libretto © S. Thompson, 2003).

I love anything that enhances or promotes the Jewellery Quarter. I was born, and grew up, within a stone's throw of the Chamberlain Clock. The first thing that comes to mind about the Quarter, is not so much the cutting of diamonds and things, it's when we used to walk up the small entries to the firms and get the smell of acid, from all the vats.

My cousin, John, who spent part of his childhood in Kenyon Street, became a jeweller. Bill Bevis, my maternal granddad, is buried there. If you walk towards Vyse Street, with Frederick Street behind you, passing the clock, with The Big Peg on you right, turn left into that first section of cemetery - that's where Grandfather Bill is buried. I like Birmingham. I actually belong to Birmingham. And I suppose, that's the reason I didn't want to leave. I just wanted to be here - I didn't want to leave my memories.

This chapter takes you on a journey of discovery around the Quarter, visiting a range of people, across a variety of professions. Some of them, including Roy O'Neill, John Bevis, Ken Goodby and Ken Schofield, have known Pat for a long time, and are already featured in previous chapters. The fascinating nature of the material gathered during these interviews, would make a substantial book. For the time being, however, we'll content ourselves with the present, more condensed version. Verses from the co-author's folk-song, *Fool's Gold* may be found, at intervals, in this chapter and the next.

Both Pat and myself are particularly concerned about the future survival of the Jewellery Quarter, hence the decision to devote a significant proportion of the book to it. These two chapters aim simply to present as comprehensive a picture as possible, through the eyes of those who have generously shared their experiences. This is not a judgemental piece, nor a critical treatise, but simply a portrait of the area – past, present and future - from which readers may draw their own conclusions.

To discover why Pat has retained such an affection for the area of his youth, we'll begin with an imaginary trip back to the Quarter, in an H.G. Well's-type Time Machine, setting the dial to a time, just over two centuries before Pat's birth.

Between 1731 and 1831, Birmingham's population had expanded, from 23,000 to 170,000, resulting in an equally rapid escalation in urban development. Engraver Ken Goodby explains: "When the Jewellery Quarter first started, it wasn't in the spot where we are, but around Summer Lane and Newtown Row, because that was the first place where town gas was introduced." William Murdock, one of Watt's business partners, (Boulton completed the trio), piped the gas in, providing a much better source of fuel for jewellers, than their former pots of charcoal and blowpipes.

Ann Colmore obtained a Private Act of Parliament in 1746, enabling the family's estate of roughly one hundred acres, to the north-west of the city, to be developed. More prosperous businessmen moved from houses on the edge of town, into custom-built residential properties, in the original Quarter. Another parcel of land was subsequently released, in Stage Two - (the area where we are taking our walk) - where Georgian houses were erected, together with workshops, in large back gardens.

The vast Newhall Estate had prospered from the outset. During the 19th century, this second area of land was converted into 'pegs' - small workshop areas and an additional phase of smart new housing began, with the requisite outbuildings. Manufacturers of buckles, buttons, steel toys and jewellery, abandoned their substandard, foul-smelling premises, in the old part of the city, and moved in with great alacrity, as soon as finances permitted.

Much of the northern section of the adjacent Newhall Estate still remains, right in the heart of the present-day Jewellery Quarter. A Jacobean mansion, known as New Hall, stood near the centre of its holding. A long straight avenue led up to the Hall, from Colmore Row, following the line of today's Newhall Street. Streets were laid out, in a regular grid pattern, from 1746 onwards, on either side of park land, then divided into rectangular plots, on which purchasers subsequently built their own houses. To maintain standards, the 120-year leases stipulated that buildings should be of three-storey design, laid out in a straight line, and constructed at a predetermined minimum cost.

Marie Haddleton, Chairman of the *Jewellery Quarter Association*, an author of several books on the subject, writes, 'Colonisation of the area began in the 19th Century. Gold was discovered in California and the domestic demand for jewellery and trinkets increased.' Details of Marie's publications are included in our Bibliography.

1913 marked the peak of jewellery manufacturing in Birmingham - 50,000 people were employed. Ken Goodby continues: "As the city swelled, the owners moved out to smarter areas such as Handsworth Wood and Handsworth: the same thing, but about forty or fifty years on. Now where are they? Sutton Coldfield and places like that." There has been gradual movement further out from the city centre, with each successive stage.

An earlier chapter described how Dolly and Frank Roach began married life in Park Road, Hockley, close to the Quarter, where Frank had set up a scrap-dealing business. Dolly recalls pushing Francis Patrick, her first-born, in his pram, along Park Road, on a hot summer's afternoon, his tightly packed head of golden curls and large blue eyes, attracting the attention of passers-by.

The Jewellery Quarter is just a few minutes walk from the city centre, its boundaries delineated by Great Hampton Street, Great Charles Street, Summer Hill, Sandpits Parade and Icknield Street, with the many and varied streets of Ladywood in close proximity. Pat spent a considerable part of his youth, within this area of 265 acres, later opening his club, *The Rendezvous*, (featured in Chapter 5), at 31 Hockley Street, by the top end of Spencer Street.

The frontages of Warstone Lane and Vyse Street have the Chamberlain Clock at their junction. The 'Golden Triangle' was the area that was predominantly retail shops, although its boundaries have changed. Much of the Quarter, including Spencer Street, is currently dominated by the respectable image of over a hundred jewellery retailers. Strange-to-think of the disreputable 'goings-on' during the previous century, in this very district! For example, the 'Direct' and the 'hookie gear', associated with the Summer Lane mob, over which Frank Roach presided, together with the antics of other 'colourful' characters, of all sizes and descriptions. The city's canal system passes nearby – an ever-present reminder to Pat, of his grandmother, Amelia's childhood.

A friend of mine, Tony Green, (whom I mentioned previously), had his business on a site where I spent some of my earliest years, in a backhouse, up an entry, between 54-57 Tenby Street North.

The two authors recently visited that location. We estimated that Pat's house would have been, broadly speaking, where the warehouse 'loo' is - behind the metal-shuttered gates! Tenby Street North was never purely residential, but a combination of small businesses, backhouses and a pub. We've spent a fair amount of time, exploring the Quarter, taking photographs and visiting various people.

There's no better place to live than Birmingham. It is a friendly, small community and if you can't get a living here, you can't get one anywhere in the world. I used to think that I'd like to be buried in St. Paul's churchyard in the Jewellery Quarter, but that seems unlikely now.

Research into the movements of Pat's family, beginning with both sets of great grandparents, reveals that they lived in Bridge Street West, Summer Lane Court, Hospital Street and Tower Street - as described in Chapter One. Pages 73 and 152 of the *Birmingham A-Z*, contain many of the streets covered in this book. Closer examination shows that the lower end of Park Road, where Pat and Dolly lived for his first four years, and Tenby Street North, (their second home), are but one diagonal square removed from each other - (1F73 and 2G73 respectively), separated only by Icknield Street.

And now for our walk! By and large we have followed a systematic route. In reality, it took Pat's co-writer ten separate visits, each lasting a day, between August and January 2004, to interview our hosts, then double-check the material. However, it's much more fun to ask readers to suspend their disbelief, and pretend that it all happened in one day. Had that *really* been the case, they'd have been carrying me out on a stretcher!

So who do we have lined up for you? We begin with businessman Roy O'Neill, followed by engraver Ken Goodby; author Marie Haddleton and entrepreneur, Kenny Schofield are near-neighbours, in Frederick Street. From Kenny's front entrance, we cross over to Albion Street, where Pat's cousin John was once a jeweller. As Chapter Nine concludes, we return to Frederick Street, en route for Warstone Lane, where we visit jeweller Rob Turley and his apprentice Nicol Dwyer. Their experiences contrast quite sharply with those of Professor Norman Cherry, Head of the Birmingham School of Jewellery, (in Vittoria Street), who opens Chapter Ten.

From there, we make our way to St Paul's, to consult the Reverend Tom Pyke, then stroll just a few yards down from the church, to Ludgate Hill, the site of *The Last Drop and The Actress and Bishop* (one-and-the-same building). Chris Millard, Paddy White and Jill White relive past days spent there. Finally, we visit the BJA, in Vyse Street – courtesy of Chief Executive, Geoff Field. Although none of our hosts would claim to be in possession of Eternal Truth, concerning the Quarter, each has his own, unique tale to tell. The Jewellery Quarter is a network, so most of our contributors either know one another, or know *of* each other.

We begin right on the periphery of the area, in Barr Street, just across from Great Hampton Street, where we visit Roy O'Neill, in the office of his large warehouse premises. As previously explained, Pat and Roy's fathers were good friends, and Roy was Best Man at Pat's wedding.

Roy explains: "I know most people in the Quarter, because they deal with me. All round this area – Barr Street, right the way down to Summer Lane, Digbeth, Perry Barr, you could buy anything you wanted, and they *made* anything you wanted. But over a period of time, they've all gone. The Jewellery Quarter itself was little rooms - workplaces. When they closed up, we used to

Map of the Jewellery Quarter - (the Parish of St Paul's Birmingham). An asterisk marks the approximate position of Pat's home, in Tenby Street North, which he and Dolly occupied during part of the war years. Readers may wish to use the map, whilst following the route of our 'walk'. By permission of Marie Huddleton.

A Second World War view down Vyse Street, before the terraced houses were demolished and replaced by the Hockley Centre, now renamed 'The Big Peg'. The ARP sign, in the foreground, points to the actual air-raid shelter where Frank, Dolly and a very young Pat took refuge. By permission of Marie Haddleton.

A 1939 postcard illustration of Tenby Street North, where Pat and Dolly had a backhouse, up an entry, with an outside toilet, one room downstairs, a bedroom and an attic. Pat recalls that sometimes his father's horse and cart would be parked outside. Courtesy of Hulton Picture Company.

A late 1950s/early 1960s view up Vyse Street, towards the Chamberlain Clock (in the distance). Nowadays, street parking isn't always necessary, as there's a multi-storey car park. Pat's grandfather Bill Bevis, is buried somewhere in the churchyard to the right. By permission of Marie Haddleton.

Marie Haddleton's birthplace, at 10/12 Tenby Street, is one of the few remaining terraced houses, typical of the Jewellery Quarter, around the 1920s – 40s. Pat and Dolly's home, around the corner in Tenby Street North, was far less salubrious! By permission of Marie Haddleton.

Albion Street Fire Station: Pat's father, Frank, managed to crawl there, from his home in nearby Camden Street. He was rushed to hospital, for a life-saving operation. According to Pat, the building became a garage repair place, and later a Day Nursery. By permission of Marie Haddleton.

The War Stone was deposited by a glacier, during the Ice Age. At one time, it was used to mark the parish boundary. By permission of Marie Haddleton.

Engraver Ken Goodby, in his Spencer Street premises, has a lifetime's experience in the trade. (His model-maker son, Eric, is working here, in the background). Ken explains: "It's impossible for the craftsman to relocate, because the Jewellery Quarter is a network of little trades." Photograph by Shirley Thompson. By permission of Ken Goodby.

The Annual Picnic of G.H. Lancaster's employees, 13 September 1913. The firm was located at 16 Hockley Street, just around the corner from Ken's present premises. The reverse of the postcard advertises numbered examples of high-class engraving. By permission of Ken Goodby.

Pat, with Ronnie Callow and two of his sons, Ronnie and Steven, taken in 2003. Steven is between Pat and Ronnie. By permission of Ronnie Callow.

PCs Phil Burlace and Michelle Birch, 'join forces' with Pat! Photograph by Shirley Thompson. by permission of The BJGF/ BJA.

Pat, with Geoff Field, Chief Executive of the British Jewellers' Association. Also in attendance was Krys Zalewska, CEO of the British Giftware Federation. Photograph by Shirley Thompson. By permission of The BJGF/ BJA.

The Plaque outside the Last Drop (now the Actress and Bishop again) tells the story. The new proprietor, Colin Woodley, is former landlord of The Railway, in Curzon Street. Photograph by Shirley Thompson.

go in there and clean them out. We'd take the floorboards up, vacuum all underneath, then put new floorboards in." The vacuumed gold dust would be taken to *Sheffield's*, smelted, refined, and payment received for it.

Roy has installed safes for many Jewellery Quarter businesses, since first moving into his premises, over thirty years ago. He and his son, Jonathan, share the concerns of jewellery craftsmen, regarding local developers. "It's right across the board," he explains. "A certain sector of the community is taking over most of the property around here. They've got that many scams on. They're knocking all the small businesses out, and it's just becoming importers and sales. There are no little factories making things now – they're all going bump. I'm trying to sell the place now."

Another mutual problem is the proliferation of derelict buildings, dismantled years ago, then left to fall into ruin. "There's one in Frederick Street that's dilapidated – the old *Feredax* building, next to the bank," comments Roy. "I've been trying to get it for years."

Recurring themes, during the course of our visits, are redevelopment, buildings of architectural interest falling into disrepair, and jewellery craftsmen being undercut, with few grants or financial support from the Associations. Conversely, we've had very positive feedback, about forthcoming projects, plus constructive suggestions for improvement.

Roy and his father have always had businesses in *this* area. Pat prompted me: "Ask Roy what 'fish' were?" "Nickel anodes", comes the reply. "An inch of nickel anode weighed a pound. So if it was sixteen inches long, it weighed sixteen pounds. They used to go to the *Hockley Chem.* (chemical works), which was on the corner of Vyse Street and Great Hampton Street/Row. These nickel anodes had a rubber section, over the hook - at the top. They had hundreds of these rubber hook covers in there," (about the size of a hand stapler top), "and the lads down at the café used to pinch a bag of them." Pat refers to these 'lads' as the 'Summer Lane Mob', in our first book.

"Each cover, weighing an ounce, would be over the top of a hook, which went down onto the nickel anode. The silver fish (anode) was sixteen inches long; they'd hang the anodes on the bars, in the vats, and fix these rubbers onto the anodes, so that when they were weighed in, each anode weighed a quarter of a pound more (4ozs.). There was a place on the corner of Vyse Street, and Hockley Street. When they got 'done' there, they found more anodes there than *Canning's!*"

Leaving Roy's warehouse premises, we cross Great Hampton Street, then into Hockley Street, passing new apartment blocks, (the former site of *The Rendezvous*), turning sharp left into Spencer Street. We're looking for engraver Ken Goodby, whom we met in Chapter 5 – (describing Hockley Street in the *Rendezvous* days). It was Pat's cousin, former jeweller John Bevis, who suggested that we contact him.

We ring a bell. Ken slides back a hatch, and in we go. Seated at his workbench, with son Eric working to his left, Ken recalls: "My father, Harold, was an engraver, like myself, but he was an ornamental engraver. He came into the trade, to work in the Quarter, in between the wars – in the middle 1920s. In those days, there were about thirty or forty thousand people working in the jewellery trade. He said that on a sunny dinnertime, when everyone came out of their workplaces to eat their sandwiches, they crowded the streets and stood around on the steps, talking to each other, and walking up and down. It was just like a Villa match turning out, because there were so many people. Of course there wasn't so much traffic there in those days. It was mainly horse-drawn. It would take you three quarters of an hour to walk from one end of Vyse Street to the other, in your lunchtime, so close were the numbers of people on the pavements and the roadways."

Ken was born in Hampton Street and lived in a backhouse (with washhouses). "There was a whitewashed country cottage on the corner, with creepers up the wall; not exactly a thatched roof and roses round the door, but it had been overtaken, time-wise, by later housing.

"I came into the trade in 1946, when I left school at the age of fourteen, starting work at *Lancaster's*, which was the main training firm for training engravers, in those days. All they did was engraving," (see the two postcards he's loaned us), "and the allied trades linked to engraving. I stayed there as an apprentice for four years, learning as a trainee and improver, until National Service, in 1950. I returned to the trade in 1952, staying at *Lancaster's* until about 1954."

Ken married, a year after being de-mobbed. Due to insufficient wages, he set up on his own. When the old jewellery factories were closing, and developers were about to move in, he discovered a lot of original equipment. "We were stripping out the old factories, and everything was being thrown into skips. For instance, there was a firm, almost on the corner of Branston Street and Vyse Street, which closed down. They'd been trading since the middle of the 1800s, making brooches and pictures, out of huge tropical butterfly wings. But they also specialised in military badges – and badges for other armies, which they'd been producing since Waterloo. There was a great star-shaped display, of all the hundreds of regimental badges they'd ever produced."

The scrap merchants went down the cellar, and bought all the old dyes. "They took the labels off and chucked all the metal tins into the back of the lorry - just buying them for scrap – for a fiver a shelf, or something daft. Then they moved up to the other room and saw the display of military badges, which went for a helluva lot of money. It suddenly occurred to one or two of them, that they'd been scrapping the dyes and stamps that made these badges. It was such a laugh, because they were in the back of this truck, trying to match them up! But that was wicked, because you realised then, the destruction that was going on, to the history of the trade, through sheer lack of knowledge."

Those premises were only a door above the present-day Jewellery Quarter Museum, itself a former jewellery workshop. Ken explains: "They simply closed the place down, paid off the workers, and left everything. If you went into these places, everything was still there – years later." It sounds like a Miss Haversham-type scene, from Dickens' *Great Expectations*!

"In the museum," he continues, "the benches are still there, the sandwich boxes and the mugs; the kettle's on the stove. It's like a ghost workshop. I've been in one or two of those places, because we used to do a little bit of tatting around for things at weekends. It's really *spooky*, because everything is so quiet. Some of them were vast – big long workshops. Over the road there was a big old firm, in Spencer Street, which produced beautiful enamelled silver brush sets, spoons and cutlery with enamel on the handles. Dressing cases and dressing table sets. They even printed their own catalogues. I've got some of their old wooden printing blocks."

Up until 1976 – the Jubilee Year – there were still plenty of manufacturers, large and small, here; and every street was a kind of village. "It had the one who thought he was the squire – (those who were doing better than the others – with new cars) – all the way down the line, to the village idiot! 'What time d'you call this – to come into work?' It was like a little community; everyone knew each other's character. If anything happened to anybody on *that* side of the trade, by lunchtime, everybody in *this* side of the trade would know about it.

"The Jewellery Trade, like everything in this country, isn't what it was. We noticed that some of the larger firms were moving out, around about the beginning of the mid-1970s. Production work decreased and some of the larger manufacturers were shrinking, due in many cases, to the import of jewellery, from cheaper labour sources, in the Far East, Poland and Spain. As old premises were vacated, so developers started moving in - taking us up to 1980." Jewellery workshops were disappearing, purchased for alternative uses. "Around about 1981/82, the first of the big slumps came," continues Ken. "The property developers and speculators got their fingers burnt. They were going to develop them into offices, according to many of the placards. But office space wasn't needed so much then, with the advent of the electronic office. So you could literally run a business from one small room, with the improved communications and printing. You could hardly walk down the streets and see the walls, in some parts of the Quarter – because they were covered with these signs!

"Then the economy picked up again, and we're back to where we were. Some of that old property has now been bought over, and converted into town flats and lofts, with tremendously high rental and value. It is space once occupied by hundreds and hundreds of little firms – if not thousands. Even if the demand for the workspace was there, it's no longer available. But what *is* concerning us, is that remaining property is being increasingly encroached on by the developers: we see it shrinking all the time. So, now, even though you have a place, you're not necessarily going to be there, if the landlord, (which could be the Council, or a private landlord), is approached by a developer who is putting a parcel of property together, to build more of these lofts and flats."

Some contributors mentioned friction between the Council and the jewellers, because the council feel that they're paying insufficient rent – which reinforces Ken's point. "It's this unfortunate perception that people have," he continues, "that because you work in the *jewellery* trade, you're making a fortune – but you're not." Marie Haddleton comments: "… it's not little men in white coats, popping diamonds into rings." "No, it's not," agrees Ken. "Maybe *retail* – yes – but we're workers: we *make* the stuff! We've got this example in our minds, (those of us who can remember back that far), of our sister trade – the Gun Quarter – just over by St Chad's - which was a mirror image of our trade. It was full of little craftsmen, working on their own, as well as the large production firms – the *BSA Small Arms*; the shotgun people like *Greenings* and *Greenalls*. They depended on the little men, who were specialists. That was exactly the same as our trade. It went into a great redevelopment scheme – and it's totally disappeared!"

A few of the larger companies have registered offices there, but Ken doubts that there's much production. "I know that it's not the warren of little craftsman that it was, when I used to visit it. I believe, somewhere, there is a blue plaque on the wall, which tells people that once, this was the centre of Birmingham's world-famous Gun Quarter. We can draw a parallel, because one day, there'll be a plaque on the wall of the *Jeweller's Arms*, saying, 'This was the centre of Birmingham's world-famous Jewellery Quarter'!"

Jewellery craftsman Rob Turley predicts that, in five to ten years, only the pubs will remain, plus one or two little landmarks. I wondered whether this might be somewhat pessimistic? Ken disagrees: "I don't think that he's being pessimistic, because it's been accelerating. The thing that's held it down, *slightly*, is that much of the property is *leased*. The workers who work in the property have leases of between three to ten years. So they're having to wait until these leases are 'falling in', otherwise, if they want to break their side of the lease, they have the difficulty of finding you a comparable, replacement property. But they are no longer re-granting leases. We'd then go on to weekly or monthly rental, with three months' notice, which is now becoming more widespread." Fortunately, as Eric Goodby and Marie Haddleton both confirm, at a November 2003 meeting, Peter Jones assured those present, on behalf of

Birmingham Property Services, that anyone who wants a lease for a property in the Quarter, can have one.

"It's impossible for the craftsman to relocate," explains Ken, "because the Jewellery Quarter is a network of *little* trades: mounters, model-makers, engravers, with a system of runners, or 'porters', taking the jewellery from one craftsman to another." Henry Savigar, Brian Webb's grandfather was a jeweller's runner and Rose Collins, Ken's mother, sometimes ran similar errands.

Ken Goodby observes: "The refuge of all old jewellers was to get a porter's job, when you packed up, because you knew the trade, were well known and you were trustworthy and honest. As it's such a network of inter-dependent, and closely interconnected trades, if you start cutting holes in the net, sooner or later, it's just one big hole. So for the self-employed jewellers and jewellery workmen to have to move outwards, no longer around the corner from each other…

"Many of the big jewellery trade firms, that have left the trade, have relocated in Taiwan, South Korea and places like that. Then the stuff is re-imported, hall-marked down at the Assay Office, with the Birmingham hallmark if they want it; it's not manufactured within the trade itself. So although you can have these great publicity schemes, it just brings people in, and a great deal of what they're buying doesn't help craftsmen in the trade."

So what precisely would help the Quarter? Is there a solution? "Everyone's been beating their brains out here," replies Ken. "It's a problem for the shops, because they also deal in repair work, and re-setting stones, and stuff that is faulty, so they *need* little craftsmen. Some have got their own staff: one or two craftsmen in back workrooms, where they can, for example, re-size a ring for a customer. Or like me – round the corner – if they want their name engraved on something."

On a positive note, Ken observes, "The things that applied a few years ago are no longer the case. Communication *is* much better now, because of the Internet and fax machines. If someone wants a name on an Identity Bracelet, or little dates or messages inside wedding rings, then I'm here to do that. You can't do it out there yet, but who knows? Maybe they will, one day."

Ken's branch of the industry may be able to hold out for longer. However, there are problems with his son Eric's branch of the trade: making models for people who cast and make rings. Nowadays, the firms that sell castings are having the patterns and the models made, the other side of the world.

3-D computer technology provides greater flexibility, for design, although, according to Ken: "It's still got a lot of bugs to iron out. They can design these lovely things, on the screen, and the technology will actually build a wax model. But the people who are doing the design, and understand the technology, aren't jewellers, who can sit down and do the practical side. So the design may be alright and the wax will be there, but if it doesn't *work* properly, it has to come back and be adjusted by people like Eric, or other model makers. Clients have obviously got to pay for the £50,000 or £60,000-worth of computer technology. We say: 'If you'd brought the design to me in the first place, I could have done it properly, and it wouldn't have needed re-adjusting.' With intricate work, you've got to know exactly what your materials can or cannot do – and what your process can or cannot achieve. So you need both types of skills."

Ken sometimes saw Pat in the *Brown Lion*, when he called in for a drink. "We knew each other just to nod to and speak to. If he was sitting with friends or acquaintances of mine, then I'd be drawn into the conversation, as we were waiting at the bar. He *is* a well-known person, around the trade." Unusually, Jewellery Quarter pub names include a range of colours; one could probably write a book on that alone!

"The chap I mentioned earlier, Albert Marson was born in the trade - in Frederick Street," recalls Ken. "His father was the caretaker of Lloyd's Bank. Marie's office, where *The Hockley Flyer* is printed, was Albert's bedroom, where he was born." Our cue - no doubt - to visit Marie, and have a chat with her, in Albert's old bedroom!

Marie's publishing company, at 22 Frederick Street, is accessed through the side door of the bank, then up a steep staircase. Marie and her son, Mark, have been very successful in improving communication between members of the trade via their magazine, *The Hockley Flyer*. We're seated either side of her desk. Photographs and memorabilia of past events cover the walls.

Marie was born in the Jewellery Quarter, in Tenby Street, seventy-five years ago, in 1929. "Where I lived, in Tenby Street, it was slum housing, although my mother fiercely kept it clean," she recalls. "There was a back entry. Apart from the fact that I wandered away from here for a time, as is inevitable with anyone connected with the Jewellery Quarter, you keep coming back. It's almost as if you've got a piece of elastic tied between you and the clock, and wherever you try to go, it pulls you back again." This analogy echoes Pat's sentiments. "Age is no escape," she continues. "I suppose the only escape really is death, because you see people around you who are so old, it just isn't true – that they could still be walking about; they're wonderful! Then you suddenly find that they've gone to the 'Big Jewellery Quarter in the Sky'.

"It was mostly slum areas, when the big jewellers began to leave, and I lived here. Then, in the 1930s, the City Fathers decided that everyone had a right to fresh air, a garden, a bathroom and an inside toilet. So they built Kingstanding, Great Barr, and all those sort of areas. I was living in Well Street at the time, and was moved out, into the fresh air. I'd got TB. Most of the kids had TB and rickets. We all moved out. It couldn't have been far off the war years at that time, because Kingstanding was built for this purpose, but during the war it was let to the American forces. So they occupied Kingstanding for a few years, before we could have it back."

Marie's two homes were distinctly up-market, compared to the little backhouse, which Pat and Dolly occupied. For a while, during the early 1940s, he lived in Tenby Street North, after Marie's family moved from the neighbouring street. He and his mother, Dolly were subsequently evacuated to Hereford, when the pub on the corner of Tenby Street North was bombed. Dolly described the bomb shelter in Warstone Lane, under the crypt, where she and Pat took shelter, when the sirens went. One of a range of photos, which Marie has kindly granted us permission to publish, features Wartime Vyse Street, and the sign to the actual Air-raid Shelter, which Dolly and Pat used!

"About twenty years ago, I came back into the Quarter again, to open up a secretarial business, looking after small businesses," explains Marie. "I was keeping books for about thirty of them, and doing all their typing etc. That was off Key Hill – York Terrace; that's why my business is called *York Business Administration*.

"I got to know the jewellers; they're very difficult people to get to know. In spite of someone saying: 'They're a friendly lot.' I said: 'I wouldn't count on that!' They're a lot of *other* things: they're loyal, and they're honest with each other, and they've got a certain amount of integrity about them; but they don't take kindly to strangers. They didn't like tourism starting up, and residents coming into the Quarter, but they've accepted that; they've been very tolerant and very good. It took me four years to get this area declared a 'full conservation area'. That actually includes taking care of the integral trade.

"I formed the *Jewellery Quarter Association*, fifteen years ago, with some handpicked directors. Before that, – my son, Mark and myself had just launched the *Hockley Flyer*, which is the local magazine." Marie delivers the *Flyer* around the streets, by trolley – as featured on a recent edition of the *Inside Out* television series. "The *Jewellery Quarter Association* does a great deal of work. Six years ago, they launched this Urban Village – *stupid* complex (excuse the extra word in the middle of it)."

Marie's area of responsibility, within the Association, is Planning and Development: "Before the Urban Village, I was invited to go onto the *Conservation Areas Advisory Committee*, who look at all planning applications for conservation areas. I'm regarded as the expert for the Jewellery Quarter, on that. When this Urban Village came about, they tried to do it behind my back, because they knew I wouldn't like it. I was kept out of all meetings, but me being me, I gatecrashed everything I could, and caused hell! I went to see Albert Bore, who's the leader of Birmingham City Council. He actually put

Paul Spooner onto me, who is the director of the *Economic Development*, and said: 'Marie is right – help her.'

"If you look at the map in my office, you'll see that there are lines drawn on it - where we actually map out the Inner Core, (where the small jewellers are); the bigger ones can look after themselves quite well. We decided that we needed to protect the Inner Core from inappropriate housing, which would force up all the prices of land, property and rents – the little guys wouldn't have survived. When the planning legislation was changed, to include this Urban Village, it lifted all the Jewellery Quarter Housing Restrictions, dating back to 1960."

According to Marie, the City Council lifted the restrictions, in conjunction with the *Prince's Trust*. "Arsenic is still the traditional way to commit suicide, and we did have a couple of suicides, when this Urban Village was announced, because they thought it was the end. We even had developers coming round, with pound notes in their hands, trying to buy buildings from the private owners. Employees were worried that their jobs would be going. So we had to do something really quickly.

"I became very unpopular with developers – still am. They say, 'Well you can't live for ever Marie.' That's their attitude. Round here, they've dubbed me 'The Queen of the Jewellery Quarter' – that's my official title. Eventually, we managed to get new planning legislation – changing what they'd done, and putting some of it back as it was. That was more than a year ago - it took me nearly four years to get that. Tears on my pillow at night; crying and crying; screaming everywhere I went."

Marie lobbied various contacts, such as the *Conservation Advisory Committee*, *The Victorian Society*, (who'd saved the area in the 1960s, from the developers), and the *Civic Society*. "I thought I was standing alone against the City Council. But *English Heritage* was behind me, watching my every move. They told me *afterwards*, saying, 'We were afraid you would stop.' Every ten years or so, the 'powers that be' decide that we need regeneration again, and we have to fight our way through it all, and survive."

I asked Marie to outline her basic aims. "The jewellery trade is under pressure, in a lot of ways. I can't stop the importing, or the innovation – it's going to happen. But my idea is 'as long as one jeweller wants to work on his own, in the Jewellery Quarter, where it's traditional, I will help him.' I feel as if we haven't got many friends, funnily enough; but the *jewellers* know what we're doing. They've scrapped the Urban Village idea now completely; the *Prince's Trust* has dropped out of it altogether."

The Birmingham Jewellery Quarter hallmark is an anchor. Since 1877, the Assay Office, in Newhall Street, has determined and controlled the regulations, about how jewellery is made in the area. A recent European

Directive, suggesting an open market, with no restrictions on hallmarking, has happily now been put 'on hold'.

Marie recently helped to put James Watt's house back on the map. "I went to see the bloke who lived there, about the building, because it was in atrocious condition. It was where Watt had his children, and it was all fields, all round here. So we got in touch with the *Civic Society*. They took an interest, and only just a few months ago, they put a blue plaque on it – 'The James Watt House'. It's just round the back here. You go past the little road – down Ken Schofield's road – Regent Street. You cross over, do a little 'dog leg', which takes you through to Regent Place. Walk down, just a little way, you'll see a red and white building, then *Deakin & Francis*, then there's a little car park and then James Watt's house. It looks very *plain*, apart from the blue plaque." The *Hockley Flyer* ran the story - just one example of why the magazine is so valued.

Kathleen Dayus, the celebrated Jewellery Quarter writer, was born in Camden Street, in 1903. She was brought up in a Hockley slum, and was left a widow, at the age of twenty-eight, with four children to bring up. She has written several books, about her life in the Quarter. Coincidentally she was one of my own publisher's top team of writers, which also includes Carl Chinn and Alton Douglas.

"She died recently two weeks *before* her birthday," explains Marie. "We arranged a party to celebrate the one-hundred-year-old clock and Kathleen's hundredth birthday. We'd printed a little book and were going to give copies to the schoolchildren – the history of the clock. It was very sad; we were very upset. She was a lovely person. I absolutely adored her. At ninety-nine she was hilarious. When you made her laugh, she'd throw herself back, with her legs in the air, and knickers directly in view. A lovely character – she was brilliant!

"Instead, we arranged a party for a centenarian cobbler, in the Quarter. The police were going to drive him around, with all the sirens going, and we'd got a great big cake. He saw his birthday, but he was in hospital when he died. So I said: 'When I get to a hundred, I don't want a party!' "

Kenyon Street Police station features in Chapter 5 – in connection with police raids on Pat's club, *The Rendezvous*.

The old station was almost on the corner of Great Hampton Street, when you turn left into Kenyon Street. Its modern replacement is in Vyse Street.

Ken Goodby, at our previous stop, recalled: "When my father and his friends were little boys, on a Saturday night, they'd go down to the bottom of Snow Hill and Livery Street. There was an old granite horse trough there, where the GWR horses pulled the wagons up to Snow Hill and back: they used to stop and have a drink. It was about twelve feet long – with the usual drinking bowl for the dog, on the corner of it.

"According to my father, all the drunks used to come wandering back to their houses, from drinking in town – singing. The policeman used to stand in the dark doorway, and as a drunk came staggering past, he'd put his foot out, trip him up and he'd sober up in the trough! If they were really drunk, they'd be dancing along the pavement. The boys used to creep up the side of the police station, where they could hear these people being put into a cell. They'd have no light on, and their boots and trouser belts would be confiscated. If they'd been particularly nasty, and whacked somebody, a couple of policeman would go in, in the dark, and set about them – stamping on their toes – and so on. Which was an even greater delight to my father and his little friends, who were listening outside!" It sounds brutal, but we *are* talking about 1901.

Marie's father, PC 77 - Richard Evan Jones, from Aberystwyth, was stationed at Kenyon Road Police Station, between the wars. "He received a merit stripe for carrying eleven people to safety, when Hockley Brook flooded. Kenyon Police Station has always had a bit of a reputation, because two of the policemen were hanged for murder – on two separate occasions. One was the famous 'Towpath Murder': the officer actually helped with the investigation – and he was the murderer!" The murder took place near Hockley. Both officers were later hanged for their respective crimes.

Marie adds: "*Advantage West Midlands* are putting money into the Quarter, for example, into this Coffin Factory, just around the corner. They're angels – actually!"

Marie's near-neighbour, just three doors away, is antique dealer and entrepreneur, Ken Schofield. He owns most of Regent Street, which separates their respective premises. Like Pat, whom he met as a teenager, Ken is a 'local boy made good'. Marie observes: "When we *do* get a problem here, we sort it out: we 'kick ass' – 'til we get what we want; I just won't let go. And Ken, I find, is in the same mould as me." He's a fellow director of the *Jewellery Quarter Association*, which Pat has recently been invited to join. "The Quarter is a fascinating place - all the way through," concludes Marie.

From the dizzy heights of his third floor, at 25/26 Frederick Street, formerly a Georgian mansion, Ken shows me a 'bird's-eye' view of the School of Jewellery, (we pay a visit later), otherwise known as the 'School of Excellence', which is part of Birmingham University. He jokes: "When Prince Charles comes, they pull all the shutters down, so that he can't see the dilapidated buildings down below!"

Ken's area of responsibility, within the *Association*, is *Tourism and Leisure*. Funding for the Information Kiosk, on the corner of Vyse Street, which he'd previously set up, is one of the recent problems he's had to resolve. It's taken nine months to re-open it, with help and encouragement from Andy Maddocks, Mike Long, Marie Haddleton and Rob Turley.

He is also keen to improve a range of facilities for the disabled. "None of us know when we're going to be disabled. We can be getting in or out of our car, fall and break our neck as easy as anything. So what I'm trying to get, is more awareness in the Jewellery Quarter, about disabled people."

Ken, who has been based in the Jewellery Quarter for eight years, is quite an authority on English Architecture. Having been at the *Antique Centre*, on *Holliday Wharf*, he came to the Jewellery Quarter, as a last stand for the antique dealers in Birmingham. "It's the only place where they can't come along and knock our buildings down, and destroy them. Because they're listed buildings. Come on – I'll show you!"

We walk across into the next room – a tastefully furnished Georgian lounge, and look out at the views. "That's the most 'un-bastardised' furnace chimney in the whole of the Jewellery Quarter," explains Ken. "Look at the contrast between the old and the new. Isn't it fantastic?" (He's referring to an old brick-built chimney, with the modern steel version, just behind it). "That's *Cookson's*. That's how they melt gold now," (steel chimney), "this is how they melted it then." The old chimney bricks look very worn, possibly Georgian – early 1800s. The rooftop views from Ken's premises provide fantastic photos, of Georgian and Victorian houses, with their workshops.

Looking at the Georgian façade at the front of Ken's house, over to the left there's a number 26 engraved in the stone work and below it the word 'Goldsmith', (presumably, the owner's occupation, rather than a surname)? "That's the factory building immediately to the left of this house. I own that too. *This* building, where we are now, to the right of the factory, was a Georgian house. People lived here. The servants in the house would have lived upstairs – there are more rooms up there. The guy who lived in the house, a Mr. Elliott, owned the button factory, at the end of the street, and another factory, on the other side. There's a massive safe, in that building over there." (We're looking out of the same window, at a rectangular brick outbuilding, down below and to the left, with a rusty, corrugated iron roof).

"If you go up to the next floor, there's only a ladder on top, but you can see a view of the whole city. But what they're doing here, in the Quarter, is using it as a 'landbank'. Rob and I are working quite closely, on a number of things. You can see that building there. These buildings are all burnt out at the back. We're in an historic monument. And what are they doing? They *talk* a lot and do nothing."

We're looking at a row of buildings: *Westminster House*, *Variety Works* and *Robinson and McKewan – Manufacturing Jewellers*. "If you went inside there," explains Ken, "it's diabolical: they're not doing anything. All they want to do is let that building fall down. What is it that Joni Mitchell sings? 'Take Paradise – put up a parking lot'. They're all historic buildings, but they're just using them as land banks. When did we clean the building out? Over twenty-five years ago!"

Ken removed the interior architectural features, which were then put into storage, for the landowners, the *King Edward Foundation/Trust*. He's done that on several occasions for them. "That was the most beautiful building, when we cleared it out. They leave it to fall down, and once it's reached that state, they can pull it down. The problem is that unless they allow the developers to make money, they aren't going to develop; they need subsidising." There are a range of different landowners, within the Jewellery Quarter. Behind these three buildings is a gigantic red crane, where new flats and apartments are being constructed. "But the developers won't jump onto these older buildings," adds Ken, "because they ain't gonna make no 'dough'."

He has been working to improve the area for at least six years. "I haven't achieved a great deal. The first Christmas lights that were put up in the Jewellery Quarter, were put up by me – last year. They'd had them before – but it had just died; there *were* no Christmas lights. I got people with a lamppost outside their premises to sponsor it." Ken got halfway down Frederick Street, Vittoria Street and Vyse Street, with the scheme. "You would be surprised, the big companies gave nothing, but the little guys, like *Delaney's* and the Indian guy, in the corner shop went: "Here you are Ken – how much d'you want? I'll sponsor two lampposts."

Meetings of the *Jewellery Quarter Association* are held at the various directors' premises, on a rota basis, when there are particular problems to solve – not to a fixed timetable. "We have an AGM," explains Ken, "but other impromptu ones as well, with various members of Birmingham City Council." As it's a huge area to cover, they each have projects. "You just go for a project that your heart is in. It doesn't matter if you win it – if you succeed – and bring it to fruition. Marie has done *so* much for the Jewellery Quarter. She's got the housing development going forward. A lot of people live here, in the Jewellery Quarter, but what we *cannot* do is squeeze out the jeweller."

How did Ken come to have a 1989 copy of the *Babes in the Wood* programme? (He later gave it to Pat, who'd played Little John in the panto). "I collect paper – documents: from an out-clearance – out of the rubbish bins. I've got five hundred boxes of paperwork!" Ken shows me a Quinton woman's 'life in a tin', (souvenirs, documents etc).

"When the church had been broken into a couple of times, I went down, and we'd got a deal going on with *Bat Alarms* – up the road here. You must understand something. If I decide to do something – you can defeat me – no problem; but I'm coming back again babe!" That's something that he and Pat have in common. Working for the community seems highly commendable. "But it doesn't always *look* like that," comments Ken. "It doesn't make me friends. Rob Turley was on the committee for CCTV Cameras and Security, in the Quarter, in conjunction with the police. He can tell you exactly how the Jewellery Quarter works."

I'm certainly going to ask him, but there's another landmark to visit first. Leaving Ken Schofield's Frederick Street premises, I cross over into Albion Street, one of several places where Pat's cousin, John Bevis once worked as a jeweller. He recalled recently: "Pat used to phone me in the 70s, when I worked by the Albion Fire station, and in Keele Passage, at the side." As a boy, he lived at 4 back of 11 Kenyon Street, attended St Paul's Junior School, and was a member of the church congregation. He recalls visiting 'Dabble', the rag-and-bone man, in Buckingham Street. "It was quite funny, because he used to be on the old 'bomb peck' – the old bombsite, and sell anything and everything – that's how he got his name – 'Dabble'. I went there with my mother, Nellie, and her mother, (my grandmother), Emily." Pat has thirty-year-old receipts from John, for gold jewellery, dating from the time his cousin worked in the Key Hill district.

Leaving Albion Street, I turn right, up Frederick Street, towards the clock, then right again, heading for number 7 Warstone Lane, at the top end, on the right-hand side. Rob Turley is a highly skilled manufacturer and repairer of jewellery. Visitors to the Quarter are able to view him, in the window of his shop, busily employed at his workbench.

You see, this craftsman, skilled and bold
With worldly cares is lumbered.
Yet still the schemes keep rolling in
And so his days are numbered.

Rob entered the trade at sixteen, after leaving school. "Just before my nineteenth birthday, I went self-employed, and I've been working for myself ever since." His first premises were down Hockley Hill. "I was working for a company, earning £11-00 a week. Then from April to Christmas, I was spending that on tools-of-the-trade - just messing around, at home. I left the company on 8 April and moved in here – when I went self-employed." Such is Rob's reputation, he is the craftsman Pat automatically heads for, when he wants to purchase jewellery in the Quarter, or have a repair job done.

Sadly, Rob is rather despairing of the present-day Jewellery Quarter: "The Trade is it's own worst enemy," he explains. "I've tried to tell them, but they won't stick together, they won't promote the industry. Why should I spend any money, or advertise, when it will benefit those who won't do anything? It's their whole attitude. If you turn round to them and say, 'Give us ten thousand quid and I'll give you twenty thousand back next week,' they'll give you a hundred grand; if there's money to be made, they'll part with their money. But if you're asking them to do anything, where's there's no profit, they won't do it."

According to Rob, there are three additional problems: lack of support from the Assay Office, on the one hand, being undercut by cheap imported jewellery on the other, and internal political manoeuvring. In a positive move to try to resolve some of these issues, he recently started a new, independent association, with like-minded people, to identify the particular needs of its smaller craftsmen members, then act upon them. On the other hand, Marie's experience has been that the Assay Office has always supported any projects in the Quarter.

"If the big boys with the money don't get together, and start ploughing in money to the trade, instead of taking it out, there isn't going to *be* a trade," continues Rob. "There'll be a pub called *The Goldsmiths' and Jewellers' Arms*, (which is its correct name - it's just been shortened). There'll be one bullion dealer, a few shops, and a couple of little manufacturers; it will be like the Gun Quarter."

How about the Urban Village idea they were trying to introduce? "Well, the developers are making money. Now it doesn't matter whether you own your own building; within a certain period of time, you're going to pass on, and that building's on the market, so it will become available." He seems to be painting a very gloomy picture. Does he subscribe to the theme of our folk song, *Fool's Gold*, that in ten to twenty years, the jewellery industry will have died in this area?

"Well, you can quote me: 'In five years' time, the trade will be dead; ten years, and it will be the Gun Quarter'." Ken Schofield thought there might be twenty years left in it. "No, it won't last that long," is Rob's reply. "Can you see that Elaine?" (his assistant). "The Trade won't last twenty years, will it?" She replies: "It doesn't *look* as if it's going to."

So it's like a Disappearing World round here? "There always will be people around here, but not as it was," he observes. "The ones that make money in this trade, are in with a pot full of money. They don't know anything about it, and all they do is buy and sell. They might as well be buying loaves of bread or bottles of milk. They're not interested. All they've got is big money – 'I'll buy that.' Everyone around here who's made money, they're not jewellers: they're individuals, who don't know anything about it."

Rob feels that the *British Jewellers' Association* should do more, in terms of investing money to support the smaller craftsmen. However, Geoff Field, Chief Executive of the *BJA*, recognises that the lifeblood of the jewellery industry *is* with smaller craft-based companies, and has recently been negotiating with the *Learning and Skills Council*, a major funding package for the next two years, which will provide free training for small companies.

"One of the interesting things is the Jewellery Quarter School," observes Rob. "If I went for a job down there, I don't have the paper qualifications to do it. You'd get twenty grand a year, teaching: hassle-free. But the majority of students there get their *City and Guilds* and the rest of it. They come out, and they hear there's a job in there, teaching. What they should be doing, is going around to sixty-year-old blokes, and saying: 'We'll pay you three hundred pounds for an afternoon, to come in and teach.' It would be more than their daily takings, so they'd have a strong incentive to do it." Later in the chapter, Professor Cherry, Head of the Jewellery School, provides an alternative perspective.

"I wanted to promote the Quarter on Valentine's Day," Rob continues, "and give away fourteen one-carat diamonds. The trade price could be £800 to two or three grand a stone, if you like. But a couple of grand a stone is going to be a reasonable thing to give away. The retail price would be something like six grand a stone. So you get local radio/TV/newspapers involved, and let them do all the promotion of it – so that's no problem. We just get the stone dealers that are in the Quarter, to donate money – or an association.

"Valentine's Day is coming up, which is a month when it's quiet for the trade anyway (14 February). So every year you give away fourteen, one-carat diamonds. The newspapers would set the competition. I also suggested, as part of the same promotion, that everyone who buys a present for somebody – would be given a camera, and have a prize, for the best pictures taken at the wedding, or on their anniversary. We could give away gold cigarette lighters in the shops. You could have them shaped to resemble a gold bar, if you wanted to. If you couldn't get a gold bar shape, and get the Gold council to promote that, you could produce cheaper plastic novelty lighters." (Shows me a miniature red fire extinguisher, as an example). "You're talking about small amounts of money – maybe twenty grand a year, to promote Valentine's Day, within the Jewellery Quarter. And you're telling me that we couldn't get that back, around here? But they won't do it."

I'd mentioned Rob's St Valentine's Day Scheme to Ken Goodby earlier. He commented: "It's a good idea. I agree with Rob on that: we *do* need publicity. But that's not to do with the little craftsmen, because people coming into the trade are attracted by the publicity and by the shops. OK, the shops, (in some cases), are feeding back jobs to the little craftsmen, but the bulk of stuff that's sold in the trade now, (I haven't got the statistics, but I'm pretty sure), is manufactured abroad."

According to Rob, "When I was in the *Jewellery Quarter Association*, I said: 'Why doesn't the Association write to the stone dealers, inviting them to participate?' Up the road is one of the top 350 companies in the West Midlands, making about £250,000 profit. It's tax deductible, isn't it? All they've got to say is 'We're chucking in £10, 000.' They'd be promoting the Jewellery Quarter."

Perhaps they don't *need* to get involved in projects to promote the Jewellery Quarter image? "They're just greedy," replies Rob. "They'll spend money on themselves, but they won't put any back in. And it's a downward spiral. The Jewellery Trade is a cottage industry, with 'mega' money, but they won't stick together – apart from all the ones with the money. You can't get them to put their hands in their pockets and promote British-made stuff."

> *Look to the future, twenty years on,*
> *When we're all old and off it.*
> *Will it be worth the sacrifice -*
> *Just for the sake of profit?*

We asked Rob's talented, twenty-three-year-old apprentice, Nicol Dwyer, for her views, as a representative of the industry's future. "I've been here about four years, and after two years went to the School of Jewellery," she explains. "I spent a year there, doing an HND in Jewellery and Silversmithing, realised that I'd already learned everything, and that I was wasting money being there. Came back down to Rob's, where I knew that I was going to learn what I need to learn. In reality, if somebody comes in, you might not even have the chance to scribble something – let alone draw it, as we were doing at the school. You haven't got the time. People don't want to pay you to *draw* it; they want to pay you to *make* it."

She speaks highly of Gaynor Andrews, the Head of the HND Department and the ND's. "From what I've seen, she's also very good in a practical sense. She can really produce the jewellery." The fact that Nicol had already gained considerable experience from working with Rob, presented difficulties: "They didn't like it when I said that wasn't the way that it was *supposed* to be done." In any event, the course was unsuitable for her particular needs. College courses aim to cater for a range of students, but there will always be exceptions.

Like Rob, she prefers making more traditional jewellery – "...although there are other 'bits-and-bobs' that I've done for other people. I've always been into art and music – I'm a musician. I went to the *International College of Music*, when I lived abroad. I play jazz guitar. I *am* artistic, but I don't have to *pretend* to be all 'airy-fairy' about it. I like to get on with it."

Nicol was introduced to computer technology, whilst working for a relatively new company – *Sude* (pronounced 'Sueday'), up in Hockley Hill. "They wanted to teach me that, and they wanted me to do certain things. But it wasn't what I wanted to do, because all they were doing was designing for a particular company – boring. You put it on as 2-D, then the computer will pick it up and fill in the rest for you." Rather like the Special Effects for action films, where they can replicate thousands of skeleton warriors, from one sketch? "I think it's pretty much the same as that; you just press a button, and it does it for you."

Like Ken Goodby, and the Reverend Tom Pyke, (whom we meet later), Nicol agrees that specialising and concentrating on more technically intricate jewellery, which the competition can't produce, may be one solution. Did she think that might be where *her* future lies? "Yes – hopefully. The more experience I get. I want to become like Rob. People go to him, because they know he knows what to do. If there are problems that people can't get around, he can, and if he can't do it, it can't be done. Rob hasn't got the qualifications, on paper, but that means nothing to the trade round here."

In Nicol's opinion, graduates from the school have difficulty in producing the turnover that companies require. "When they take the graduates on, that person might be all well and good making the 'one-offs', but that's all they can do. There aren't many young jewellers who can sit down all day, and make loads of different stuff." Professor Norman Cherry will later tell us that, in his informed opinion, this is a mistaken view.

According to Rob and Nicol, few graduates from the school have actually succeeded in business, in the Quarter, although this doesn't tally at all with information supplied by the School. "There are two guys with a place called *Mocame*, on Vyse Street," explains Rob. "They've done the HND like I did. Then they got the money together and started their own shop. They're the only two that I know who seem to have done any good. There's another girl who wanders around; she's doing OK and maybe a couple of other girls, who're maybe doing OK – but other than that… A lot of them are Japanese students, who go back home."

Like other creative occupations, people frequently do it for the love of the job. "After thirty years' experience, you're lucky if you're earning two or three hundred pounds a week. "There's no money in it," explains Rob. "I do it because I want to do it," adds Nicol. "When I'm doing it for other people, I kind of lose the will. I can't be bothered. I like working here with *Rob*. I'm really lucky.

"This is my station (her workbench). I work with Rob and Elaine O'Carroll, but I work by myself at my station, although I'm close enough for Rob to look over me, to see what I'm doing. I think my future's bright – to be honest. A lot of older people around here are saying: 'Trade's bad and trade's that.' But I don't see it in the same way as they do. Maybe it's because they've got years on me, and they can see it? I'm sure, as time goes on, in ten years or so, it will get better. I'm not going to feel bad about it.

"I've got my ideas that I want to do, Rob's got his. Put the two together and God knows what you come up with! I think, to be honest, in a few years, when some of the tat's squeezed out, and the one's who can't make it here have left, and you're left with the ones who can… (To Rob) I'm positive that you'll still be here."

It's been estimated that by 2005, there may be about 5,000 residents living in the Quarter, judging by the new building schemes. "It's good for us to have all those people around here," observes Nicol, "because as well as spending money on their houses, they can come and spend it on jewellery. Now we've got this new jewellery shop here, *Clearwater*." (A new Spar mini-market has also just opened, next door). "So it will bring more people down this end, and they're building more stuff over there. So it can't be bad."

Does she think that the trade can live harmoniously side-by-side with the residents? "I don't think we've got much of a choice, because they're not going anywhere – and neither are we. I've got four years behind me, in a trade that I'm good at. I really do love it – (there's not many people of my age around here that do). A lot of people have found it strange that I'm a woman as well – it's a predominantly male trade, and I'm starting to overtake people and learn more – because of Rob. He and Ken Schofield have got a lot of confidence in me. I like Ken: he's completely 'off the wall'! They really do believe that I'm going to succeed."

Chapter Ten –

AS THE VICAR SAID TO THE BISHOP...

In terms of someone feeling that concerned about their business, I think that there are people who need to know that. People like the Jewellery Quarter Partnership need to know that; the city's Economic Development Department needs to know that. They don't need general statistics. They need real stories, about real people, so that they can actually work at what needs to be done.

The Reverend Tom Pyke

Seeking an alternative viewpoint, to Rob and Nicol's, we turn right out of *Turley's Jewellery Repairs*, heading for the top end of Warstone Lane. Here, we take the first turning on the right, past the clock, to consult Professor Norman Cherry, Head of the Birmingham School of Jewellery, in Vittoria Street.

The professor, who has been Head of School for over eight years, is a Sean Connery 'sound-alike' (and somewhat 'lookalike'!), although unlike his fellow countryman, he doesn't hail from Edinburgh. "I'm actually a Glasgow man, but the accent doesn't sound too much like it. I lived in the southeast of Scotland, for a long time." The information he provides is definitely an 'eye-opener'. By the end of the visit, I'm left with the impression of a dynamic and forward-looking relationship between school and community.

Seated in his office, I ask Norman Cherry whether the majority of graduates from the school become designer/makers, rather than going into apprenticeships? "No, you have to bear in mind that there are something like five hundred students here, at any given time; of which, roughly-speaking, two hundred are full-time students and three hundred are part-time," replies Norman Cherry. "Now, of the two hundred full-time, we're talking about something like six different courses." He describes these in ascending order:

"There's a full-time National Diploma, which is very much craft-based, and those tend to be the people who will go and work at the bench. There is a Higher National Diploma, in Silversmithing and Jewellery. In the past few years, since it's been directed by Gaynor Andrews, the HND has become increasingly industry-focused, and is working very closely with companies, in terms of Live Projects; the introduction of CAD and CAD/CAM, (that's Computer-aided Design and Computer-aided Manufacture). We're doing that in conjunction with one of the major software companies – *DelCam*. Their stuff is rapidly becoming the industry standard."

For designers and designer/makers, of the future, there is a three-year degree course, (Bachelor of Arts), designed to develop and educate. "Although some of these people are working in industry, at the bench, mainly they are designers – the creative talents, which will move our industry forward," explains Norman. "The jewellery industry encompasses everything, from mass manufacture, through to small batch production, to 'one-offs'. That particular course is able to cater for that broad church."

There are three HND courses: Silversmithing and Jewellery, Gemmology and also Horology, (that is, watches and clocks); the latter two are the only courses of their kind in the entire world! For developing creative thought to a higher level, there's a Masters Course - *MA Jewellery, Silversmithing and Related Products*. "Those last three words are very important," observes Norman. "It means that people are operating in areas that include Accessories, Interior Lighting, aspects of fashion, and aspects of small-scale industrial design. So there's actually a wide range of activities taking place here.

"We don't have a House Style: you would never be able to recognise a Birmingham graduate, by the style in which they work, because everybody is encouraged to develop their own particular creativity, which I think is very important."

At the time of writing, the School has seven or eight Ph.D. candidates, the first of whom has recently qualified; others work in conjunction with the *Jewellery Industry Innovation Centre* – just across the street. The *Centre* includes three major activities: Research and Development, Technology Transfer, and Consultancy. "We have people who are looking at the application of lasers to colouring and patterning of metals," Norman explains. "Some Ph.D. students are looking at historical and critical aspects of jewellery. One candidate is exploring the relationship of the mathematics of 3-dimensional form, to the actual complex structures that are being manufactured: it's a *very* interesting one; it's taking very profound mathematical theory into the range of practice – which is very important."

The *Jewellery Industry Innovation Centre*, a particularly important part of the School, is supported mainly by European funding, and has been operational for almost seven years. "It has put *so* much into the West Midland Jewellery Industry, in that time," Norman explains. "I can assure you that the industry would be a pale shadow of its former self, if it weren't for the contribution that the centre has made. In simple terms, we have pumped about eight million pounds-worth of expertise into the local jewellery industry, in that period: an incredible amount of money. Nobody has actually had to pay for the expertise and advice they've been given."

The current project is *New Product Development*, whereby Innovation Centre staff go out and work with West Midlands companies, particularly in the

Jewellery Quarter - either as technologists or designers. European funding covers all of the West Midlands area.

According to Norman: "Companies tell us what they think the problem is, and the *Innovation Centre* staff will then advise accordingly." Two Industry Liaison Officers, (one of whom actually works out of the *British Jewellers' Association*), work closely with the companies, which range from self-employed, to three hundred employees; that covers every jewellery company in the West Midlands. Many companies have already benefitted from this scheme.

The School has also assisted graduates to work, within the industry, through a Business Incubation programme. The professor explains: "It's in a 'fallow' year at the moment. In fact, the presentation I'm doing this afternoon, is about the next stage of this incubation development. The programme operated for about seven years, and offered one year's support to graduates. It was open, not only to Jewellery and Silversmithing graduates, but also to those from other creative industry areas. It gave graduates a year's support, inasmuch as they had free workspace, business training, mentoring, and the opportunity to show at two major trade shows, in the UK.

"So that gave a lot of people a wonderful kickstart, in setting up their business. Now somewhere around 120 people benefitted from that scheme, while it was operating, and of those, about 90% have stayed in the Quarter. Most of them have set up businesses. That's the *whole* point, it's about establishing viable, design-led businesses."

The writer referred to previous information that only a handful of successful young business people are making headway in the jewellery business, within the Quarter itself. Also, to reports that most of them have been obliged to go outside the area to achieve success. "Well, some of them are not so young now," comments the professor, "but at the last count, there were just under a hundred micro-businesses within the Quarter, and about 90% of those came through the Incubation Scheme. There are others elsewhere in the West Midlands, but most of them settled within the Quarter."

So, in fact, these are very encouraging figures? "Incredibly – because that's the future of the industry. It's *not* in supplying nine-carat mass production jewellery, at the lowest unit cost; that's the work that's going out to the Far East."

Norman sees the jewellery industry as a microcosm of British industry, where we were all encouraged to buy British, because it was cheap – even if it fell apart in six months! "It's taken until fairly recently for British industry to understand that what was really important was about *value* added and *perceived* value added. The jewellery industry is coming up slowly on the rails, to understand that that's the message, as well. It's no accident, that in the last twenty years, the growth industry in British jewellery has been in the designers, designer/makers, and the design-led companies. It's not the guys who are supplying catalogue shops, and struggling, and having to outsource to China and Thailand, and so on.

"The *key* is about value added: producing products that are interesting and have their own quality of uniqueness. I don't think it's even necessarily about intricacy. During my last visit to India, in January 2003, I saw some very intricate, high quality jewellery. So India is not just about producing 'El Cheapo' – it's also capable of producing quite high quality. We have an immense store of designer talent and designers who understand how to marry aesthetics with technology: what you need is innovative technology *and* innovative design. Designers are essential to the whole process; design is absolutely intrinsic to the whole manufacturing process, and companies that are successful are those which understand that; whether they're in Britain, Germany or America, or for that matter, in China or India.

"We are a very prominent part, both visually and practically, of the Jewellery Quarter. This is a landmark building, for a start, which, ten years ago, kickstarted Regeneration within the Quarter," explains Professor Cherry. "We have very good relationships with a big chunk of the local industry – perhaps not *all* of them – but most of the major players. A number of the courses within the School do Live Projects (in effect, consultancy work), with these companies. Often, the products designed do actually go into production. Some of the HND students' designs caused quite a stir, on the stand of a major manufacturer, at last year's *Spring Fair*, at the NEC in Birmingham.

"The Jewellery Industry Innovation Centre is the main conduit for relationships with industry, but then equally, our part-time classes are available, to members of the trade and they do *send* a lot of people. There are, roughly speaking, three hundred part-time students, made up mainly from people in the trade, who come in to do technical classes; for example, for the *Gemmological Association Diploma*, for *City and Guilds* certificates and so forth."

About half of those part-time students are from the Quarter itself. There are also people travelling a hundred miles, for one day each week, just to come to one of these classes. "Furthermore, there are a series of short courses, entitled *Easter School* and the *Summer School*, because the school is open all year round – apart from Christmas Day, Boxing Day and New Year's Day. We run a whole raft of very concentrated classes, over the Easter period, and for the first four or five weeks of the Summer Break – (so-called!). Those attract people, not just from all over the UK, but from elsewhere. The staff that we employ, to teach those classes, are all internationally recognised specialists; we import staff from Germany, Italy, the States and elsewhere, to teach these."

Professor Cherry dispels another myth, by confirming that skilled craftsmen from the Quarter teach at the School, adding: "All our part-time courses are taught by people from the trade." How about reconciling creative design with the high turnover rates required by industry? Rather than producing an exquisite ring, being able to fashion twenty, within a short space of time?

"There's no problem with that at all, although it's a cultural thing. When an employer comes to see the work of a student, at the end of a year, and he or she sees a lot of very creative, visually-exciting work, the potential employer's job is not to say: 'Oh – far too outré – I couldn't make use of that!' But he *should* be saying, 'My God – how creative! How can I use this creativity, within my particular area of work?' "

The School receives regular feedback, from potential employers. Norman comments: "It's the student's job to say: 'I have to demonstrate how creative I am, in order to get a job, and make my contribution.' Now, students from the Far East understand that, and Eastern employers understand far better what they need and what they can make use of."

Thus it seems that for industry to flourish, it's not simply skilled craftsman who are needed, but those who are 'ahead of the game' – in creative terms: producing new designs and keeping up with the latest trends. Indeed, actually creating the trends. "It goes back to what I said at the beginning," explains Norman Cherry. "It's about 'value-added' and marrying innovation design with innovative technology."

Does he think the future of the Jewellery Quarter is a bright one? "I think it *can* be, but that depends how creatively minded people want to be. The answer, as I say, is not about trying continually to produce work, at lowest unit cost. It's about producing work that is different - which people want to buy, and pay good money for. And there is undoubtedly a market there. In terms of national and international trends, there is less interest in the more traditional patterns, and *more* interest in contemporarily influenced design. Manufacturers need to be awake to these international trends. You cannot continue making what you made yesterday, last week, last year, twenty years ago, and still continue to think that you're making what people want – because they *don't* want it any more." There are a number of shops around the Quarter, selling contemporary jewellery.

Would Norman describe the worries expressed by the majority of our hosts, about the future of Jewellery Quarter industry, as largely unfounded? "Oh no – they're not unfounded. I think the worries have to be there. I mean, I have grave concerns. But it's about the way that people *tackle* the problem, and it's about being *proactive* before the event, not *reactive* after it. If you're reactive to events, then you're lost. If you're proactive - if you actually *create* a situation for yourself, then you will be successful."

Does he have a long-term solution for keeping the Jewellery Quarter alive? He suggests that one means of producing value added products might be to:

"… work with people like us. You use design; you use innovative technology; but you use them *together*. What we *plan* to do, is to set up a *Centre for Design Excellence*. That will give us the opportunity to bring the *Innovation Centre* the *Business Incubation Scheme* and one or two other activities, all together on the one site. But we would plan for it to be adjacent to the School: that would give us an opportunity – again - to work even more closely with the local industry, and really *develop* the Jewellery Quarter as a place which is recognised for high quality jewellery design production. But work which is of today, not work which is rooted in a century ago.

"Our current plan is that, by next year, we'll have a new region-wide scheme up-and-running. I'm leading a consortium of six universities. We will provide, in *various* centres, throughout the region, *including* the Jewellery Quarter, a new Incubation Programme, which will run for three years, on a kind of tapering subsidy basis. Beneficiaries get 100%subsidy as before, for the first year, 50% for the second year, and 25% in the third year. My belief is, by doing that, they'll be in a position where, if they want to, they can start employing people, maybe even *before* the third year period. You've got the opportunity there, or the conditions, for a really exciting design-led business development."

The provision of graduate living accommodation for a limited period of time might provide some incentive to remain with the Quarter. Norman comments: "I *understand* that there are *plans* for some live-work space, but nothing specific as yet. It's difficult, because it's becoming more expensive to live here, and unless you've got very heavy subsidy, I don't know that you can make live-work terribly cheap in the Quarter, for people. I would *like* it to be cheap; it's important that people can live and work here, but there are clearly cost restrictions.

"A significant percentage of graduates from the School move out of the area. "You've got a school here, which is international: 15 – 16% of my students are non-UK: they're coming here, literally, from all over the world. Of the remainder, 50% don't come from this part of the country anyway. They're coming to us from as far north as the Orkneys, as far south as the tip of Cornwall – or the Channel Islands, for that matter. A helluva lot of British jewellery graduates are working in countries like Italy and Germany. An increasing number are going further afield: to the States, to the East. Obviously most of the Eastern students tend to go home, because they're on a government bursary, and they're expected to return, to benefit their country."

Are there, nevertheless, sufficient numbers of jewellery school graduates starting businesses in the Quarter, to maintain future trade? "Already we've got over 90 micro-businesses, most of whom have come through the school." So provided they continue to prosper, there's every reason to hope that they'll keep the trade alive within the Quarter? "That's the whole idea," concludes Norman. "That's what we want to see happen."

Heading swiftly along Vittoria Street, then on, to Regent Place, I pass a street that conjures up private family 'ghosts'. My deceased father, Harry Wareing's ancestor, Bernard Wareing, ran his own business in the Quarter, for fifty years, from 1877 to c1927, *Bernard Wareing Ltd.* was located at 70 – 76 Northwood Street, on the right-hand side, just past the Caroline Street junction.

If you've got your back to Caroline Street – and you're looking down the hill, which it's built on, towards town, across the church, there is a tunnel, from the church, to the buildings on the left, (there was a domestic situation, relating to the church, on the other side of the road). We used to collect scrap from all round there – and from the right hand side as well. The buildings housed either priests, or church personnel of some kind.

St Paul's was erected, partly funded by a gift of £1,000 from the Colmores, and three acres of land, which the family donated, for the church and cemetery, consecrated in 1779. This new place of worship, conveniently located at the centre of the grid, in the area designated St Paul's Square, inevitably increased property values considerably. The church and Square, remain an integral part of the Jewellery Quarter community to the present day, and a well-known landmark.

We're here at the kind invitation of The Reverend Tom Pyke, whose reputation already precedes him, via Ken Schofield: "Tom will be one of the bishops of Birmingham – eventually. He's probably in his 40s. Great guy. He has a beer, a fag - you know what I mean? He's one of *those* guys. But unless something is done in the Jewellery Quarter…"

Tom observes: "There is a temptation to see residential development, in the Jewellery Quarter, as making worse the situation for manufacturing jewellers, and also the retailing jewellery shops; but that is to look at things completely on their head. In fact, the situation is that the decline of the jewellery industry is a matter of world economics - we're suddenly part of a much bigger market than we have ever *known*; even at the time of the British Empire, the Jewellery Quarter didn't know that sort of market. Suddenly, we're competing against local markets in the Pacific Rim, whose daily rates are probably what people would be paid by the *hour* here. It becomes very difficult, certainly to do the *mass* production, which was how the Quarter made its name: it was a place where mass production, in nine-carat gold particularly, was taking place.

"So all of that has filtered off to the Pacific Rim – and to India. Craftspeople in those countries are doing wonderful jobs, producing fantastic jewellery. The challenge to the Jewellery Quarter, it to find a new *sort* of market; producing goods that other countries have not got the facilities or the technology to make.

"It always strikes me that the jewellers have amazing *elbows*. It seems a funny observation, but to be able to sit at a jeweller's bench, and to be able therefore to have that sort of precision of control, with what you're doing. It's a tremendous thing. The jeweller's bench has been the same since medieval times – and before. It's like that because they've just tuned it and tuned it, until they can get that sort of precision.

"Here in the Quarter, we've got the leading School of Jewellery in Europe," (as we've just discovered). "They're doing things within an Innovations Department: loads of designing and computer prototyping, where they can have a 3-D image on a screen, which they can then produce as a wax moquette, within twenty minutes. Now that's an extraordinary development."

Like his three or four predecessors, Tom is both vicar and Industrial Chaplain. "There isn't just *that* distinction; I find that I'm working with three groups of people. One group is the workaday parish: the jewellers, financial advisors, small architects, surveyors and people like that. They're here from nine to five each day, and probably at the end of the day, they go back to the suburbs. They may well be involved in church parishes at the weekend, in Solihull – and that type of area. For them we have a service once a week, on a Wednesday – that draws them in. That's rather interesting, because you begin to draw on the experience that people have, from all over Birmingham. It's not just a local thing any longer – it's fascinating. At the Christmas Lunchtime Carol Service we half fill the church – which is about 350 people. At five minutes to one, there's nobody there, and you think: 'We've done it this time – we've not advertised enough!' Then suddenly – whoosh! They all come in, and at about five past one, they're all standing there – ready to sing!"

The second group of people is the residential section. "They are *legally* the parish – because if you live within a Parish boundary, you are truly parishioners. Whereas our congregation tends not to be – they tend to be coming from elsewhere. In four years, we've suddenly gone, from being a typically depopulated city centre parish, to actually being the largest truly city centre residential population in Birmingham. When I came, in 1999, there were in the region of 350 residents only, in the Quarter. Now it's in the region, we think, of about 1500, and I think it's going to be 5,000 before you can blink, really! So it's a big number of people.

"It's only really beginning to be a community *now*, as our Community Web has got going, (which is a sort of super Residents' Association), working right across all of the apartment blocks. It's run very efficiently, as a Public Limited Company. I'm a Director of it. We're actually committed to ensuring that the jewellery crafts *stay* in the Quarter."

Marie points out that *The Jewellery Quarter Association* shares that same objective.

"It's one of those things which gives the place its value," continues Tom. "To have a rather large area, simply called the Jewellery Quarter – and no one can remember why – completely destroys the reason why many of the people have moved into it; which is actually because they *like* being side-by-side with these things.

"One of the things that I had never experienced before I came here, is the way in which a business community can compete with each other, yet cooperate with each other, at the same time. Typically, what happens is that people will compete for a big order. Then when they've got the order, they find they can't actually fulfil it. So they then employ the people they've actually been competing with, to help them fulfil it. That's a very typical Jewellery Quarter way of doing it. And I'm sure that in the past, there were runners going to and fro' with bits of work, all the time."

Sadly, the church has suffered two recent burglaries; Ken Schofield describes it as 'desecration'. "My experience, over the last few months," explains Tom, "after I'd recovered from the shock of our burglary, was that I was able to say: 'Actually, we were very lucky.' The attitude of the jewellers was that this is *their* church and it had been spoilt, which shows how fondly the church is held, in their estimation. Ken was brilliant – really, really helpful. Yes, we were broken into before. The police were able to catch the person involved." An alarm system has now been installed.

Tom is even more concerned about attacks on people, during early evenings, or weekends. "We have shocking robberies in the Jewellery Quarter. We've had somebody doused with petrol, and someone standing behind them with a cigarette lighter, threatening them and telling them to open the safe. So there are some nasty incidents.

"I think it's greed. When it *does* happen, it's a lot more threatening than you would get in a normal residential area – where you get burglars going into houses. These are actual robberies, rather than burglaries. That's one of the key things. What I'm saying about the industrial or residential deserts, is that crime thrives on a situation where people aren't around. The very best protection for businesses is actually to have a residential community around here. It goes the other way as well. Absolutely the best protection for residential communities is not door phones, or big gates on car parks – that just creates fear. I think it's having a working community around, and people who are vigilant."

He has been reading *The Hockley Flyer* for four years. "I've only just realised that the key bits are actually the adverts! There's very little editorial, but if you read the adverts, it's *fascinating* what other people are doing." (He describes a particular innovation).

The third congregational group sounds even more interesting: a youth group who grew up together. "They tend to be people who were born and/or lived in the Jewellery Quarter. Or, in one case, they came to a 'make-do and mend' group, which was run at the church, during the war years. Then in the 1950s, when the parish was depopulated, and a lot of the poorer housing was removed, these people were moved out to other areas, such as Perry Barr, Great Barr and the Ladywood end of Edgbaston, but kept coming back to the Quarter. Families who want a family funeral often ring me, and I'm thinking: 'Well, why are you ringing me from there?' And that's why.

"The congregation is quite unusual for a city centre church, because they have a *real*, strong interest in what's happening in the Quarter, and really feel that it's important; getting the mixture right is a real matter of concern and prayer for them." Most of this group are now sixty-plus. *"Very* often," observes Tom, "there's a wedge driven between a church congregation and the community that actually just happens to be in. You see this all the time: there's nothing that connects them. Here, there is a *lot* that connects them.

"I'm trying to get the church to actually reflect the age profile of the Quarter, as it *now* is. So we're gradually encouraging younger people to come and use the church, as well. We're providing church services that are different – using video and recorded music – and things like that." Ken Schofield recently described how innovative some of these services have been!

Tom's duties as Chaplain are "… all about relationships: meeting somebody once, then again and again, and gradually getting them into a sense of being comfortable with you." How would he tackle the hypothetical case of a jeweller with financial problems, who can see his whole life's work disappearing before him – having devoted everything to it?

"There's a real role for saying to somebody: 'I want to hear what you've got to say, because, actually, I want to go and talk to somebody else, about what you've got to say.' I mean, one of the things that typically happens here in the Jewellery Quarter, is that people talk to each other, but they don't *listen*." Sometimes he'll act as intermediary:

" Often what happens is that I go to a person's workshop, where he tells me that someone has done (or said) something dreadful, and that he's feeling really sore about it. And you say, 'Really? That's not the person I recognise.' So immediately, I go to the other person's workshop and say: 'What did you say last Tuesday? And why is that particular person so angry about it?' And then come back."

Marie said that there's always been a conflict between the smaller jewellery craftsman and the City Council, who feel that that they should be paying higher rent. "I think there is a prior position – even before that – which is that there are a lot of private landlords who are sitting with locks on the doors of their premises, because they're just waiting for a better offer. You see great big padlocks on so many *beautiful* buildings that could easily be used for workshop space, and always were, in previous times. But somebody is just waiting for a better offer – that is certainly a force that is fuelled by the atmosphere of redevelopment in the Quarter. Although, having said that, it's also restrained by the very good Development Plan that we now have. So we're not going to get residential development in the industrial heartland."

The concerns we've discussed are reflected in the general mood of the area - when Tom visits craftsman, in his capacity as Chaplain. "I think there is a spirit of not *desperate* depression, but a long-lasting depression, which *is* there. It's a sort of feeling, that the trade is slipping away." Rather like a disappearing world? "Yes it is. I think there are key things that can actually keep that at bay.

"For example, the whole business of good education, within the Quarter, and actually training jewellers who are of a fantastic standard – who are good at design; the jewellery trade has been slow in taking on board the changes in design - not just of innovative techniques, but also design as well. I think this is actually true across the world. Retail jewellery that one sees imported from Taiwan and all the rest of it, has a similar old-fashionedness about it. Every jewellery shop on every High Street is the same. I suppose I speak as a man. But you look at an engagement ring – basically, they're all the same; there isn't any innovation and design.

"We have had, for a long time, the leading school of jewellery in Europe, here in the Quarter, teaching people the principles of good design; teaching them to use innovative techniques, and the basic craft, to a very high standard. And we're producing graduates, year after year, who are *stunning* jewellers. What we really want to be doing is to make sure that they find a home in the Jewellery Quarter. I don't know what that will take. It probably needs money to be provided - for free workshop accommodation.

"That's really important. If we can say: 'Well, here are a hundred workshop units, which are produced year after year for graduates, so that they're not going off, but have a home, here in the Quarter.' " In Tom's opinion, the community has a responsibility to provide the opportunity for graduates to actually practice what they have been taught. "I don't think we're talking about the apprenticeship schemes, in this context. It's a case of giving people their head and saying, 'You have a dream – follow it. Whatever it takes, in terms of resources, if you can visualise what you want to make, we will find some way of providing support for you.' "

Tom also identifies the communal way in which work is done, in the Quarter, as a key factor: (the way in which people compete for an order and then actually 'farm out' the work to their competitors). "It's crucial that we keep the critical mass of jewellers. Because there comes a point at which, when we start losing polishers, setters, and so on, the rest of the community can't operate either. Then we start farming stuff much further afield than we need to; whereas in the past, it could all been done here in Birmingham."

The St Paul's District recently won the *Silver Gilt Standard Award* for *Britain in Bloom*, plus an additional award - *The Royal Worcester Spode Trophy* for outstanding excellence or merit - all the more remarkable, because it was their first year of entry.

> *So if you'd like a present for*
> *Your wife or son, or daughter,*
> *Preserve our Heritage - it's yours and mine*
> *Come down the Jewellery Quarter*

Following my conversation with The Reverend Pyke, the co-writer heads down the hill, to investigate a commemorative plaque on the outside wall of a famous Ludgate Hill pub:

Roger Fewtrell (initials RAF aka 'Bomber'), and one of the well-known Jewellery Quarter kids, Chris Millard, turned the former factory premises on Ludgate Hill into 'The Last Drop' pub, near the last public hanging in Birmingham of a warehouse guy, who'd been found guilty of murder. It's fifty yards from St Paul's Church.

Chris Millard's family jewellery business, *L.Woolley*, originally in Warstone Lane, involved three generations: "My grandfather, my father, myself and my brother. I was never qualified, but I could *do* it – it's something you learn. I started with my dad, when I first left school - working in his polishing shop. At that time, everyone was paid 'piecework'. The first thing I was given was 22-carat wedding rings, which get very hot when you polish them. The only thing I was allowed to do was to polish the insides.

"So after a week of this, and ten plasters, one on each finger, (blisters and everything else), I went to get my wages. My dad said, 'Here you are,' and he gave me a fiver. I said: 'What the hell's that?' He said: 'Well, I bring you to work in the morning, I buy you a sandwich, I buy you your lunch, and I take you home at night, so that's what you get!' " Despite Chris's attempts to resolve the situation, his father was adamant: "You only get a decent wage when you're qualified. You're just an apprentice at the moment." "I said, 'Well, you know what you can do with the job, don't you? You can stick it where the sun don't shine!' And I walked out."

Chris eventually returned to the business, after trying other occupations. "I came back, (although I never really wanted to be in it), because my brother, Mickey, had worked for my dad since he left school. He's four years older than me. I got a phone call from my dad saying: 'You can either come here and work, and have half the business, or you can do what you want to do, and your brother gets the lot.' Well, brothers being brothers, we always hated each other, as kids.

"The family business grew, so we moved out of Warstone Lane, and opened a factory in 1980, in Ludgate Hill. It was *Rose's* old shoe warehouses. We put a huge vault in. If you go down into the cellars now, the vault's still in there. There are no safes in there, but there's a big safe door, like a vault door in a bank. As you open that – you walk in, and there's a gate, like a prison gate, to an old cell." That was their stronghold. The name 'Ratners' is inscribed above the gate – (the people who made the safe - nothing to do with the jewellers).

The factory was on four different levels: "There was the basement, where the vault was, where we used to do the posting," explains Chris. "Then there was the ground floor, which was the Casting and Stamping Department. The first floor was where they used to do all the setting, soldering and polishing. The top floor was for offices."

Around 1986/87, he converted this same building into *The Last Drop*, with 'Bomber' – (Roger Fewtrell), as his licensee. "Bomber's a bit older than me. Him and Eddie used to have a club called *Rebecca's*, which was a tremendous place to go. On Saturday mornings, Bomber and I would meet Pat for breakfast, at a place called *Denny's*, in New Street, just up from the Gym - he was a Superstar then."

According to Chris, "Public hangings used to be held at the end of Ludgate Hill and Lionel Street, where Snow Hill Station is now. The criminal was brought down from the church, down Ludgate Hill, then across the road, to be hung. So we were using a little bit of journalistic license. The name of the pub was a 'play-on-words': the last drop of booze, and the last drop of your head! When we opened, we had a big mural on the wall, which was a picture of this last public hanging. All of the faces of the people watching were caricatures of the directors of *Ansells*, the brewery. The MD of *Ansells*, at the time, was being hung!"

Paddy White explains: "When Chrissie left *The Last Drop* it was closed for a while, then the brewery refurbished and re-opened it as *Lloyds On the Square*. That didn't do very well, so after it had been closed, for at least a year, we bought the lease from the brewery, Carlsberg/Tetley, who had become the head leaseholders."

Prior to interviewing the vicar, I stopped for a drink, (non-alcoholic, of course!), at *The Rope Walk* pub-restaurant, adjacent to St Paul's. The manager explained that the premises were on the site of a former rope works; rope from the factory was actually used for the Ludgate Hill hangings. "I can imagine," comments Chris. "The building on the corner, down from the church, the buckle-makers, which is now the *Bucklemaker* restaurant, used to be the nunnery for the church. When we first moved down to Ludgate Hill, that same building was derelict - burnt-out. No one would touch such a weird old place, because so many people had died in it!

"I was twenty when I came into the trade and I got out in 1995." His brother, Mickey, still runs a jewellery factory, under their former family business name of *L. Woolley*, in Warstone Lane, (where he previously had a business called *Mylords*). *The Gold Factory*, in Branston Street, is another of his businesses. Both brothers became interested in car racing. Chris subsequently became twice winner of the Porsche Support Race for the *Birmingham Super Prix* - in 1989 and 1990, the latter being the final car race to be run on the streets of Birmingham.

Paddy White and George Cullen continued to work in the Quarter, until tragedy struck. "George was killed in a car crash, around 1983," Paddy recalls. "I hadn't seen him for many years, but strangely enough, a week before he died, I met him in the Jewellery Quarter – in the *Quarter Club*. This was a long time after the *Rendezvous*. Things had become very disjointed: I'd gone my way, he went his. The *Quarter Club,* just around the corner from the *Rendezvous* site, later became *Branston's Club* - which my nephew owned, and Jill helped run – much later on." The drink with George, resulted in one of those: 'I'll look you up, and I'll give you a ring,' type of situations.

Like Pat, Paddy was a keen sportsman, for many years. The following weekend, he returned from a National League water polo match in the Cardiff, to discover that George had been in a serious car crash. He went down to what was then the General Hospital in town, where George was in Intensive Care: "He died the following day - it was terrible. With the whole friendship thing 'the proof of the pudding' is that forty years on, Pat and I are still friends – without being in each other's pockets - *true* friends."

Paddy and his youngest son, Patrick, also had offices in the Quarter. "We ran the *Actress and Bishop,* for approximately ten years and only recently relinquished it," he explains. "At one stage, I hadn't had any contact with Pat for years, but was driving up the hill with Patrick, towards the office. Subconsciously, I saw someone walk across; I didn't give it a second's thought at the time – drove in. Got into the office. As soon as they told me that he had been in looking for me, I realised – it was Pat who'd walked across in front of me!"

Paddy's wife, Jill, recalls: "I was in the *Actress and Bishop*. BRMB Radio DJ, Bobby Hunt was there – a really good guy. We used to chat to him. He came over the one night and said: 'Are you Beecham's?' I said: 'Hang on!' He said: 'Are you known as "Jill the Pill"?' I said: 'Yes, but not for the reason you're thinking!' He said: 'I do *know* the reason.' One of his uncles was friendly with Pat Roach, and he must have been talking to them. I said: 'I can't believe you!' I called Paddy over – and he was in fits of laughter. I laughed when Pat called me that in the café, the other day." It's a nickname Pat first gave her, when she began working for him, all those years ago, at the *Rendezvous*. The *Actress and Bishop* became *Bonedangles* for a while, but has reverted once more to The *Actress and Bishop*, under Colin Woodley, former landlord of the highly successful music venue, *The Railway*, in Curzon Street.

In July 2003, Pat and I had a meeting about this book, at *Angels Restaurant*, Warstone Lane, close to where his young life first began. Pat had also arranged to meet Ronnie Callow there, later, prior to being collected by his chauffeur, and driven back to London, to continue the final month's filming of the fourth series of *Auf Wiedersehen Pet*. It was one of those occasions when Fate lends a hand. Pat had mentioned, on several occasions, that he would like to include Paddy and Jill in our new book. Then suddenly - right on cue - they both walked in for a coffee; simply because Jill had decided to visit the Quarter, to have her watch repaired!

These two chapters have been somewhat complicated to write, because there are so many variables and different viewpoints involved, and a cross-section of at least eight contributors to include. To put so many viewpoints together, in a condensed version, has been quite a daunting task!

We conclude our chapter with a visit to the BJA, (The British Jewellers' Association), at their headquarters in Vyse Street. Pat and myself were present, in company with the Chief Executive of the BJA, Geoff Field, Krys Zalewska, CEO of the British Jewellery and Giftware Federation and members of the local police force, who were launching a crime prevention initiative.

1987 marked the centenary of the Association, which was originally founded as *The Birmingham Jewellers' and Silversmiths' Association*, by a group of businessmen. They were concerned about 'the prevalence of crime and insolvencies, the lack of training and the poor state of business'- (to quote from the BJA's official history, compiled by Shelley N. Nott FGA).

Pat was a special guest of the Association. We began the proceedings by taking group photographs of those present. Our host, Geoff Field, the Chief Executive, kindly took Pat and I on a guided tour, of what is a *most* impressive building. Looking out of the window of the upper room where we were assembled, Geoff observed: "This graveyard is built on the site of an old sandstone quarry, so the land drops away very sharply, about fifty yards from here. What they did was tunnel backwards *underneath* this part of the cemetery, to put catacombs in, because the cemeteries in Birmingham were under so much pressure. They literally didn't have enough land to bury all the people. So there are coffins *stacked*, all underneath this land – in the catacombs."

These date back to Dickensian times – or thereabouts. "You can still walk around the entrance," continued Geoff, "although they're all sealed up now, but there's quite an elaborate brick and concrete structure: go and have a look later. There was a chapel, which became unsafe and was demolished, where they would carry out the funeral services, and then lower the coffin underground."

Geoff showed us some of the silverware, on display in the BJGF cabinets, specially made, and presented on a variety of occasions. "Every so often The British Jewellery and Giftware Federation, which is our parent body, commission a piece of silver; usually from someone in the Quarter, as part of our Silver Collection. We have several exhibits made by *Deakin & Francis* and, *A. Edward Jones*, for example." Krys Zalewska, subsequently sent us a copy of the BJA History Book. We saw a range of items that afternoon, including:

A silver mace, with ebony shaft, made by *C.J. Vander* of London, presented in 1965.

A three-handled silver Loving Cup, commissioned to commemorate the marriage of His Royal Highness the Prince of Wales, to Lady Diana Spencer, on 29 July 1981, in St Paul's Cathedral, made by *Wakely and Wheeler*, in 1981; a silver condiment set, inkstand and silver gilt chalice, manufactured by P. Nicholas, in commemoration of the Millennium of Saint Dunstan. Also, a pair of silver candlesticks, presented in 1976, made by *Maida Brothers*, London. A silver Loving Cup, made by *A. Edward Jones Ltd*, a famous Jewellery Quarter firm, purchased in 1962. Quite a few of the items on display have been made by London manufacturers, which is only to be expected as the BJA represents both London and Birmingham members.

There is a pair of candlesticks, made by Matthew Boulton, Birmingham 1798, presented to the BJA, by Mr. H.G. Tandy, in 1935. A silver compact, with the BJA coat-of-arms was particularly interesting, and a silver trophy to commemorate the Golden Jubilee of the Birmingham Jewellers' and Silversmiths' Association, made by *Deakin and Francis*, Birmingham 1937. This was commissioned before the BJA changed its title to 'British', in August 1946. Also of note, is an exquisite cigar casket with escolian handles, made in 1956, by *Deakin and Francis*. Decorated with the BJA coat-of-arms, it was designed by J.M. Ricci and presented by Birmingham City Council.

As the other guests departed, Geoff escorted Pat and myself into the Federation Boardroom, which seats about fourteen people. "We hold all of our meetings here, but we also let it for private functions, etc. This is very unusual – a clock that we commissioned for the Millennium, designed by a guy called Robin Kyte, a lecturer in Jewellery at the *Sir John Cass School of Art*, in East London." It looked like a cross between a globe and a ship's sextant, or compass - highly unusual, and of very imaginative design.

Although Geoff has only been Chief Executive for a couple of years, he has already discovered that the place has a lot of history. Pat asked about the Association's responsibilities. "We have six hundred members - jewellery manufacturers, wholesalers and suppliers, diamond dealers, bullion suppliers – that sort of thing. So we represent the people who supply the High Street jewellers' shops," explained Geoff. "Some are manufacturers, quite a few of them are now importers – sadly – but that's the 'name of the game'. We have about 120 members in the Jewellery Quarter, so 20% of our members are here. As we started as the *Birmingham Jewellers and Silversmiths' Association*, this is where we've always been, if you like. But actually, we've got more members in London, including Hatton Garden, than we've got in Birmingham. As London's such a big city, I suppose that's to be expected.

"We're the national association; I spend quite a bit of time down there." Pat observed: "I can see now that it justifies what you've got here." "We've even got nine or ten companies up in Orkney: a very thriving little jewellery industry," Geoff continued. "There *was* a London group, but eventually they merged. It's always been the *Birmingham Jewellers and Silversmiths' Association* – then it became the *British Joint Association*. But it's always been the BJA."

With regard to developers having a more dramatic impact on Hatton Garden, than on the Birmingham Jewellery Quarter, Geoff observes: "It's natural pressure, isn't it? Hatton Garden is between Clerkenwell, the City and Holborn, in a very fanciable area. When buildings become available, they attract developers, because people will pay a lot of money."

A further exhibit, labelled *Timepiece for the Millennium*, is the latest addition to the unrivalled BJGF collection of silverware, built up since 1954. Geoff recounted the story of a young man who, in the sixties, was sent up to the Jewellery Quarter, to choose a watch for his 21st birthday. "Even then he had to get a *permit* from somebody in the trade, to allow him, as a member of the public, to come and buy from someone in the Quarter."

Geoff directed our attention to an oval-shaped silver tray, on the boardroom table, reading the biblical inscription engraved on it: " 'Woe onto them that are wise in their own eyes.' That's from Isaiah Chapter 5, verse 21." In other words – don't be conceited!

We examined entries in the Visitors Book, which Krys found among other artifacts, and has now put on display. There's an entry for 6 May 1948, when Queen Elizabeth the Queen Mother and her husband, George VI had visited the BJA. This ties in nicely with our Coronation Street Party photo of Anderton Street, for these same monarchs, taken the week before Pat's birth.

Gazing out of a BJA window earlier, Pat commented: "Some of these graves are ancient - we must take a look at them." Later that afternoon, before twilight fell, we did precisely that, although, sadly, for a second time, we couldn't find Grandfather Bill's grave. We also visited the catacombs, where I made notes. The entrances, as explained, are now cemented up. On the lowest of the three levels is a large commemorative plaque, warranting further investigation. But we'll reserve that for another occasion. For the time being, our visit to the Jewellery Quarter, a place so dear to Pat's heart, is complete.

Then if by chance in the future you stray,
Down by the churchyard, early,
You won't find that old craftsman there,
A-weepin' for a memory - a-weepin' for a memory…

A number of issues have been raised, some of which can only be clarified through in-depth research. Although there are still many problems to resolve, if the Quarter is to survive and prosper, it's abundantly clear that there are many talented, caring and resourceful individuals, working hard to maintain its unique qualities.

Chapter Eleven –

GOODNIGHT VIENNA

Now you can imagine me keeping a promise, can't you? I said, "Listen Bigun, don't you leave me roastin' here, all night long, because I'll be Danger Man." I was completely fearless Shirley, he'll tell you – the Bigun!

Billy Sutton

And now, Ladies and gentlemen, for something completely different – as they say!

For a few minutes we're leaving the UK behind, to head for foreign climes. We present you with a Double Bill – Bill Bridges and Billy Sutton. You've met them in previous chapters, as close friends of Pat's. Such is their collective sense of humour, they could well form a double act!

Bill Bridges, (a.k.a. Wayne Bridges), a former World Heavyweight Wrestling Champion, was featured in Chapter Eight. His wife, Sarah Bridges, is current holder of the British Heavyweight Bodybuilding title, for 2004. Billy Sutton, (known as 'Sutty' to his friends), is a Brummie, originally a 'fly pitcher' and flower seller, who has led a highly eventful, often-traumatic life. Pat uses his own version of the nickname – 'Sooty' – because the glove puppet in *Sooty and Sweep* was always getting into scrapes!

Between 1986 – 1995, despite being a recovering alcoholic, Billy was honoured twenty-two times in America, for his work with youngsters; fourteen awards were from the Miami Police, for his work with young drug offenders, who were *far* more willing to take advice from a recovering addict, than from social workers. Gary Stretch, former boxing champion-turned-film star, has first-hand experience of Billy's effectiveness, both on the drugs scene and with sports. Speaking on *The Carl Chinn Show* (14 December 2003), he explained just how successful Billy had been, and spoke of their friendship and his high regard for him.

Billy introduced *Little League* football into Britain and broadcast his own Saturday morning radio programmes about the sport, from *Pebble Mill*, for ten years. It was there that he first met Carl Chinn, who is currently writing Billy's biography.

In 1996, 'Sutty' was honoured by the City of Birmingham, at a sit-down celebration for a thousand people! The guests included judges, police chiefs, mayors, the stars and his family, including two former wives. Pat was among those friends invited on stage to say a few words. Billy also has the distinction of turning down two OBEs, on a matter of principle!

In *If – The Pat Roach Story*, we devoted Chapter Seven to Pat's international wrestling career, including winning the Cup in Hanover, in1976. Subsequent research has revealed the degree to which Pat understated his success abroad: namely, achieving and maintaining star status for almost two decades. Charting Pat's foreign tours, is a fairly complex process. To simplify matters, for all concerned, his co-writer has compiled the following Table of Events, placing countries in *alphabetical*, rather than chronological order:

Pat's wrestling tours abroad:

Country/Continent	Approximate Date	Wrestling/other Companions
Africa (South)	Pat undefeated in South Africa. Toured Cape Town, Durban, Johannesburg and Pretoria; became good friends - Willie Grové (Groovay) and family.	
America/ Canada	Los Angeles 1971 &1974/75	Wayne already in Canada on a different circuit. Pat touring alone.
Austria	c. 1965	Billy Sutton
Germany	1970s	Pete Roberts/Johnny Kincaid
	1976 – cup in Hanover	Johnny Lees
India	early 1970s	Wrestled Dara & Randhawa
Japan	1971 & 1975	Killer Kowalski, Wayne Bridges, Pete Roberts

During six weeks in Japan with Wayne, Pat was undefeated. Wayne confirms Pat was invited back to Japan many times, but was always fully booked, wrestling elsewhere.

In addition to tours of Germany (Berlin), America – (Los Angeles) and Japan, Pat also has many stories to tell about wrestling in countries such as New Zealand, Turkey and the West Indies.

The two Bills 'join forces, later in this chapter, to recall memorable trips abroad with Pat. But first we begin with the recollections of three famous wrestlers, *Killer Kowalski*, Dara Singh and his brother, Randhawa.

John Hayles, a.k.a. *Killer Kowalski*, has been a good friend and wrestling colleague of Pat's for many years. The summer of 2002 wasn't too good for him…. "with knee problems (the result of too many knee drops off the corner posts). However, I had the operations, came out of hospital and then into rehabilitation.

"Pat and I often did the German Tournaments, during the 1970s, together with Pete Roberts and Johnny Kincaid, mainly working for promoter Paul Berger. These were in Hamburg and Berlin, and consisted of six weeks – seven days a week. They were run twice a year, during spring and autumn, so quite a lot of time was spent in Germany." Unfortunately, Johnny Kincaid was sacked while they were in Berlin, so Pat called a strike in protest.

"Berlin was a good city to be in," recalls *Killer*. "Of course, these years were during the existence of the Berlin Wall, but West Berlin was a bright, highly active city, in the middle of a drab Eastern Germany. Travelling there was a bit fraught, if going by car - enduring the checkpoints. So the favourite mode of travel was to fly in. Pat came down once in the Rolls-Bentley. This, of course, caused amazement with the East Germans – not used to seeing anything but the Trabants, made in the East.

"I remember Pat turning up in Hamburg, just a visit, on his way through to a Hanover tournament. He called in at the digs to see Pete Roberts and myself. He said: 'How about a cup of tea?' To which Pete said, (ever the joker), 'I forget who we lent the tea bags to.' Pat's remark was unprintable! However, I think he ended up with a 'cuppa'.

"Hamburg was also a good city to be in. When you are in one place for six weeks, it is easy to get fed up with your surroundings and the company you are living with. No problems with our group. Pat and I would often go off after the evening's wrestling, to a jazz club, of which there are many in Hamburg."

Film star and former *World Heavyweight Wrestling Champion*, Dara Singh wrestled in England in August 1957 and stayed until May 1958, performing in venues around the country. Birmingham, he recalls was the only place, at that time, which would stage matches on Sundays. Jack Taylor referred to him in glowing terms, in Chapter Eight.

Dara became *Rustam-E-Hind* (Champion of India) in 1954, when he defeated Tiger Jaginder Singh, in Bombay. He defended his World Championship title against Lou Thez in London, in 1957, but the result was a drawn match. They had a rematch in Bombay, in 1968, which Dara won. In 1959, the year after his first visit to Britain, he won the *Commonwealth Heavyweight Wrestling Championship*, from George Gordienko, in Calcutta. Dara retired as the unbeaten *World Heavyweight Wrestling Champion*, in 1983. In the interim, he made return tours of Britain in 1966 and 1972, although Pat wasn't sufficiently experienced to wrestle him at that stage.

The *Birmingham Bull* (as Pat was sometimes known) and the *Rustam-E-Hind* eventually 'locked horns' when Pat toured India, in the 1970s. Dara subsequently wrestled with Pat in Birmingham in 1978 or 79 and on three other occasions: in Bombay, Gauhati, and Canada. In Bombay, Dara wrestled with many famous opponents, including *Giant Haystacks*. He continues to make television films there, both as an actor and a director. Dara makes the point that, (unlike India), to the best of his knowledge, Pat is the only English wrestler to have become a fully-fledged film and television actor.

Dara's brother, the celebrated film star Randhawa Singh, was *Heavyweight Champion of India* from 1968 until 1988. The brothers continue to live in close proximity, and maintain regular contact with one other. Like Dara, Randhawa regards Pat with great affection, and respect, and has kindly written the following letter, especially for this chapter:

'After my schooling, I left for Singapore for further studies, in 1953. Since my brother, Dara, was already a successful wrestler in Singapore by then, he had to come back to India for tournaments, leaving me behind with his guru. The guru was impressed with my physique and inspired me to take up wrestling as a profession. By then, in the mid-fifties, wrestling had become a rage back home, and when my brother got to know of my training in Singapore, he asked me to come back to India and start rigorous training. After four years of rigorous training, I wrestled for the first time in India, in 1957, in Delhi, against Charles Gamech of Australia. On the same card, my brother Dara wrestled with Primo Carnera, a former world famous champion boxer turned wrestler.

My wrestling career lasted thirty-one years and I finally retired in the year 1988. I won the Indian Championship in 1968 and defended the same until my retirement, without losing a single match. I was also the Indian tag team champion, along with my brother Dara, for many years.

In my career of thirty-one years, I wrestled throughout the world with famous wrestlers, such as King Kong, John Da Silva, John Quinn, Hay Stack, David Taylor, Bill Robinson, Ray Apollon, George Panchiff Gordienko, and Ricky Dorzan of Japan. All of these were famous defending champions of their respective countries and last, but not least of course, the famous wrestler, Pat Roach.

I enjoyed every match against Pat, since he was a skilled and very fair wrestler, and was known in India to be a gentleman wrestler. About the stabbing incident that you've mentioned, well as far as my memory goes, the incident did not take place at the Vallabh Bhai Patel Stadium in Mumbai, but in Gauhati (Assam). On the particular day, there was a huge crowd in the Nehru Stadium - something close to seventy thousand people. There was a stampede after the match, and in all that mad rush anyone could have been hurt. The temporary bamboo carriers could have caused the accident.

My favourite match? Well, wrestling has been my passion. I cannot recall a particular favourite match, since every match was a favourite, and played with the same intensity. Now - about my film career. Well, I worked in about thirty-five movies, out of which I played the lead in twenty; some of which were mythological movies and some fantasy action movies.

Right now I am enjoying my retirement. I do have my own farms and business, but most of my days are now spent taking care of my health and diet, by doing yoga and light workouts. After my retirement, my son, Baljit Singh

Randhawa, *did* carry on the wrestling profession for a while, and became defending champion for five years. But unfortunately, for the last seven years, there are no wrestling matches held in India.

I do hope my contribution to your book is of good help to you. My best wishes are with you.' He signs the letter - 'S.S. Randhawa'.

In addition to Germany, John Hayles also toured India with Pat, (including the time of the stabbing incident), and the Far East: "Pat and I went to Japan round about 1975. What a hard place to ply your trade. No holds barred – you took your life in your hands, wrestling those 'Japs'! Food was always a problem. If available, a plate of chips cost £5-00. For two guys the size of Pat and myself, it was a game getting enough food. Sushi, whilst being quite tasty, is not substantial enough, and you can get fed up to the teeth with rice!

"We were never really able to spend much time in the towns in Japan, as most days were spent travelling, and by the time you got to the town, it was time to put your boots on.

However, Pat was always great company and I thank him for his years of friendship."

I loved judo – I was a First Dan, and was in Japan, when that story happened to me that can only happen on a movie, or you read about in a book. Where you're in the 'dojo' – the gym if you like, and you see, literally, a little old guy with a wispy beard. He stood there and he was a 'sensa' – a teacher – and he dumped me all over the place – just like a fantasy or fiction. He had me on the end of his fingertips. As I am now, I was six feet, four-and-a-half inches tall, and, in those days, probably seventeen-and-a-half stone; very fit – and he just dumped me. You couldn't believe it!

Perhaps it was poetic justice? Readers may recall the reverse side of the coin, described in Chapter 6, by Pat's friend and colleague, Paddy White, when Pat decided to teach him the finer details of the sport: "And being the silly Paddy I am, I've gone: 'I'll have a bit of that.' " It ended with Pat flipping him over onto the floor, like a baby.

Wayne Bridges (a.k.a. Bill) confirms: "Pat was very successful abroad." The former World Heavyweight Champion has first-hand experience of this, as he and Pat have wrestled in countries such as Japan, India, Canada, USA and the Middle East. He recalls a memorable occasion, when the two of them were wrestling in Osaka, a southeastern region of Japan, south of Kyoto, near the Pacific Ocean. It involved a Japanese Grand Master.

"This chap came into the dressing room, and he was asking for Pat, who happened to be on the ring – working. So I said: 'Oh, he won't be long.' And you know the way I joke? – I said: 'He's boring the people at the moment!' So he said (Japanese accent): 'Oh no, no. Pat Roach – big force to be reckoned with! Great honour for me to be here.' When Pat left the ring, the Grand Master greeted him with a very low bow. I said: 'He's not that good, is he?'

The Master replied: 'Oh yes.' Pat later told me that he'd got his Black Belt within two years."

Until that precise moment, in 1971, Wayne knew nothing about Pat's previous success – "And I'd known Pat then, for probably seven years! He said, 'I've played about with judo – a bit.' The next thing I know, he was doing these judo matches and demonstrations – in judo jackets. Even the promoters didn't know about it! They realised that he was so good – now we're talking Japan here – the 'home of judo'. So what they did – they put a price on Pat's head: meaning that he was open for offers; from anybody: you didn't have to be a wrestler! I mean, you could just come on in, and if you beat him, there was a price on his head; he was out there, on a tour, for six weeks. Many tried, but Pat made short work of them. But, ever the gentleman, he helped them up and applauded them."

Pat then took the situation, (as he often does), a stage or two further. "For any young wrestler to even be allowed to *train* as a wrestler," explains Wayne, "what he has to do, to start with, is 500 free squats. Until he can do that, he can't even think of it. And they get one chance at this; if you fail the first time, forget being a wrestler.

"So Pat was standing there, watching these young lads. There were a dozen of them, in the ring. A seasoned wrestler was going around with a bamboo 'kendo' type of stick, and he was whacking them on the head – 'Come on, that's under a hundred – keep going!' So Pat got in the ring and joined them. On the next night – at the next town, he banged out a *thousand* free squats. Then he brought something else in, which they still use in Japan today. (I've got friends in Japan, so I know that they still use this method).

"What Pat used to do – he always carried a deck of cards" - (Pat recently explained that he was in fact, emulating a practice, originated by Pete Roberts). "He turned the top card over; the Ace counted as 15, the King, 14. So you went from 2 to 15," continues Wayne. "If you turned the top card over, and it was an Ace, that would be 15. So he did 15 free squats. You turned the next one over and if it was an 8, you'd get up and do 8 'push-ups', or 'press-ups'. And without stopping, he would go through the whole deck. Now that takes quite a lot of doing – and they still use that method in Japan today. It was free squats, push-ups, free squats, push-ups; so with each new card, you'd alternate between the two kinds of movement. So he was *extremely* fit – Pat."

Wayne also recalls that Pat used to use Yoga, to enable him to stick pins through himself. A photo in our previous book shows him wearing a false beard, attached by that method – it doesn't bear thinking about. Wayne declined Pat's invitation to try it for himself!

He confirms: "*The Killer* was a close friend of Pat's too. (Pat even introduced John to his future wife). The only two countries that I visited with John were Germany and Japan. We went to Germany about five or six times together, and once to Japan. All the other trips that I did were without *The Killer* - America, Canada, East Africa, and so on.

"What you *must* have, in the wrestling business, is a supple back. So what you do is – you hit your foot up against the wall, and come out with your other foot, and you stand there. The object is to lean your hands back against the wall, and go down the wall – to give you a supple back. It was in Japan that Pat said to the trainer: 'Get me – for tomorrow – a strong car tyre, off a wheel, which is easier for them.' And what they did – they had to bend backwards over this car tyre – to give them a supple back – instead of them going down the wall. It's *much* safer, because if your back is going to go, you still have something there to support you – and they still use that method today. In fact, I think gymnasts use that now.

"There's a fella who lives in America now, *Judo Al Hayes*; he went out there in the mid-70s: very successful." Bill explained how Al Hayes and Pat first met. "I hadn't long been in the business at the time, and the two main bodies were *Dale Martin's* and *Paul Lincoln Promotions*. They were both jostling with the smaller promotions, to get Pat to come with them. *Paul Lincoln Promotions* got hold of Pat first, and put the offer in. So Al Hayes was part of *Paul Lincoln Promotions:* there was Paul Lincoln, Ray Hunter, Mike Marino and Judo Al Hayes – they were the four governors of *Paul Lincoln Promotions*.

"They got hold of Pat first, through Jack Taylor, because Jack used to work in conjunction with Paul Lincoln, but then Paul got so big, Jack sort of 'fell by the wayside' with him. They were the first to proposition Pat, so he went with *Paul Lincoln* first. Sadly, Al's suffering from chronic arthritis. Whereas he used to be 5 feet 11 inches and 16½ stone, he's now only 5 feet 3 or 4 and 140 lbs. When I talk to him on the phone, he's exactly as he used to be – but obviously, when you see him, he's not. He lives in Texas."

Wayne recalls some of their American wrestling venues: "What happens when you're in America – when I went there, they said that they would give me every opportunity to go Main Event – because that's where the money is (you're on a percentage of the house). So they put you in around the middle of the bill – so your money's still very good. Even if an American has been Main Event in another territory, (American State or area), when he comes to a *new* territory, he doesn't naturally go Main Event: he goes in around the middle of the bill, and they give him every opportunity to lift himself. So he could have been Main Event everywhere he's been, be he won't come in there at that level.

"Now the point of me telling you this is, when Pat came in, this *particular* promoter had only seen Pat twice. By this time, I was Main Event, but it had taken them four months to lift me to that position – every opportunity that could be given was given to me, to reach that stage. But when he saw Pat the promoter said: 'Do you know Pat very well?' I said: 'Yes I do.' He said: 'Please tell him to come and see me, and if he'll come for me, the week after next he's Main Event.' "

To do so meant breaking the rules. Did Bill ever witness that happening to anyone else?

"No – never. The only other two people who came in Main Event were the World Champion and André the Giant, who was over 520lbs, and 7 feet tall. But he wouldn't stay, you see? The World Champion would only be in that territory for a week, then move on to the next territory; but everybody knew the World Champion. He'd send a videotape in so that it could be played on TV in that territory, three weeks before he was due to come in, so that everyone knew well in advance. But apart from that, no wrestler, other than Pat and André, ever went straight in on top."

This was in 1974 or 75, so Pat had a well established international reputation, when this exceptional offer was made. When I suggest that Pat had been wrestling for at least ten years or more by then, Bill quips: "About sixty years I think!

"I can give you another example. I was in Canada. I'd been there about six months, and become very well established, and had the *Pacific Coast Belt* there. Pat came into Vancouver, in an opposition, if you like, with some Indian wrestlers. Such was the impression Pat made on the promoter, he came to me and said: 'Do you know the English chap, Pat Roach?' Because the Canadian promoters, (Sandor Kovacs and Gene Kininsky – Kininsky once held the *Heavyweight Championship of the World*), both wanted to get Pat to work for them. He was only on a *tour* of Canada, so he was going to appear in Vancouver, for instance, twice, and then he was going to move on to say, Toronto or Calgary, and they were going to do a tour.

"But I went to Pat, I was earning a phenomenal amount of money (I mean, I had a license to print money – then). I said: 'They want you here, and they'll give you every chance.' Because Pat had this sort of 'gift' with audiences: he was *instant* – you didn't have to build Pat up. It was a certain kind of charisma, you see. He said: 'Well, how long for?' I said: 'Well, they want you to stay for a year.' But he just wouldn't – he won't leave England for a year.

"I know for a fact, Arnold Schwarzenegger asked him to go to the States. I knew Arnold when he was eighteen. He was living in a partition, really, in a gym, in Munich. He was a nineteen-year-old boy then. He was always a bodybuilder, although he was very strong, as well. Pat did movies with him and he then made Pat the offer – to come to America. Arnold and Pat were in *Red Sonja* and *Conan the Destroyer* together. But he wouldn't leave England. Even Arnold calls him 'Big Pat'." With Arnie's recent election to office, Pat can now rightly claim that he once 'Body-slammed' the Governor of California!

Wayne has a comprehensive series of photos relating to Pat's wrestling career, although as Pat observes, the majority of published photos somehow always show him on the receiving end, which, one can only suppose, makes it more interesting! Wayne explains: "This was because Pat was rarely on the receiving end, so when he was, it was camera – click, click!" One example of Pat, in customary control, is included in this book; the remainder we hope to include in a future book – *The Pat Roach Book of International Wrestling*. The final one in Wayne's collection is of particular significance. "I told Pat that the only way that I was going to defend the *World Heavyweight Wrestling Champion Belt*, against him, was if he would come to the match, dressed in the same attire that I have on in this picture – to wrestle me." The photograph is captioned: 'Wayneta Bridges' – so we'll leave that to your imagination!

Wayne also wrestled in East Africa. When Pat wrestled in South Africa, there were certain stipulations: "To prove that you were worthy of being a professional, you had to wrestle their top Amateur Heavyweight," Wayne explains. "If you couldn't beat him, you couldn't get a job – you couldn't wrestle at all."

Wayne also reveals that Pat was the highest paid wrestler *ever*, in Germany. "Pat *still* holds that record, (it hasn't been broken up to today – I'm sure), of the highest paid wrestler *ever* – to work in Germany – that includes Americans, Japanese – everything!

"Even up to the present day, his fee has never been equalled." How can he be absolutely *certain* about that? "Because it hurts me to say it! It was common knowledge."

Pat recalls that 'Kaiser', the promoter, was involved in the deal. "Paul Berger came over here, looking for talent, and saw Pat at *Belle Vue*, Manchester. He wanted Pat so badly," explains Wayne, "that's the fee he offered him, and it's never been equalled since. Paul Berger," (mentioned on several occasions in our wrestling chapters), "had the larger venues in Germany, Austria and all around there. He was able to offer more money that the other promoters who wanted Pat. It was such a high figure, because he wanted Pat *exclusively* for himself; the other promoters couldn't equal it."

Before the second member of our double bill takes centre stage, Georgie James, Pat's friend from his early Ladywood days, has a few introductory words to say:

"Billy Sutton the madman? Flower seller, loves a drink – or he used to. I think he's stopped now." (He's been on 'the wagon' for many years). "He used to get out of his brains!" continues Georgie. (Pat adds: "… and his trousers!"). Georgie's nightclub, the *Spider's Web,* was one of the venues where Billy used to 'play up', (as he calls it). "He *certainly* did, confirms Georgie, "dancing on the floor, swinging the microphone around at the band; stripped naked. Messing with some of the girls on the dance floor – he was a nightmare! But a crackin' fella – a lovely fella. I couldn't walk down the street without him – "take these for your wife!" Flowers – always putting them into my hand; very nice fella. He went to America, didn't he? The Miami Police made him an Honorary Colonel. In the late 80s he arranged football games and boxing matches, between American and English kids. He used to bring youngsters over from Miami, to box the Birmingham lads."

Billy, who eventually achieved his own celebrity status, recalls visiting Pat's Hockley café – *The Fly-over* –('many moons ago'), announcing that in a couple of days, he was off to Spain. Billy tells the story so well, that you'll only find the *occasional* interruption, from Pat and myself!

"All the lads, like Johnny Hart, used to go to Spain," explains Billy. "I was the one who always missed out - I had to stay in Birmingham, for some reason, to play up, and I never got to visit Spain. But this was a time when I was definitely going. I promised 'Harty' and all the rest of the troops, that I would. But of course, when I go to see the 'Bigun', he was talking about going on his own and it didn't take long for me to change me mind."

According to Pat, their transport was an American Convertible. "Yes – the 'Yank' a Galaxy 'Drop-head," confirms Billy, whose use of the Birmingham vernacular makes Pat sound like Prince Charles! Pat describes the car as 'a bit of a gas-guzzler' - it consumed *so* much petrol! The two friends reached Vienna, and discovered that the wrestling was at an ice rink; the stadium was next door to the rather plush, *Intercontinental Hotel*.

"The promoter's name was Blemenshutze," Billy recalls. "In those days, I was about nine-and-a-half stone and everybody nicknamed me Terence Stamp. I had black hair, a moustache and that – and I was a 'ringer' for Stamp. (I've met him of course, but over the years, it became a burden). Roachie thought it would be a good idea for me to wear a tracksuit, with 'Elstree Studios' on the back. When we get to Vienna, the bullsh** will be that I'm over there, learning the wrestling business, because he's preparing me to appear in a wrestling film!"

Pat points out that it was Billy's idea really! "That was the 'pitch' – you got it? Of course I looked such a ringer for him and with me being with the 'Bigun', nobody ever questioned it at all," continues Billy. "The first part of it was that we'd both got a few quid, and we stopped at the *Intercontinental* – a very nice hotel to stay in."

Jimmy White lent them a tent. "The thing was if there was any situation where I'd got to start training, to keep the nonsense up, which eventually became a bloody reality, we needed a tent. But of course, the Bigun and me had never put a tent up in our lives! We went to the stadium, Pat introduced himself to the wrestling promoter, I think we got there on a Thursday or Friday – and his first bout was on the Monday.

"Now, just outside Vienna is an inlet; the name escapes me at the moment. It was a beautiful part of the year, when we were there. As we got to this inlet, Pat recognised a lot of the wrestlers, with a lot of birds round them, but me and him were milky white – like ghosts. These German and French wrestlers were all bronzed up, with all of the birds round them. Him and me looked like a right pair of lollipops! So what he said was: 'What we do son, we'll get to the other side of this island, have a few hour's sun, then we'll make a guest appearance and introduce ourselves.' So that's what we did: we camped up on the other part of the island; me being jet-black I tanned up quickly and the Bigun did - eventually. We went over and introduced ourselves to the rest of them – and they were lovely people.

"This first fight, he fought a Belgian called Mark Breston, who was as bald as a badger, about 6-foot one, and had a neck of about 26 inches on him – I'm not joking! Of course, this was straight wrestling. It was once a year, in front of Vienna Television, and went all over Germany – everywhere! Of course, I had to be his 'second' in the ring. It was so 'straight', they had police outside with automatic sub-machine guns! So nobody could get at the wrestlers or impose on them. When your bout finished, you were taken back to your changing room; once you'd changed you were escorted away, so that the punters couldn't get at you. It was very high security.

"When we got back, to get changed, we got to the 'Yank' outside, luckily parked right outside the stadium." That evening, Pat and Billy visited a very famous restaurant called *The Scotch Club*. "The bouncers and the manager of the club recognise who he is, give us a nice entourage downstairs. Roachie spends about ten minutes with me. He says: 'Now Sut, whatever you do, you're a stranger here. Don't start performing like you have at the *Cedar*- it's a different ball game. Promise me you won't play up!' Having recognised some friends at the table in an adjoining room, on the way in, Pat planned to join them for a while.

Which brings us to Billy's comment, at the beginning of this chapter. Unfortunately the Bigun *did* leave him unattended! "During the course of the evening I'm getting plenty of large vodkas down me. On the stage there's a trio. Because my stage act in the *Cedar* or the *Rum Runner*, years ago, used to be doing Jerry Lee Lewis – *Tell Me What I Say*. Then I'd finish up on the stage, doing the mike action: going to beat the guitar player with the mike, throwing the mike up in the air, catching it. Oh, I used to be a master at it – he'll tell you – the Bigun!

"I got myself up on the stage with this German trio, I said: 'Jerry Lee Lewis,' so they start beating it up; then all of a sudden, shirt off, trousers off. The place is full of birds, like you've never seen in your life. Because this was the in-scene, with all the Viennese, you know? So now I'm down to my underpants!

"The geyser on the piano was in his early forties; the other kids were in their early twenties. As I glide over to him, (singing) 'Oh when the pianist plays that song,' I dive on him and his toupee falls off. He's got a full toupee on top of the mike, and he's bald as a badger!

"All of a sudden, down the stairs comes the Law – with sub-machine guns! I've not even got a pair of socks on now, bear in mind! There's murders! One's got me underpants, one's got me shirt, and one's got me trousers! They're pushing me up this flight of stairs with the back of their guns – the barrels – right? I get up to the top/restaurant part - bear in mind, I haven't got a pair of socks on! Now all of Viennese Society is eating there in the restaurant, all dressed up, evening suits, full gowns on."

Think about it readers – (if you can stand it); I *couldn't* have made this up, could I?! "Monkey suits – right?" continues Billy. "All of a sudden, as I'm looking through the restaurant, outside, I see the 'meat wagon'. Well I've been in plenty of them in my life, haven't I? So I know what's coming – I'm going to be 'banged-up' in the meat wagon! As luck would have it, Jake Zatuski, who was one the great German wrestlers, (and finished up befriending me and Pat), is in there with a couple of other wrestlers - recognised me. They get hold of the Vienna 'Law', saying, 'Crazy – he's not used to drink,' bang, bang, bang, right? And they persuade the law to let me go.

"As this is all going on, the Bigun walks back into the room, and all of a sudden he's onto me. You know he gives you that 'deep' look? He's got his arms together, like a schoolteacher, dressing me down. He's going: 'What a f***ing treat! The only club in Vienna and you get the ticket, the first night!' "

After about five days, Pat and Billy were 'skint'. "He's gone through all his money, off the promoter, so now the next move is, we've got to get to a campsite outside, I've got to get into strict training, and this is the way we were going to operate. We go to Link, a place just outside Vienna, beautiful countryside. We see this massive big caravan site and holiday park advertised. So we pull in, and through the gate there's a bungalow. Roachie pulls up, the fella comes out. We say we want to stop for a few days – no problem - 'Get yourself organised and pay me when you come back.'

"So we're driving through this holiday park, we pull up outside one of the tents, the Bigun gets out and they're all a load of New Zealand birds. (We're coming to the best part now). Opening the boot – all these birds are posing outside, getting a bit of sun on them. We lift the tent out, which is a big size, out of the back of the boot, put it onto the ground. All of a sudden he gives me the forlorn look – well? He said: 'I don't know how to put a tent up.' I said, 'I'm an international playboy. I'm not used to camping. What's all this malarkey?' "

Neither of them had a *clue*. "So we're having this moody ruck, when all of a sudden, a little German kid comes up and says: 'Me can do.' So there we are – two grown men." Pat recalls that the boy had something wrong with his eye. "All of a sudden this kid gets this bell tent up, which was in two sections, bang, bash, wallop – done," explains Billy. "And what do you think the Bigun gave him? An orange! I've never been so embarrassed in my whole life!"

The kid looked at me as if to say: "What a cheapskate!"

"Of course, that's the meanness of him – the Aston face. I hope you're listening to this Roachie! Now we've got a camp bed and the 'cobblers' is – I've got to start doing some road running. Pat said: 'All that stripping and running round as a street kid – you've got to be as fit as a fiddle! What I suggest we do is put our tracksuits on. I'll park up a mile outside Vienna, on the main road.' "

I said: "Now 'Soot', what I want you to do is just have a gentle jog, in the front. I'll tag behind – in the Yank." We were a short distance away from the city, but it was a very warm day.

"I've done about half a mile on, with all the booze inside me," continues Billy. "Of course, I'm 'cattle-trucked'! I haven't trained for years and it's all starting to come out of me. So now I'm into the equivalent of New Street, on a Saturday morning Shirl, and the roads are packed, either side. Of course, he's 'pipping' the horn and there's punters waving to the left and there's punters waving to the right, and I'm doing my Mr. Terence Stamp bit. I'm waving to the left, waving to the right, when all of a sudden I go into a bus stop! Spark out in the middle of the road! The Bigun gets out of the car and birds are standing over me. He's looking at me – towering over me. He couldn't believe it."

Undoubtedly, Pat was thinking: 'Oh no – not again!' (to use the polite version). "He dragged me up and put me on the front seat of the car. He's slapping me on the face to bring me round. I mean, you've seen the size of his arms! He doesn't 'arf take liberties. Anyway, crash, bang, wallop, that was the end of that exercise. We get back to the site and he says: 'You go and have a mooch and I'll get a bit of kip.' I go down to the local beer garden and get plenty down me.

"I arrive back about ten o'clock at night. Well it's pitch black and I'm absolutely 'laggin', and I'm starting to howl like a wolf! So I'm inside now and of course, as you know, the bell tent has got one single pole inside; he was in the back part and I was in the front. So I'm howling and my arms are going everywhere. All of a sudden I howled and jumped up and the bloody tent came down on me! I'm out of the tent, my eyes are absolutely white and I frighten the life out of him! I was howling like a bloody werewolf. At different times in his life he has backed off me when I've gone over the top. This was one such exception - you know?"

The next day I said: "Son, I've never seen anything like that in my life – like that with you last night." And of course, we'd got the problem of putting the tent up again.

"Eventually, he performs fairly decently there; we drive all the way back," Billy recalls. "We drive back on the Friday and on the Saturday my sister was getting married. Now, she was in a bit of the social set, my sister Madelaine." On the return journey, the gearbox packed up. "Thank God we got back – that was a right load of hassle. That really came together – I'll give him full credit; he nursed the car and he got us back."

If I'd only known – Georgie James had actually got a car over there in Vienna at the time, but we didn't find out until later.

"Anyway, that was the end of the Vienna tale. We come back to England, get back to the coffee house, go over the road to get our 'barnets' cut. We got changed and my sister's getting married over at Wootton Wawen. We miss the ceremony, but we both arrive at the reception. Then afterwards, everyone went back to my father's house – God bless my father – he died thirty-three years ago. But we went back to my mother's house, which she still lives in on her own, at 23 Simon Road, just off Hollywood Lane. Mary's been in that bungalow for about forty-seven years now. So we get back and the neighbours, who lived about seven doors away, had a beautiful piano. The old man said to Roachie: 'Pat, would you give us a hand to get the piano down?' " According to Pat, he was one of a group of six or so men who carried it to the house.

"You know, three days later, it took seven of us to carry it back? We had a good 'free and easy' with it," recalls Billy – "the old singsong, Summer Lane . style, at my parents' house after the wedding. Pat lay down, the length of him, in my mother's lounge, drinking vodkas, and it hit us, because we'd had a long play-up over there, a long drive back –then the wedding straight after. My mother had half an acre of two beautiful lawns outside. We had the double bay windows open as well, you see." In those days the area was still quite rural.

Billy and Pat sometimes talked in Birmingham backslang when they were in Vienna, which was confusing, to say the least. Pat recalls that Billy used several different versions of backslang. For years afterwards, his German friends still asked, "How's Awowa?" – their nickname for Billy!

"Jake Zatuski did all the stunt work for Hardy Kruger in *The One That Got Away*," recalls Billy. (We mentioned the film in our first book, because Pat watched it over in Ireland, with Hardy, although no one in the audience recognised him)! According to Pat, Jake owned a club, somewhere in West Germany. "He is one of the wrestlers who Pat fought in Vienna," explains Billy. "He did all the baling out and the ice part, in Hardy's film - going from America to Canada. Pat knew him very well. They were a really great set of people."

Chapter Twelve –

A MAN FOR ALL SEASONS

He told me what his greatest wish – I wonder –do you know? He said: "Mother, before you die, because we've got to be sensible, it's got to be talked about, I want to be able to tell you, I'm going to be a millionaire." Now I'm praying to God: please help Paddy to grant him his greatest wish, because he never stops – he works so hard.

Dolly Roach

Pat has a determination and strength of character, which more than equal his physical stature. It's a quality that has helped him conquer the earlier disadvantages of his childhood, and later, to overcome all manner of difficulties.

Despite sometimes being on a short fuse, generally speaking, he has a tremendous regard for the needs of others, coupled with a desire to lend a hand, provided those involved show sufficient drive and determination themselves. No one gets a free ride with Pat! There are numerous examples of this, from our many contributors to date.

Pat has fought, all of his life: that's why he has managed to achieve so much. He's a very forceful character; if there's a job to be done, he'll see it through. The 'mighty presence' that you feel when you're in Pat's company, is only part of the picture. The true situation is far more complex and intriguing. There's another real *character* inside him … Just waiting to be discovered … If, in the course of reading this book, you have caught a glimpse, from time to time, of this other, rather more *private* persona, then our book has gone some way towards achieving its objective.

Sarah Bridges, film actress and current British Bodybuilding Champion, whom we mentioned in two previous chapters, describes Pat very well:

"I was seventeen years old when I first met Pat, at a pub in Greenwich – *The Prince of Orange*. My first impression of him was that I thought he was a god. I was frightened to talk to him. I was very shy anyway. I was only – like – nine-stone and seventeen years old. What makes this man so popular and such a Superstar, is that he is the same with whoever he meets. He can rub shoulders with such people as Harrison Ford, Ryan O'Neal, Arnie, Ursula, Sean Connery, and he will be exactly the same, and give the same attention, to a young lad on his first visit to the gym. I'd known Pat for only a couple of months, when he put out his hand in friendship, to help me, and fifteen years on, he's *still* helping me. I never once had to ask; he's always been there for me. Every audition I've been on I've got the job, due to Pat's advice and help."

Paddy White comments: "I've known Pat for many years and my view of him is - really *sound* guy, quite private – very *clever* guy, in terms of survival, for a start - and you mustn't underestimate how intelligent you've got to be, not only to survive, but to be successful, as well."

According to Ronnie Callow, Pat always puts a tremendous amount of thought into what he does – he considers all of the angles beforehand; whereas others might jump into a situation, without much thought.

During the course of our book, we have visited the Jewellery Quarter, Ladywood, Balsall Heath, Lozells, Sparkhill, Winson Green, Sparkhill, Aston, and many other areas, which hold special memories for Pat.

We've two further books planned as co-writers, which are already partly written. One is about the four *Auf Wiedersehen* series and the other will be *The Pat Roach Book of International Wrestling*.

In Chapter Eight, Pat explained that he had been Chairman of the Birmingham Branch of *Equity* for a good few years. He's still a union member, attending meetings, when time permits. Branch Secretary, Len Edwards, describes a fairly recent show. "He did the *Auf Wiedersehen* show at the *Saddler's Club*, Walsall, on 29 May 2002 and also came to a couple of our branch meetings, and gave us advice about a further way of raising funds. He was suggesting that we should find a first-class Charity to support, and do the thing jointly. So that's what we did with this *Auf Wiedersehen* Show. Pat did his 'take-outs', in conjunction with the 'Hospice'. He sold a number of books too, I might add (you're talking about his eye to business) – nobody's fool!

"You've got to *know* the man," Len continues. "You don't expect a wrestler – even an ex-wrestler – to be as profound as Pat is. Invariably, when Pat was Chair, any issues that came up, where people wanted to speak about it, he'd say: 'You've spoken on it once, that's it.' Invariably, after one or two short deliberations with people, he'd cut 'straight to the chase', bang his gavel and say: 'We'll move on.' "

That tallies with Wayne Bridge's description of Pat's approach at the *Annual Wrestlers' Meetings*. He said that Pat keeps order, in the nicest possible way. If anyone is waffling on for too long, he'll find a way of cutting them short, but often in a humorous way. This enables the proceedings to move forward, without actually offending anyone; he's very good with people.

"In that respect, he was a great Chairman," recalls Len, "because meetings have to be controlled. He would get through the agenda always – bang, bang, in an excellent way. If somebody wanted to prolong it, by going on and on, Pat would have a very nice little way of wrapping it up, tying it up, and moving on; very very good."

As a biographer, I have to present both sides of the picture, so I'm obliged to ask you about the more negative aspects of his character. Pat won't mind in the slightest. Len replies: "I can't think of any, off-hand." Did he recall any situations where the left-wing, right-wing differences, which Pat has mentioned, came into play?

"I can't think of specific instances. I do know that on numerous occasions, over a number of years, both as Chair, and since he held the position, whenever Pat had something to say about an issue, quite frequently, it was a different *side* of the argument - something that no one else had thought about. Where we were 'chunelled' and red was red and black was black, Pat would come up and find white. And you'd think: 'Well, I never thought about that.' "

It's the same, working with him as a co-writer; he'll approach a situation from three or four different directions. Although, I take a reasonably diverse approach myself, he's absolutely brilliant at it. (In effect, we're talking about different versions of 'divergent thinking' here - the hallmark of the creative personality).

"He came to one of our meetings," Len continues, "and he gave quite a talk to our members, (certainly within the last three years). He was advising potential and practicing actors about the best ways to promote themselves, to get parts, and how to avoid the pitfalls that he'd found. He was passing his own experience on to them.

"It was a general talk, but I remember him saying that if you start asking for too much money, then you don't get the job. If you have a part, and you're successful in that, you become known in that part, and the rate is – whatever. If you start asking for more, on another production, you don't get the part, because the funding is controlled. I think he lost a few parts that way, where others were intervening, on his behalf."

Sarah Bridges recently explained how Pat's advice has enabled her to further her career.

"Yes, if you want acting roles, you must stick with that," Len elaborates. "It's no good, if you've got a few bills to pay, and think: 'Oh well, in the meantime, I'll do a bit of extra 'walk-on' work.' You'll be known as an extra walk – on: it won't help you. You must persevere, in the direction in which you want to go."

If he were asked to describe Pat to someone who'd never met him before, what would he say? "A warm-hearted, highly intelligent individual, and I suppose, a 'Man for All Seasons' really. For example, if you need help, he'd always be there: if not financially, certainly in a helpful way. Pushing you in various directions, or getting people to give you a ring."

This is the most difficult question of all: what, in your opinion, are Pat's faults? "Well, at times he can be a bit brusque, I suppose. If he's pre-occupied, or he has problems, then he could be a bit sharp with you." He's said himself, that sometimes people think that he's rather arrogant, although those who know him really well realise that he isn't.

Len explains: "Although he can *appear* off-handed, that's not the true picture. If you met him afterwards, and he felt that he had been, he would come and apologise to you. He's a straightforward guy, is Pat. If he hasn't got time for you, invariably it's because he's too busy - or certainly in the past. He's got his fingers in so many pies and after all, he's got a living to earn, you know?"

Pat thrives on variety too. He's the type of personality who likes to have several different projects 'on the go', at the same time. "He's not afraid of telling you, if he thinks you're wrong. He doesn't 'suffer fools gladly' does he?" comments Len.

Several of our contributors have said that as a result of past experience, Pat's also very quick to 'suss out' if someone's taking him for a ride: he's very good at summing people up. "He's a man who 'knows his way around', is Pat," Len concludes, "because whatever the situation, generally speaking, he's been there before. He's experienced it through other people, or seen it happen to other people."

Whichever district of the Midlands you hail from, (or beyond), we hope that you've enjoyed this trip through our twelve chapters. We hope to see you again, perusing the pages of our wrestling book, or perhaps, on an imaginary film or television set?

So until then, *Auf Wiedersehen,* from both of us...

SELECTED BIBLIOGRAPHY

Biography

If – The Pat Roach Story – by Pat Roach with Shirley Thompson (2002).

See also Jackie Pallo's autobiography, under 'Sport' section.
The Treacle Stick – by Helen Butcher (1999).

Historical

A History of Greater Birmingham – down to 1830 – Victor Skipp (1980).

Discovering Birmingham – An Introduction to the City – by Jonathan Berg.

Handsworth, Hockley and Handsworth Wood – compiled by Peter Drake (1998).

Ladywood – by Norman Bartlam (1999).

Old Ladywood Remembered – Victor J. Price (1987).

The British Jewellers' Association, 1887 – 1987, 100 Years Of Service –
by Shelley N. Nott, FGA.

The Jewellery Quarter History and Guide, (2nd Edition), - by Marie
Haddleton, (first published 1987).

The Chamberlain Clock, 100 Years of Keeping Time – by Marie Haddleton
(2002).

Historical Records and Maps

A map of Ladywood, 1907, (previously published in 'Ladywood' – Sutton
Publishing Ltd. 1999). Reproduced by kind permission of the author, Norman
Bartlam.

The Parish Of St Paul's, Birmingham, (previously published in 'The Jewellery
Quarter'). Reproduced by kind permission of the author, Marie Haddleton.

Miscellaneous/Reference

Proper Brummie – A Dictionary of Birmingham Words And Phrases – by Carl Chinn and Steve Thorne (2002).

Sport

You Grunt, I'll Groan, by Jackie 'Mr. TV' Pallo.

Two Wrestling magazines, compiled and published by Jack Taylor: 'Wrestling', and 'Wrestling Whirl'.
'The Good Old Days' by Jack Taylor (previously published in the Middlesborough-based 'Fanzine' magazine).

Newspaper articles and magazines

The Birmingham Post and Mail

The Birmingham Post

The Sunday Mercury

The Brew 'Us Bugle (various editions) – magazine of the Ladywood History Group.

'On the Ladders with Dad' – article by Brian Webb, (first published in Carl Chinn's 'Old Brum' supplement of the Birmingham Mail, 9 September 1996).

The Hockley Flyer (various editions) - Mark and Marie Haddleton.

INDEX